Praise for

Change Proof

"Thinking about change often brings up in us rolling panic and a sickening fear of the unknown. Adam Markel turns that on its head with *Change Proof*, offering leaders an opportunity to confidently adapt to, and even pursue, change. Take the opportunity to build resiliency in yourself, your relationships, and your business. A must read!

—Marshall Goldsmith, *New York Times* number-one
bestselling author of *Triggers, Mojo,* and
What Got You Here Won't Get You There

"Adam Markel's *Change Proof* tackles complicated topics with simplicity and exceptional storytelling. It's an important read for leaders building resilient teams."

—Brian Halligan, cofounder and executive
chairman of HubSpot

"Adam has done it again with *Change Proof*. Resilience, real-life solutions to chaos, and practical ways you can use them to learn and lead in your organization."

—Garry Ridge, chairman and CEO of WD-40 Company

"A three-step process to keep driving toward your vision—spectacular!"

—Phil Town, CEO of Rule One Partners and *New York Times*
number-one bestselling author of *Rule #1* and *Payback Time*

"How do you make sure your folks are crushing it without getting crushed in the process? Adam Markel's *Change Proof* is a guide for building resilience into the very fabric of your team. It's hard to imagine a more important book for our tumultuous times."

—Steve Farber, author of *The Radical Leap* and
Love Is Just Damn Good Business

"In *Change Proof*, Adam Markel artfully explains how to thrive in the face of constant 'change.' The concepts are universal and apply to readers at all stages of life. By weaving together game-changing wisdom with engaging storytelling, Markel charts a path for us to become more resilient and upgrade our lives."

—Mark Gober, award-winning author of
An End to Upside Down Thinking and board member
at the Institute of Noetic Sciences

"The first book on change to invite readers to be emotionally engulfed in dramatic uncertainty, and then rationally receive the tools to effectively deal with it. If this book were a movie it would feel like *Raiders of the Lost Ark*. Get ready for a wild ride."

—Chip R. Bell, author of *Inside Your Customer's Imagination*

"Adam Markel is a terrific storyteller, and his new book, *Change Proof*, will have you ripping through the pages to find out what happens. Along the way he will teach you—painlessly—how to deal with change. Read it now if you want to thrive in the post-pandemic world."

—Dr. Nick Morgan, president of Public Words, Inc.,
and author of *Can You Hear Me?*

"Adam Markel's *Change Proof* is like talking with your best friend through your toughest times and getting life-changing advice you will share with someone else in need someday. I highly recommend reading this book!"

—Lisa Garr, host of *The Aware Show*

"*Change Proof* is pure wisdom. Adam shares powerful lessons from real experiences to teach us how to convert fear, stress, and uncertainty into rocket fuel for resiliency!"

—Todd Kane, author of *Hide & Seek*, speaker,
and inclusive strategist

"The need for resilience and agility is more important now than ever before, and these characteristics are going to become even more important as we move into the future. In *Change Proof*, Adam Markel provides the recipe for developing these characteristics so that you can be the driver of your future instead of the passenger of it."

—Ryan Gottfredson, consultant, trainer, speaker, and coach

"The only true constant in life is change. Revealing his own trials and tribulations along the journey of life (with some of the most daunting arising when we think we have it all figured out), Adam beautifully lays out what is required to be authentic and effective in a perpetually changing world. Our fantasies have to die so that our dreams can come true. If you are a human, this is a book for you!"

—Reed Diamond, American actor

"Long-term and sustained resilience is needed now more than ever before. I completed 112 marathons. I lost a child to suicide. Adam taught me how to be resilient—regardless. Deposit what Adam teaches you in *Change Proof* in your subconscious and see how it will help you move forward one step at a time."

—Dr. Peter Neiman, pediatrician, health coach,
and bestselling author.

"Adam has done it again with *Change Proof*. Resilience, real-life solutions to chaos, and everything else you would want from a powerhouse business development book."

—Dr. Ivan Misner, Founder of BNI and
New York Times bestselling author

"There are few certainties in life, but the fact that things change is one you can count on. Adam Markel's new book, *Change Proof*, will give you the tools and strategies needed to not only deal with changes that occur, but to embrace them . . . and thrive."

—David Meltzer, cofounder of Sports 1 Marketing,
bestselling author, and top business coach

"Wow, *Change Proof* is awesome. I began reading and couldn't stop!"
—Dawson Church, PhD, CEO of Energy Psychology Group

"A delightful read packed full of real-life stories you will immediately relate to and tools you can actually use. It's time to kick stress to the curb and, as resilience expert Adam Markel puts it, become Change Proof."

—Sandra Joseph, Broadway star and author
of *Unmasking What Matters*

Change

Proof

Leveraging the Power
of Uncertainty to Build
Long-Term Resilience

Adam Markel

New York Chicago San Francisco Athens London Madrid
Mexico City Milan New Delhi Singapore Sydney Toronto

1 2 3 4 5 6 7 8 9   LCR   27 26 25 24 23 22

ISBN   978-1-264-25898-7
MHID   1-264-25898-4

e-ISBN   978-1-264-25899-4
e-MHID   1-264-25899-2

Library of Congress Cataloging-in-Publication Data

Names: Markel, Adam, author.
Title: Change proof : leveraging the power of uncertainty to build long-term resilience / Adam Markel.
Description: New York : McGraw Hill, [2022] | Includes bibliographical references and index.
Identifiers: LCCN 2021049714 (print) | LCCN 2021049715 (ebook) | ISBN 9781264258987 (hardback) | ISBN 9781264258994 (ebook)
Subjects: LCSH: Resilience (Personality trait) | Change.
Classification: LCC BF698.35.R47 M35 2022 (print) | LCC BF698.35.R47 (ebook) | DDC 158—dc23/eng/20211217
LC record available at https://lccn.loc.gov/2021049714
LC ebook record available at https://lccn.loc.gov/2021049715

McGraw Hill books are available at special quantity discounts to use as premiums and sales promotions or for use in corporate training programs. To contact a representative, please visit the Contact Us pages at www.mhprofessional.com.

McGraw Hill is committed to making our products accessible to all learners. To learn more about the available support and accommodations we offer, please contact us at accessibility@mheducation.com. We also participate in the Access Text Network (www.accesstext.org), and ATN members may submit requests through ATN.

*To all those courageous enough
to embrace the unknown.*

Contents

PART IV
Change-Proof Software

Preface
The Suck

Life changes in the instant. The ordinary instant.
— JOAN DIDION

Imagine it's 1981. You're on a bus out of Queens, headed east on the Long Island Expressway. It's smack dab in the middle of a heat wave in the hottest week of the summer. The air-conditioning of this rolling crate gave up years ago, and the windows are forever stuck closed. You're only 10 minutes into the ride, and you'd give your right arm to feel even the slightest bit of a breeze. If the neighborhood pool were ever open you'd be there, but it's been closed all summer.

As you leave the city and career into tree-lined suburbia, you sit still and quiet, breathing through your nose, trying not to be carsick from the rocking of the bus and the exhaust fumes snaking through the vents. In spite of the heat, your family makes each other laugh arguing about breakfast or Star Wars or baseball or whatever will keep their hearts excited about your destination.

Finally, just when you can't take anymore, the bus skids to a stop on a spit of land on Long Island called Jones Beach. You wade through the other city-dwellers, dodging suburban station wagons in the parking lot until you burst onto the sand and are greeted by the thunderous blue surf slamming into a shoreline filled with a screaming wall of humanity.

Literally, it's as if a Yankees game ended, the final notes of Frank Sinatra singing "New York, New York" echoing into the sky, and the entire stadium decided, as one, to go to the same half-mile section of beach. Actually, two Yankee Stadiums full of people.

Imagine the sensory overload! One hundred thousand people! Every skin tone imaginable, slathered in oil and lotions; footballs, handballs, baseballs whizzing by your face; the crack of a thousand beers and sodas being opened at once; all five New York boroughs crammed together on towels and blankets; the smell of charcoal grills and sizzling meat mixes with the salt in the air; and the lifeguard whistles that pierce through the symphony of the senses.

Exuding calm, cool confidence, these lifeguards are the lords of the beach sitting on their thrones. They all sport mirrored shades, tans as perfect as the bodies, forever twirling whistles lazily around their fingers. They're watchful, alert, ready for anything.

In the lifeguard code, a single whistle says, "Hey, you there, get away from that spot." Two whistles say, "I'm going in the water." And three whistles say, "All hands on deck, we're going to lose someone."

In a few short minutes that someone is going to be you.

For now, the whistles are silent. At last, you find a spot near the lifeguard tower that's too small, but it'll have to do. You get your towels down, fighting the family behind you for space while your own family continues to bicker. Everybody gets a snack. And a drink.

You whip your shorts and shirt off. You step out of your sweaty shoes. It feels amazing, so good, in fact, that you don't even mind that the sand feels like the surface of the sun. Hopping as quick as you're able, you leave your family behind and navigate the labyrinth of towels, blankets, and umbrellas between you and the sweet coolness of the water.

Your feet hit the water line, you feel air and the sun hit your skin, and for the first time in weeks, you realize you've been holding your breath. You exhale. For a moment, the entire odyssey feels worthwhile. You close your eyes and feel something that feels like relief.

Then when you open them, the water around you that moments ago was bright blue, is now blue-green around your shins. You don't give it another thought as you wade out, feeling the tide pulling on you like an excited child. "Come on! Come on! Further out!" You don't notice it at the time, but you'll remember later, an odd sound, fizzy, like someone's opening a seltzer bottle in slow motion.

Without a thought, you dive under, into the waves, into the spin cycle of another universe, pulling yourself out with your hands in the sandy bottom until you emerge, exhilarated, into the sun. Turning, you look back, to wave to your family.

But hang on a moment: You can't find them. Scanning the shore, you bounce on your toes and realize you've drifted away from the lifeguard tower by almost 40 yards to the right and even farther from the shore. What's more, the water that was once brilliant blue is now almost brown.

OK, time to head back in, you think. Except now, your feet can't find the bottom. You strain your toes to find even a grain of sand. Nothing.

Fine, this is fine, you're going to be fine, but you're going to have to swim, so you put your head down and do your best version of the front crawl, making 10 or 12 strong strokes back to safety.

Then you raise your head, your arms heavy, chest heaving with the effort to realize you're even further out than when you started. A bronze lifeguard stands at the shore waving you in, blowing her whistle. But you can only see her like you're looking the wrong way through binoculars. Her bright blue and gold swimsuit seems a mile away and getting farther. Desperately, you're trying not to panic, but your body feels like a stone and no matter what you do, no matter how hard you swim, you're headed out to sea. You gasp for breath, but splutter out a mouth full of seawater.

Then there they are—Tweet! Tweet! Oh goodness, there are the two whistles! The beach version of DEFCON 1. People are running, yelling, pointing in your direction. You try to wave, but you can't raise your arm. Each stroke, each movement, sapping what little strength you have left. To make matters worse, you're getting a little bit of water with every breath.

When you woke up today, not any part of you thought this was going to happen. A minute ago, you were on the shore! Now you're breathing salt water. You're now in it. For real. Full-blown panic. Every part of your brain is screaming, flashing red lights, like a submarine in a deep-sea dogfight. Every single molecule of your being, your mind, your body, your heart, and your spirit is dedicated to fighting like hell to get back to shore, to get your feet on solid ground, but the people on the beach are getting so small now, no matter how hard you struggle, it seems like help, if it does come, will be too late.

Still, even though you know it's pointless and the water is almost above your head, you keep struggling to get back to shore, to safe ground, your arms and legs kicking uselessly as you're carried out to sea. As you slip beneath the waves, the deepest part of your panicked brain is telling you, "Keep swimming. Don't give up. Whatever you do, don't give up. Don't ever give up. Keep fighting. . . ."

• • •

That's what it feels like to get caught in what lifeguards call "the Suck" otherwise known as a rip current; a powerful water flow that arises seemingly out of nowhere, pulling sand and water and anything in its path out into deeper water. They usually come in the period between high and low tide, they're the number-one cause of lifeguard rescues, and they kill close to 50 swimmers in the United

States every year. The unlucky ones perish because they panic and fight like hell to survive, which is a normal, human reaction. The lucky ones not only survive, but they thrive in the current.

> In our lives, "the Suck" can happen at any time, in a variety of ways, and usually when we least expect it.

100 Pages of Your Life

On August 6, 1926, a 21-year old American swimmer named Gertrude Ederle set out from the coast of France to swim the 21 miles across the English Channel. She learned how to swim in Highlands in central New Jersey.

On her first attempt to swim the English Channel, she was nearly halfway through the journey, when she was abruptly taken out of the water by her coach who saw her floating face down in the water and wrongly assumed that, because she was a woman, she was in distress and thereby not capable of making the swim across.

Gertrude Ederle was furious. She wasn't in distress, she was merely resting in the water. She hadn't come all that way to swim to the middle of the English Channel. She declared that if she ever set foot in French water, she wasn't going to give up until she stepped out of English water.

A year after she was pulled out of the English Channel, Gertrude Ederle returned and in 14 1/2 hours, she was the first woman to swim the English Channel. In the twelfth hour of her swim, in a nearby support boat, her new coach saw that the winds were becoming unmanageable and called out to Ederle that she should abandon her quest for greatness. She simply raised her head out of the water and asked, "What for?"

Two simple words expressed that resilient young woman's spirit. She was asking, "I've come this far. Why would I stop now?" She didn't yell. She didn't scream. She didn't need an inspiring speech. She just decided *not to quit.*

I wrote my last book, *Pivot*, in 2016. Back then, the world looked completely different than it does today. At the beginning of the book, I set out a marker that was a 50-page challenge. The reason why? Here's what I wrote at the time,

> *Because when you read 50 pages and move on, you're not just giving up on a book; you're giving up on yourself. You may not realize it, but your 50-page habit is rearing its head elsewhere. What else are you "50-paging" in your life? Are you 50-paging your relationship? Your parenting? Your health? Your finances? If you're only going two chapters deep in your life, you're only going to get two-chapter results. "Fifty-page syndrome" is just another way of saying quitting. Don't do it.*

The book you're reading now is about using your resilience to become change proof through all of life's uncertainties so you can leverage them for their creative opportunities. Change-proof resilience is about using change rather than change using you. So with that in mind, I'm setting down a new marker: 100 pages.

If you can't make it to a 100 pages, how are you going to keep yourself, your family, and your business afloat in the relentless current of the history in which we're all living? Blow past the 50 pages. Don't even think about it. Give it 100 pages. If you're willing to stick it out to the hundredth page of our story, you will find yourself becoming resilient.

CHANGE-PROOF POINT

▶ If you think about quitting, just ask yourself, What for?

PART I

Choose Change Before It Chooses You

The only way to make sense out of change is to plunge into it, move with it, and join the dance.
—ALAN WATTS

CHAPTER 1

How Change Changes Things—and What to Do About It

Making Friends with Change

We have to make friends with change.
—RAM DASS

Like the rip current, everything in life isn't always going to go according to plan. No matter how well-manicured your plans, they are going to change.

The Tao says it perfectly, "Life is a series of natural and spontaneous changes. Don't resist them; that only creates sorrow. Let reality be reality. Let things flow naturally forward in whatever way they like." That's a painful lesson I had to learn after one of the foundational success stories of my entire life.

In 2016 I wrote a book called *Pivot*, which became a bestseller. The book was about reinvention, a guide to transforming your life when your life no longer fulfills you. If you were unhappy in your work, your body, or your relationships, *Pivot* defined a path you could follow—a way to bridge the gap from where you were to where you wanted to be.

The book also described my own successful pivot from miserable and burned-out attorney to the engaged CEO of one of the world's largest personal development training companies. That was where I found myself when *Pivot* hit the shelves that spring. They were heady times, and I was on a roll. There were book signings and sold-out keynotes. Speaking engagements to thousands of people. I lectured to the Fortune 500 and shared the stage with people like Michael J. Fox, Jack Canfield, and Larry King.

And then the wind changed.

• • •

The summer after *Pivot* launched, I was in Paris for my wife Randi's fiftieth birthday. It was a beautiful place to celebrate a milestone, and we were delighted to be joined by our four adult "kids."

While we were ostensibly there to celebrate, I had a secret agenda of my own. I was coming off the end of an exhausting round of book promotions, piled on top of my ongoing job as CEO, a role in which I also ran many of the company's most critical training events. I was spent—deeply tired and desperately needing a break from work and some restorative time with my wife and kids. My secret plan was simple: enthusiastically spend magical time with my loved ones, while at the same time sleeping as much as possible to emerge rested, recharged, and restored. All without really revealing to anyone that I was teetering on the brink of burnout. Again.

• • •

Of course, it was a ridiculous plan, and I wasn't fooling anyone. Our second-born daughter Lindsay, who had just reached a milestone of her own by graduating from UCLA, called me out as we sat in a café on a beautiful Parisian street.

"Dad," she said, "I'm really worried about you. You were this miserable workaholic lawyer. You left that, and now you help people see the damage they're doing to themselves and those around them when they try to make things work that just aren't working." Lindsay is never one for beating around the bush. "Now, look at you," she continued. "You're a workaholic again. You're miserable. You're ignoring a lot of signs that this is all tougher than it ought to be. And you're the one that's oblivious to the damage."

Ouch. Lindsay's worries weren't entirely unfounded. The incident that had kick-started my pivot from lawyer to CEO had been a trip to the hospital with chest pains. (A day, I realized as I sat across from Lindsay, that was a lot like the very one we were experiencing at that moment.)

I fessed up. I told Lindsay she was right. I was working too much. My health was deteriorating again. I was becoming unhappy. "But the good news," I told her, "is that I'm an expert on reinvention. I'll sort it out."

Then I did nothing of the sort. What I did do, instead, was what I'd done as a discontented lawyer. I circled the wagons. I put my head down. I went back to working harder. Again.

A few weeks later, my wife and I were at a work retreat, and the issue came up again. We both knew things weren't working with my business partners, who didn't see eye-to-eye with me on the direction of the company. Randi and I agreed: we needed a pivot plan to exit the company.

"The good thing," I told her, "is that I'm a pivot expert. I'll sort it out." In that moment, I really believed it.

And then I immediately went back to work, doubled down, and ignored everything we'd just discussed. Again.

●　　●　　●

A few months later, I travelled to Los Angeles for a six-day business training in front of a sold-out audience. These almost weeklong events are an exhausting and adrenaline-inducing roller-coaster ride. Six days on a stage requires you to be "on" for hours at a time and that's just the time on stage. The moment you step off the stage you're in demand. Evenings are a combination of dealing with the demands of running a multimillion-dollar company, socializing with event attendees, and prepping for the next day, which usually starts before dawn with more prepping and work.

In contrast to the exhaustion, of course, is the sheer power of what's happening: people transforming right before your eyes. It's a blessing to be a part of it—a priceless gift to know that you played a small part in someone's pivot toward a life that holds true meaning for them. It was those transformations, those reinventions, that kept me going.

About halfway through the week, I got a message: my business partners from Asia were flying in to meet with me at the end of the event. When they arrived, we arranged to have lunch, and as I sat there I realized exactly why we were meeting. I remember closing my eyes for just a few seconds before the scene unfolded. I was calm and the voice inside my head just said "embrace the pivot." It took just a few minutes to clarify the details. We disagreed on the direction of the company. I was being replaced as CEO. And just like that, it was over.

I left the hotel, overwhelmed with emotion and spiritual dejection. Facing a long and lonely drive back home, I called a close friend. It turned out he was driving, too, winding his way down a mountain road in northern California. The cell service was terrible, and his voice faded in and out. I didn't even get a chance to tell him what had just happened—I could barely hear him. Abruptly, the static ended and there was a brief moment of clarity. Then, completely unprompted, he uttered the words I'd said to myself earlier that day. "Adam," I heard him say, "Embrace the pivot."

And then, like a mystery movie that suddenly goes to a commercial, the call cut out. I tried to call him back, but voicemail was all I got. I finished the long drive alone, with those now familiar words ringing in my ears. Embrace the pivot.

By the time I got home, however, I'd forgotten both the call and those words; reality had begun to set in. I walked into the house and sat alone in the dark. I thought, I'm 51. I'm getting fired. We have a mortgage. Bills. We still have kids to go through college.

What the hell am I going to do?

• • •

It was Groundhog Day, all over again. The months that followed were trying. There was the discomfort of continuing to show up at work for a time to keep the company stable and the team focused while my "exit" was sorted. Then there was the constant uncertainty of when things would officially end, what would happen next, and how we'd manage in the interim.

Strangely, the most difficult part of those months wasn't the stress of the mortgage, or the bills, or even keeping the refrigerator full. That was all very real, but it was like a surface layer of concern; underneath was a deeper anxiety that I couldn't put my finger on.

One morning it hit me. That sick feeling in my stomach wasn't really the worry about being able to provide for my family. It was the fact that I was right back where I'd started.

The more I thought about it, the crazier it seemed. I'd been an angry, overworked, unhappy attorney. Then I'd left that to become, in the end, an angry, overworked, unhappy CEO—just as my daughter had pointed out. Not only that, but during my time as CEO, I'd been ousted from the job by my so-called partners, not once, but twice.

Time and time again, it felt like I'd pivoted, reinvented myself, and then somehow wound up right back where I started.

I was on repeat. I was living in my own personal purgatory. Change. Stress. Change. Stress. Repeat.

That, I realized, was the nagging anxiety. It was that whispered voice in my head saying, why bother? You're just going to end up in the same place again.

To make things worse, I was supposed to be the "pivot guy." I was the reinvention expert. I actually wrote the book on the subject. And yet here I was, a failed example of how to do just that. It was awful. Was everything I stood for just a sham?

I spent a few miserable days in that vortex. I began to think, maybe it's true. And if so, why fight it? Why go through all the effort if the end result is the same? Why not just go back to being an attorney?

Maybe that's just how life is, I thought. You can't count on anything. Everything is transitional, like so much ethereal dust. Nothing stays the same. I was discouraged, overwhelmed, and losing hope by the day. And then things changed again.

• • •

Earlier in the year, I'd spent several days in the studio recording the audiobook version of *Pivot*. Now, I walked out the front door of my house, pressed play on my phone, and listened as my own voice said, "*Pivot: The Art and Science of Reinventing Your Career and Life*, by Adam Markel."

I nearly dropped my phone. For an author, revisiting your own words on the page can be strange. But to listen to yourself read your own book? Ugh. Moreover, there was a surreal irony to the experience. Here I was, in the middle of a pivot of my own, listening to me giving pivot advice to . . . myself.

Yet, in almost no time, the awkwardness fell away. What was at first my own voice reading a book, quickly became the words of a close advisor, a consigliere who knew me better than anyone. And so I started to walk. And I listened.

I did a lot of walking that week. I walked by myself. I walked with the dogs. I walked the beach, the trails, the streets. And through it all, I heard my own voice in my ear. By the end of the audiobook, I knew two things for sure.

The first was that, despite what my anxiety-fueled brain had been telling me, *Pivot* was something I was proud of. The book's model for change was effective. It worked. And I knew it worked because by the end of the book, I had a plan in place. I wasn't a sham, a fake, or a snake oil salesman. This approach to change was something I really, truly believed.

The second thing I knew was that I needed to write another book. One that would deal not with planned, predictable, and infrequent change, but one that would help people build resilience in the face of rapid, near-constant change. One that could help inoculate them against what I was beginning to think of as a whole new kind of pivot.

As 2019 drew to a close, I did not fully realize how true that would be.

On Guard: The Problem with Chronic Change

I'm far from the only one to feel the winds of change. You've almost certainly felt them too. If you're "normal," which is to say you're human, you've probably experienced a few of these feelings lately:

- Anxiety about the future of your job or business
- A feeling of increasing workload and/or decreasing time
- Worry for the future of your children or other loved ones
- Difficulty sleeping, relaxing, or enjoying downtime
- A lack of purpose or drive
- Inability to "keep up" with new tech and social changes

With rare exception, almost everyone I speak to experiences feelings of unease or anxiety in one form or another. In my work with thousands of people around the world, however, I've noted a singular, significant change in those feelings. Rather than occurring during periods of significant change—a job change, a divorce, or a new business—those feelings now seem to be a near-daily part of life. Once upon a time, for example, it was typical to hold one career your entire life. In recent decades, we began to come to terms with the fact that we might pivot once, or even twice. Now? Career and business pivots are becoming less an event and more a steady state. Remember the old saying, "the only certainties in life are death and taxes"? You can now add "change" to the list. Uncertainty has become the new certainty.

Change has become chronic. That poses a dilemma for good ol' *Homo sapiens* like us. As you'll see in the pages that follow, chronic uncertainty is something that we don't tolerate well. We're wired to seek certainty—to fill gaps, understand, and predict. And when we can't, there are consequences—in particular, stress. From stress, as night follows the day, comes sickness.

Now, stress and its associated challenges are piling up all around us. We're neck deep in change, and the tide is heading the wrong way.

Embracing Change

Pivot offered a solution for part of this problem. It was about how to make big changes, and it focused on creating a deliberate "plan B" for the seismic shifts in life—the things that we might experience only a handful of times. The pivot when you change jobs. The pivot when you emerge from the ruins of an old relationship and begin something new. The pivot when your startup runs out of runway and you need to reinvent your business for a new market before the next payroll.

Those pivots are not always predictable, but they do tend to share some common traits:

1. They're often a big deal. They're a significant sea-change in business and life. They have epic consequences. They're job changes, partner changes, business changes, health changes.
2. They're highly visible. As a result of their relative impact, you can see them. You can't always predict them, but there's a tangibility to the cancer, the firing, the failure, the divorce, and the corresponding recovery, job search, reinvention, and new relationship.
3. They happen infrequently. There are only so many monumental career changes, partner changes, and business changes in life. They're pivot points in our path that send us off on a new phase in life.

They are, in short, big, loud life and business changes. They're what I think of as macro pivots—large, loud, and less common.

But I was beginning to discover this other type of pivot, the micro pivots, and they shared their own set of common, yet nearly opposite traits:

1. They're often small. Micro pivots are made of things that were often unnoticeable. Tiny things. Minor slights, bits and pieces of negative news, unexpected expenses or obligations. Small things that send a day or a week in an unpredictable direction.
2. They can be hard to identify. Often, these things were hard to pin down. "I might lose my job in the restructuring next month" is a tangible, real uncertainty. A vague but persistent sense of anxiety, on the other hand, is abstract and hard to diagnose.
3. They happen all the time. These tiny micro pivots weren't occasional. They happened every day, often many times. They were frequent and chronic.

Don't let their size fool you. These little pivots—the constant demands to make decisions and take action in the face of change—stack up big. They can compound into one long infinite pivot—a state of what feels like near constant, uncontrollable change that can erode your health, wealth, and happiness.

These two types of pivots—the micro and the macro—require a shift in how we tackle changes, one that mirrors a shift in how change is happening in the real world. We're now faced with not just pivoting by design, by creating an intentional, deliberately created plan B for our personal and professional lives, but also pivoting by default: learning to manage near-constant change in a sort of moment-to-moment ongoing pivot.

Those two pivots are very different. One requires deliberate and well-executed planning, and the type of clarity and momentum I described in *Pivot*—a skill set that we still need and always will.

The second, however, requires something different altogether. It requires that we develop an awareness and mindset not just for tackling constant and unexpected change, but as Ram Dass says, for making friends with it.

As true as "embrace the pivot" is, it's not complete, not nearly complete. Why? Because 2020 happened. A global, macro pivot for humanity that required daily micro pivots of us all. The most uncertain year in decades. The year the uncertainty wasn't selective about who it touched. The year everything we knew or thought we knew got sucked out to sea. As 2019 gave way to 2020, none of us had any awareness of what was about to happen to our global community. I know that I didn't.

A friend of mine has an eight-year-old son and one day, not long ago, he asked his son how he would remember this year and how he will someday describe it to his children. His son thought for a moment and then he said, "I won't. I'm going to forget about 2020 as soon as I can."

*It's your reaction to adversity, not adversity itself
that determines how your life's story will develop.*
—DIETER F. UCHTDORF

Every New Year's Eve, if we're able to, we host an intimate party at our house. It's our ritual for ending one year and beginning another. It grounds us as a family but also lets us express our gratitude for the people in our lives who make us who we are. New Year's Eve 2019 was a magical time. Remember how you felt that night? Do you remember where you were? Who you were with? What you were eating? Drinking? What music were you listening to? Whom did you kiss at midnight? Given all that's happened since then, it's hard to remember, isn't it?

On December 31, 2019, Randi and I were gathered with a group of family and close friends. As we do every year, we were indoors, and telling stories, playing music, singing, and laughing into the night. On occasions like this, we hug, we kiss, and dance. Maybe we pray together or cry, if someone's experienced a uniquely painful year.

The point is, no matter what we do, the guiding principle is loved ones together indoors touching and breathing together. It's a simple but necessary expression of joy that most of us, if we're lucky, participate in every year with our communities. We commune together. We share a spiritual experience just by being together.

That New Year's Eve night at the end of 2019, as the clock struck midnight, Randi and I, in our own way, lit a candle to curse the darkness. We celebrated the fact that we get to be souls in human bodies having this amazing journey together.

Little did we know that this would be the last time for a long time that we would be able to do this simple act. Little did we know how much we were taking it for granted at the time. It feels like it happened a decade ago.

For Dr. Peter Nieman, the turning of the year from 2019 to 2020 would be worse than everything that would follow. On January 1, 2020, he and his wife discovered the body of their son, Ben, who ended his life after a long battle with depression. I was blessed to be able to speak to Peter at length about how he and his wife, Corrine, were able to move on after such a tragic loss.

This is what he said:

> *When we lose a spouse, a child, or a leg, or whatever we may lose, can we grow from it? Can we let it develop? Can we make that choice? I often think of how I would define resilience.*
>
> *I got it one morning again when I was running. It was such a beautiful day. The birds were singing. Where I live, if I look to the west, I look at the Canadian Rockies. I was running next to a body of water. I looked up, there was the moon setting toward the east. I thought about this. Here I am training for my next marathon, and this is a mental marathon we're going through. The definition for me of resilience is to train our mind. We have that choice to train our mind, to have the capacity, almost like fitness. Do I have the capacity to stay strong and to continue this thing, and to move forward? When life gives us what we didn't want or didn't choose?*

I can't get over how beautifully Peter phrased this. Here I was, complaining about this or that, falling down bad news rabbit holes, bemoaning yet another Zoom call, and this man faced the worst nightmare a parent can imagine. Every child is a miracle. I have four children. Until 2020, so did Peter. Now he had lost one to depression. What if that happened to me? How would I survive?

I honestly didn't know. But then, it occurred to me: despite the abyss of pain he was sitting on top of, he found a way to make meaning out of it. In the short term, Peter and Corinne had experienced the kind of short-term tragedy and upheaval that exists only in our worst dreams. And yet, they could see their loss within a long-term context. They could find their way because they fixed their eyes on the horizon and allowed the loss of their child to find meaning in their lives and in their hearts.

That's what we all need. Meaning. But where do we find it? And once we find it, how do we keep it so that it's a light for us in our darkest moments? How can Peter's experience inspire and challenge us to make meaning out of this terrible time when we've faced so much uncertainty? How can we look beyond the short-term problems and challenges that drag us down every single day and instead see ourselves and our lives in a long-term way? How do we run marathons in a culture that constantly demands that we sprint? How do we survive the rip current?

And then a word Peter used jumped out at me there in the context of his loss and the losses we've all faced in the past year—*resilience*. Resilience is what we mean when we speak about being change proof in our lives and in our business. In *Pivot*, the word that kept coming up again and again, without me realizing it, was *resilience*. For me, resilience is about how to take all the uncertainty, the pain, the loss, and the upheaval and turn that into something better. To make it mean something. That's when I realized what book I needed to write. In effect, I was already writing it, I just didn't know it yet.

Peter Nieman and the events of 2020 taught me that resilience is the energy that fuels the "big P" pivots and our micro pivots as well. It's where the literal rip current becomes the metaphor that can bring us to the moment where we truly become change proof.

For most of the last year, it's as though we've been swimming our lungs out, but the safety of the beach just gets farther and farther away. We feel like we're losing contact with who we used to be. We feel exhausted, burned-out, and worst of all, isolated, from our communities and ourselves. With our faces covered, we're lonely and anonymous in familiar neighborhood streets.

We've been terrified that we're a danger to our families and our friends. Friends and strangers alike might be carrying a deadly airborne disease. The world feels like it's changing fast, too fast, for us to keep up. Every day, reading the onslaught of news is like drinking water from a fire hose.

We've had the global pandemic that changed *every* aspect of all of our lives; we've been through a summer of racial unrest unlike anything we've seen since the 1960s; we've lost people close to us and even if we haven't, we've had a running tally of the sick and the dead in the bottom corner of the newscast; food lines stretch for miles; we've had to work from home on Zoom calls while our children go to class on their own computers; we can't even leave the house without a mask; then when we do, we have to pass the boarded-up businesses of folks who've lost everything. As normalized as these things have become, it seems like we're living in a surreal kind of dream.

We want to wake up. We want the strange distortion of reality to be over so we can just get back to normal. We want to be back on the beach. We want things to be the way they used to be.

But they're not. Over the course of 2020, the strangest year of our lives, we've seen suicidal ideation go up among the young; alcohol consumption has spiked, along with recreational drug use; our social support systems have gone dormant; and there's almost no difference between our work lives and our home lives. Dividing us from each other, our leaders have failed to keep us informed, safe, and alive. On and on, the current keeps swirling.

That's why we need to discover what resilience is and how to discover it within our hearts, minds, bodies, and spirits so that it doesn't just get us through this time, but through the rest of time.

• • •

I've felt battered by what's come at us. I'll bet you have too. That's why you're holding this book. Physically, mentally, emotionally, and spiritually, we're running on empty and the engine lights are blinking red. It's like we've had to survive a rip current in a hurricane.

And yet that's not the end of the story. Not even close. In spite of what we've lost, we're finding grace and hope in the unlikeliest places. Now, as the storm clouds dissipate and the sun begins to shine again, we feel the faint stirrings of hope. Hope that we're finally through the worst of it. We hope we are resilient.

But even though the storm has moved off, we're left with the damage. We have to pick up the pieces of our lives and we know we have to put them back together again, we just don't know where to start.

Canadian philosopher and author Matshona Dhliwayo writes, "The storm only comes to teach you how to skillfully sail your ship." If the present has taught us anything, it's that we're all facing the same storm, but we're all in a different boat. Some are in huge, indestructible aircraft carriers, some are in luxury yachts, some are in elegant sailboats, some are in leaky rowboats, while still others are adrift on a floating piece of wreckage. We know what the storm looks like now. The question for us is not, "How do I survive the storm?" The question is, "How do I thrive?"

Make no mistake, 2020 was a difficult year for every single person on the planet, but it's not the last challenging year we'll face. We need to be seaworthy. We need to leverage uncertainty and find the creative opportunity within it. We need to be resilient.

That's the resilience journey we're going to take in this book. You may be reading this by yourself, but we're going to take that journey together.

CHANGE-PROOF POINT

▶ To make friends with change, you must learn how to identify and manage the small, often hard-to-see micro pivots that occur every day.

CHAPTER 2

~~~~~~

Got Your Back

Lifeguard Lessons

*Whomsoever you see in distress, recognize
in them a fellow human being.*
—ROYAL LIFE SAVING SOCIETY MOTTO

Remember the movie *Top Gun?* The truth is, it bothers me at a level I don't quite understand: that this big, bold, loud, brassy 1980s popcorn flick about fighter planes and jingoistic American culture is now considered, by the youth of today as kind of slow, cheesy, and retrograde.

To me, it's Kenny Loggins, beach volleyball, and never leaving your wingman. It reminds me of being young. It especially reminds me of the fundamental refrain that's the story's theme: You never leave your wingman. I'll say it again: You never. Leave. Your wingman. Cheesy as it is, it's got a key lesson for us in the world of business.

Let's be blunt. You're a business leader. You're in the C-suite. You sit at the big desk making the big decisions. You've got an ego. Of course you do. Otherwise, how would you be where you are? You're used to going it alone. You're used to the idea that your ideas are the best ideas and if everyone just followed them, then your company would be at the top of the big board on Wall Street.

• • •

I've been insanely lucky in my life, endlessly blessed, to meet and talk to some of the most interesting people in the world. No matter where they come from, without fail, all of them have been teachers and mentors to me.

But none of it would have been possible without the foundational knowledge and experience I got on the summer shores of Long Island with the greatest crew of men and women I've ever had the pleasure of working with. It was a diverse group of people from every kind of background. Lawyers, teachers, emergency medical technicians (EMTs), and insurance salespeople. Careerwise, these were all folks committed to lifeguarding while they were simultaneously committed to something else. Even New York City firefighters would come out and work with us on the days they were off from the firehouse.

They took me in, treated me as one of their own from the first time I stepped onto the beach as a young man, with no experience, trying to earn a few extra dollars before going off to my second year of college in the fall.

I was 19. It was my first summer on the crew. I'd avoided the least challenging assignment, the pool. Nobody wanted that. You just slathered your nose in white lotion, put on a big hat, and stowed your whistle for the day. Without rescues to run, the only real challenge in the pool was staying awake.

Despite my rookie status, I'd scored the plum assignment of a chair in Field 4 known as the Central Mall. There were six fields at Jones Beach, each about a half a mile long. We dealt with all kinds of crazy stuff. Lost children. Drug overdoses. There could be fights. Drunks who overestimated their ability to swim. We had to be ready for anything. And that was just on the land.

In the Atlantic, we had thousands of people in the water at any given point in time, on a weekend. A hundred thousand people on the beach and thousands of people in the water. When the waves were strong, when the rip currents were springing up like weeds, we would have to make rescues every hour. Sometimes we'd easily make more than 100 rescues in a day.

These were serious rescues. We'd get in the water when we could tell when swimmers weren't at their best. We called them "Stones," which isn't the nicest name, but we got adept at spotting them and keeping them safe before they knew they were in danger. We got used to the look on their faces, a combination of a little bit of panic and a little bit of uncertainty. It was usually the overconfident guys who got out a little too deep for their skill level.

On a rescue, we would swim sideways, parallel to the shore to get out of that rip current. We would get in there with buoys and sometimes other equipment like surfboards and move masses of people. Often, people were panicking. You'd have to get people calm and get them on that life preserver. Sometimes you'd have to get your arms around them. It was a dangerous situation.

The most dangerous part of the rescue is when you first get to the swimmer and they're scared and embarrassed, and they don't want to lose face in front of their friends. At that moment it's possible for them to take you down with them. Like a stone. Hence the name. I was there for seven years in total and we did it successfully every single time—except one.

One awful time that rocked our worlds and changed my life forever.

It was a day like any other. There wasn't anything particularly foreboding. We were simply running our hour shifts: an hour on the stand and an hour down. That's how we maintained our focus. I was off the stand at the time, grabbing a quick bite to eat and a chat about the Yankees when I heard three whistle blasts. Then three again. More insistent this time. Our adrenaline spiked—three blasts meant someone was missing. As I ran to the shoreline I saw the one thing that strikes fear in the heart of every lifeguard—a crowd of people pointing at the water. Nothing good comes from that.

Our crew leader, Bob, sent us into the surf in a line perpendicular to the shore. I had only a month's experience at that point, but I knew what we had to do. In our line, we dove down, more than 10 feet into the swirling current to search for the missing swimmer. Down, search, up. Down, search, up. It was exhausting work. But we kept going for more than an hour.

We didn't find him.

Bob gave a single blast, calling us back in, even though none of us wanted to admit defeat. We didn't want it to be real. In our hearts we knew the truth, but we were still holding out for a miracle. Bob gave the blast again. One by one, our legs and lungs spent, we trudged onto the sand. Our hands and our hearts were empty.

I was just a kid, still in my teens, and I hadn't even had a full summer on the lifeguarding crew. I honestly questioned if this was for me, if I wanted to keep going. On the faces of the adults on the crew, I saw the same sentiment. As a crew, our mantra was, "No one goes down on our watch." That's the lifeguarding code. If you lose someone, you're no good to anyone. For us, it wasn't just a mantra, it was a way of living. But in reality, for most of us, death was an abstraction. Something you knew was real but didn't think about. Now, on a hot July day, death was a cold reality sitting on our hearts.

Before we closed the beach for the day, Bob gathered us together as a crew. We stood in a circle, but unable to meet each other's eyes. I was afraid I was going to start crying myself. At that moment, I felt like a little kid. I just wanted to go home. To curl up in bed and just forget about the whole thing.

Bob had us close our eyes. We paused and stood in silence for as long as we could, accepting the responsibility for what happened, and honoring the memory of the life that had just been cruelly snatched out of the world.

Then Bob spoke. He told us we had to learn something from this horrible experience. To make sure no one went down on our watch again, we would have to be impeccable. And the only way we could do that was if we had each other's backs. We had to ask ourselves some tough questions to know if we had really done everything we could do.

And then he said, "No one goes down on our watch." I have to admit, I was slightly perplexed. Someone had gone down on our watch. Maybe it wasn't our fault. But it happened. Was it all just a lie?

Sensing our wavering confidence, Bob said it again, with emphasis, "No one. Goes down. On. Our Watch." I'm leaving out at least two salty F-bombs. We knew what he meant. Just because something tragic happened, just because the unthinkable happened, we still had a job to do. If we were going to do it to the best of our ability, we had to choose to move forward together—as one. We had to have each other's backs.

It occurred to me much later that just because we lost someone in the water, it didn't make our mantra any less true. It made it more so. We had to own our failures just as we had to own our success. Truth is truth, no matter what happens. On the beach that day, Bob taught me an important lesson that I'll never forget: you can't change what happens, but you can change how you respond to it. We came together and made a choice.

As lifeguards, we had to be at 100 percent all the time or we risked someone drowning. To do that, we practiced what I now refer to as resilience training. We would work an hour on the stand in a very intense, focused way, sometimes making rescues. Then other lifeguards would spell us for an hour so we could take a break, eat, swim, run, or just relax.

Switching back and forth between intense activity, focused performance, and periods of rest and recovery is how we build muscle in strength training. It's also how we build resilience.

I imagine many of you in whatever it is you're doing, whether it's a part of your personal life and the rituals of personal activities or it's in connection specifically with business or entrepreneurship, you have to have tremendous staying power. To be successful in the long term, you have to be prepared to leverage uncertainty.

CHANGE-PROOF POINT

▶ Every time you've got someone else's back, you build up more and more resilience for yourself.

CHAPTER 3

The Change-Proof Model
Pause, Ask, Choose

In a chronically leaking boat, energy devoted to changing vessels is more productive than energy devoted to patching leaks.
—WARREN BUFFETT

Over the years, I've built a very consistent ritual into my mornings, a simple series of practices that I do almost every day. They ground me and help me prepare, mentally, emotionally, and spiritually, for the day ahead. There's one ritual that I cannot miss, no matter what. That ritual always begins the same way: I sit up in bed each morning, I put my feet on the floor, and I say, "I love my life."

Over time, that ritual has transformed from a ritual into something almost automatic. It's a habit. Even on days when I'm swirling down the vortex of indecision, I still wake up in the morning and almost without thinking, say, "I love my life." In the weeks after I was replaced as CEO, in spite of the rootless despair I was feeling, I still said it. But like all habits, that was only going to last for so long.

One morning, just after my feet landed on the floor, I wondered for the first time if it was actually still true. I paused. And I asked myself, "Am I just saying it, or do I truly love my life? Am I just covering up for something deeper?"

The answer came immediately. Yes. I knew I loved my life. Just not all of it.

But if that was true, if I truly in a harmonious way loved my life, then I had to love my entire life. The ups and downs. The unexpected twists and turns and roadblocks. For better and for worse, as my wife and I had told each other in our wedding vows.

Then just as a precaution, I stayed in that place, grounding myself. I tried to imagine myself waking up in the morning and saying, "I love the good parts of my life, but everything else sucks and I hate it." I wanted no part of that. Because it wasn't honest. Even though I was expressing love for my life, I was taking those words for granted. Just like we do with our family and friends sometimes. We say, "I love you." We say it without thinking. We say it without living it.

On the edge of my bed that morning, I knew I had to go all the way and really love my life, perceived warts and all. I had to take the bad times with the good. I had to look change in the face, and I had to choose to embrace my life in its fullness. I had to choose to love life more than my precious ego.

It was just four simple words that integrated with what had begun on that tragic day at the beach, and added themselves to my friend on the phone in the mountains, saying, "embrace the pivot." Years and moments all came crashing together in my mind, my heart, my spirit, and my body. And then, clear as a bell, I heard three words. Those three moments in time equaled three words, the three words that would become the entire thesis for this book: Pause. Ask. Choose.

For me, amid all the uncertainty of 2020, those three words were the turning point. It was, in the parlance of the book *Pivot*, my "big-D decision," a moment of clarity characterized by commitment and action.

If I couldn't outswim uncertainty, if I couldn't avoid change, and I couldn't always plan for it, then I had one remaining choice. I would learn how to embrace it. I had to take all the uncertainty the world was facing and find a key to unlock it.

I waited. I wanted to see if it was real or just a product of my own anxiety. Maybe I misheard the voice in my head. I closed my eyes and focused on my breath. For a few breaths nothing happened. And then I saw them. This time I saw them in my mind, three bright white words in block letters emerging from a field of darkness: *Pause. Ask. Choose.*

I didn't fully realize it at the time, but I had experienced the three-part pause, ask, choose sequence 30-plus years earlier. It was what Captain Bob had our lifeguarding crew do the day someone got sucked into a rip current and disappeared on our watch. In the moments that followed that awful event, he broke it down into those three stages that helped us bond together and move forward as a team. That's the DNA code of this entire book. It's the basic building block of the kind of resilience we need to stay change proof in this world (and the next).

Coincidentally, if you're ever swimming in the ocean and you find that you're caught in a rip current, then this tool at the very least will help you get back to the shore. So rather than a story that your friends tell about you for the rest of their lives, it'll be a story you tell your friends for the rest of yours. Then you can tell them that this book literally saved your life.

Pause

Caught in a rip current, with alarm bells clanging through your head and heart, it's a natural human impulse to swim, to fight what's happening. You're out to sea so you swim to shore. Easy, right?

The thing about the rip current is there's nothing you can do about it. Literally. There's nothing you can do. You don't know when it'll pop up and once you're in it, you do not, I promise you, have the swimming ability to fight the movement of the ocean. Even an Olympic gold medalist like Michael Phelps or Kate Ledecky couldn't swim through that. And that's the point: it doesn't matter how hard you work, it doesn't matter how hard you fight against a rip current, you are not going to win. In this case, your effort is not going to save you. In fact, the opposite is true: your continued effort will kill you.

So what do you do? Easy. You stop fighting. I can hear you saying to yourself, "Wait a minute. Stop? If I stop, then I'll die."And you'd be right. It is true, yes, if you do nothing, you will die. In this case, the pause is not about "doing nothing" when you're in the Suck. It's about having an awareness of how much energy you're expending and how little it's getting you. It's like they say, "If you keep doing what you're doing, you'll keep getting what you're getting." In life, sometimes more hard work isn't going to get you where you want to go. It's the effort that's killing you.

It's counterintuitive, but you have to pause. You have to know at that moment that the first thing you do is stop what you're doing. It's the hardest thing to do, to take that pause, because the risk is so great. It goes against millions of years of human evolution. Again, it's that voice in your lizard brain telling you that survival is the only option. I'm here to tell you that it isn't.

That day at Jones Beach the day a swimmer went down on our beach, we were rocked. Bob knew we could just leave the beach as individuals, making our lonely way home, each in our way, trying to piece our feelings back together. He could have said, "They're adults. They know the nature of this job. It happens.

Chalk it up and live to fight another day." He could have left us to stew in our own juices. He knew we already were.

Like all true leaders Bob didn't do that. He stopped us. He made us gather together in a circle. The pause, the circle, was about recovering what we had lost. In this case, it was the loss of life. What Bob recognized though was the more insidious loss, was the potential loss of confidence. If we lost our confidence as a crew, it could have long-term effects that could end up leading to more accidents. We needed to pause, to reflect, so we could learn together and move forward.

The context that Captain Bob established that day was one built on learning, not punishment. It was being part of a "watch your back" versus a "got your back" environment—a culture of leadership based in trust. Bob trusted that we could learn the lessons and grow in the process and that long term we'd all be better for it.

As a leader, when there's adversity, you're going to have the impulse to point fingers. Find the person responsible and assign blame. But the way forward for tomorrow's leaders isn't to create or perpetuate cultures of fear and resistance, but to cultivate learning. Growing, individually and organizationally, requires learned lessons, not punishment. We have to adapt. And *adaptation* is just another word for *learning*. The pause gives us the space to reset and learn.

For many, today, 2020 maybe was the worst year in memory. An airborne virus put a pause on everything. Sports, movies, school, work, bars, and restaurants. We had no choice but to "shelter in place" for an indefinite period of time. We can't act like that didn't happen. And really, there's no benefit in blame. It happened. It's been rough. Now what? If we're going to come out of this truly change proof, then we have to acknowledge what happened and reset ourselves to grow from it. We have to pause and learn.

Ask

Once you pause in the Suck, then you have only just begun to live. After you stop struggling against the current, the next step, the ask, is where you determine exactly how you live. It's a simple procedure, all you have to do is lift your feet and float on your back. That's all. The current will take you where it wants to. That's what you do when you ask. This is where we find purpose. Or to be more specific, this is where you frame the meaning of what you're experiencing.

As the leader of our lifeguarding crew, Bob didn't ask a question. He made a statement. Twice. A statement he expected us to hear. "No one goes down on our watch." One simple, declarative statement. That was all he had to say. And though it wasn't a question, it created a space for us to ask the questions we needed to ask ourselves about what happened and what we were going to do about it. By creating space for us, he charged us with filling that space with accountability. It was our chance to reset.

That's what living through a pandemic has done to us too. Maybe you've lost loved ones. Maybe you lost your business. Maybe you're struggling to work from home and teach your children at the same time. Maybe you've been socially distant and isolated from your community. Whatever it is, no matter how bad, how ugly, or how tragic it is, our resilience journey is about coming to terms with the fact that fate or God or the creative force that binds the universe together or, heck, even random chance is looking at us and saying, "No one goes down on our watch."

The question is, "What are we going to do about it?"

Choose

So you're in the Suck and you've done the first two steps. You stopped struggling against the current, you lifted your feet, and now you're floating on your back looking at the sky. What now?

The rip current you're riding is moving perpendicular to the shore, moving fast, but it's not going to take you out into the shipping lanes. The top of it is swirling in concentric circles outward from the flow of the water, like a fountain, so that means it'll spit you out eventually. All you have to do is ride the movement, stay above water on your back, and trust that the current will eventually release its grip.

So what do you do? Relax your body, your breathing. Recover your energy. You'll need it for the swim home. When it spits you out, swim parallel to the beach, and as you're able, make your way back to safety. Instead of the rip current happening to you, now you're happening with it. Again, it's the difference between resistence and growth. You're being resilient.

That's the lesson Captain Bob taught us that day. He made us pause, gathered us as a unit to acknowledge the tragedy that had happened, charged us with accountability, and then sent us home.

That night, I remember lying in my bed, looking up at the ceiling, trying to put together the pieces of the day. I was trying to see if there was something I could have done differently. Or better. If only I had been in the right place at the right time. Maybe I could have saved a life. Wasn't that what I was there for?

And then I thought about it more closely. I was only 19. This was way beyond my pay grade. Naively, I thought that being a lifeguard meant I'd look cool on the beach, get a great tan, meet some interesting people, and maybe chat up some girls. At the very least, I'd earn some good money to take back to college with me in the fall. That was as far as I had thought about the entire experience. In no way did I think I was going to be confronted with the reality of death. When you're young, death is as distant a reality as Saturn's rings. The truth is I wasn't prepared for what happened that day at Jones Beach and the thought of going back there made my stomach drop.

Then I realized the gift that I'd been given by Captain Bob. He left the decision to all of us. He left the ball in my court. That meant I had to choose to get in my little red car and drive out of the city to Jones Beach the next morning. If I wanted to avoid confronting my own failures or weaknesses, then that was my right. If I wanted to face them, the members of the team, and Bob, then that was also within my power. The point is it was my choice. No one else was going to do it for me.

So that's what I did. I woke with the dawn, had a quick breakfast, got in my little old Honda Prelude, and I went back to work. Everyone else did too.

For seven summers after that one day, that awful day in July, when I was only 19 years old, we never lost anybody again. That's a pretty impeccable track record. It was a testament to the fact that we can continue to do something for any length of time and not just do it and complete it, but complete it at a very high level. We could achieve a gold medal level of performance because we faced adversity in the circle together.

That's where we find ourselves as we crawl out of the wreckage of Covid-19. We lie in our beds, trying to put the pieces of normality back together, spinning in the fear, anxiety, and despair that we feel dragging us down into the depths. We might be worried about money, family, our health, and the things we used to depend on to get us through the dark times that have gone away.

It's our right to drown. It is every human's right to control their own destiny. For good or ill. Or we can stand up, look each other in the face, and choose to be resilient. We can pause, ask, and choose. Taken together, the three steps of the model give us a simple, repeatable formula for becoming a resilient agent of change, instead of a victim of it.

So much of the philosophy of resilience is about bouncing *back* because that's literally what the word means. A substance is resilient if it has the ability to return to its original state. But with this simple tool, we'll be able to bounce *forward* more like a slingshot that uncoils with greater velocity.

In the next section we'll learn more about change-proof resilience, what it is, and how it's integrated into the four most important realms of our human experience.

CHANGE-PROOF POINTS

▶ To pause is counterintuitive, but necessary because that's how you reset the space where you're making change as opposed to change making you.

▶ The ask is where you reframe the opportunity to ride the wave of change instead of fighting it.

▶ The choose is where you ritualize your recovery for higher performance in the future.

PART II

Becoming
Change Proof

CHAPTER 4

The Power of Choice

Leveraging Your Relationship to Change and Stress

*When I look back on all these worries, I remember
the story of the old man who said on his
deathbed that he had had a lot of trouble in
his life, most of which had never happened.*
—WINSTON S. CHURCHILL

Meet Josh. He's in his late thirties and works as a midlevel executive for an enterprise software company. He's married, with a daughter in grade school, and a nice suburban home. Josh isn't so different from a million other white-collar professional dads. He has a moderate commute—tolerable on a good day, terrible on a bad one—and not only is his job demanding, but his clients and direct reports span enough time zones that his workday, in reality, lasts about 16 hours.

Weekends, Josh is "off," but that time is often spent playing chauffeur and coach for his daughter, catching up on work around the house, trying to stay connected with their other on-the-treadmill friends, and inevitably, sneaking in some work—reviewing contract bids, catching up on email, delegating, and the like.

Josh actually loves his job. But for about the last five years, he has been feeling, in his words, "stretched thin." The competitive landscape of the software business is changing quickly. He's not sleeping like he used to. He occasionally wakes up in the middle of the night worried about money, work, and the seemingly endless list of things he has to do. Lately, those worries seem to have been compounded by less concrete troubles. Is the world going to hell? What's going on with the economy? Does his daughter have a future ahead of her?

Last week, for the first time, he went to see a counselor. His wife suggested it after she found Josh sitting in his car in the garage, on the verge of tears—for reasons he couldn't seem to articulate. The counselor seems to think he might need an antidepressant. Josh and his wife both think it's crazy for Josh to take medication—after all, their life is amazing. They're so fortunate. Shouldn't they just feel grateful and enjoy it? How can Josh be depressed when they have everything they wanted?

The trouble is they're not enjoying it. Josh hasn't told his wife, but he's suffering even more than he's let on. His heart sometimes races for no reason, and he's short of breath. His stomach is bothering him. He occasionally has fits of rage during his commute. For Josh, life feels out of control and increasingly less hopeful.

Now meet Emma. Like Josh, she's pushing 40. She has twins—a boy and a girl—and a partner. They live in a neighborhood not so different from Josh's. A different city, but remarkably similar in many ways.

Emma runs a small business with 20 employees. It's been, in her words, her "third baby" for the better part of a decade. She's heavily invested in that third baby in time, money, and emotion.

Like Josh, Emma is fitting a lot into the week. Her business—a boutique consulting firm for companies bidding on large government contracts—has a lot of moving parts and requires a lot of hustle to keep the lights on. She's been trying to grow it enough to hire someone to take on some of her managerial duties, but it hasn't been easy. Instead, like Josh, she uses early mornings, evenings, and weekends to squeeze out extra work in between hustling the twins from here to there and keeping the family train on the tracks.

The business is highly uncertain. It has grown steadily, but there have been times when they've been close to the financial brink, and every federal election signals another potential change in the wind that could, with a swipe of the pen, wipe out everything that Emma and her partner have worked to accomplish.

But the strange thing is this: for all the stress and uncertainty, for all the endless to-dos and late nights and long drives, Emma feels *alive*. She loves it. She doesn't always sleep as long as she'd like, but she sleeps *well*. Like a baby. For Emma, life is like choosing your own adventure, one day at a time.

Emma and Josh. The same . . . yet different. They have similar financial lives. Their days have similar rhythms. They both get seven 24-hour days, and they use them in remarkably similar ways. They both have heavy demands on their time—both personally and professionally. They face similar levels of uncertainty in their work.

Same busy schedules. Same financial burdens. Same work pressures. In all of the typical areas that we associate with *stress*, Emma and Josh are strikingly similar, and so it comes as a shock to discover how differently they *feel*. Emma, by all accounts, is thriving. Josh, on the other hand, is barely *surviving*. If you gave Emma an eighth day in the week, she'd give you a high-five and rush to the office or take the twins swimming. If you gave Josh an extra day, he'd use it to curl up in the fetal position. What's going on?

To answer why Emma is so successful in the face of uncertainty and change, and Josh isn't, we first have to understand what uncertainty and change really mean for us in the first place.

Change = Uncertainty = Stress

It's been almost a century and a half since the first telephone line and switchboard were created. That early system, a miracle of its time, allowed people to talk to one another in real time, without being within earshot. As remarkable and world-changing as it was, however, it still took almost 75 more years to put phones into the homes of 50 million people. That's a long time. Consider cell phones; they hit the same user milestone in just 12 years. And things only sped up from there. The Internet? It connected 50 million users in just seven years. Facebook did it in three.

There are a number of forces driving this rapid change—among other things Moore's law (the doubling of transistors in a circuit every two years), Metcalfe's law (the exponential increase of a network's value as it grows), and simple population growth. They all point to the pace of change accelerating. Your sense that change is speeding up is well-founded.

But the fact that we can explain change doesn't mean we tolerate it. The problem with all this rapid and ubiquitous change is that it's *stressful*. As a species, we're wired at a neurological level to be on guard for change. Why? Because change means uncertainty. We have a deep-rooted drive to make sense of things and predict the future. We like to know where our next meal is coming from, and whether that noise in the bush is something we can eat or something that can eat *us*. When we can't fill in all the blanks—in times of change, in other words—our brains respond, often as if our survival is on the line.

One study looked at how fearful test subjects were of an electric shock. The subjects who *knew* they were getting a more intense shock showed less fear than those who thought they might get a milder shock but didn't know for sure. Another study asked participants to play a computer game in which they overturned rocks and were given an electric shock when a snake appeared. Similar to the first study, stress levels increased with uncertainty. When it comes to change, it seems we're wired up to get fired up. We often respond to uncertainty as if we're in danger. We get *stressed*.

Like me, you might feel at first that this idea of change-equals-stress doesn't quite ring true. What about good changes? Things like love, and great jobs, and shiny new houses?

Those things may be wonderful, but they can be just as uncertain. Consider, for example, that while moving to a new home, starting a new job, getting married, and having a child often top the list for life goals for many people, those same things often land in the list of reported top most stressful changes in life as well. Whether change is big or small, positive or negative, it almost always comes hand in hand with uncertainty. And that stresses out our brains.

We know from the science that Josh and Emma are experiencing stress as a result of uncertainty. Yet that still doesn't tell us why Josh is considering medication and Emma is eagerly looking ahead to even more challenges.

A Different Look at Stress

In 2013, health psychologist Kelly McGonigal took the stage at TED and described the results of a study in the United States that was not only counter to what most of us believe about stress, but also helps explain the Josh and Emma paradox.

The study tracked adults for eight years, and asked them, among other things, two questions:

1. "How much stress have you experienced in the last year?"
2. "Do you believe that stress is harmful for your health?"

Then when all was said and done, the researchers checked to see who was still alive after eight years. (No one ever said stress research was cheerful.) As expected, people who reported a lot of stress in the previous year, based on the first question, had an increased risk of dying—a whopping 43 percent increased risk, to be specific. If you watched the TED talk, at this point you were probably, like me, nodding along, and thinking, "Yep. Makes sense. Stress is bad. It's so bad it *kills* you."

Then McGonigal dropped the bomb. It turns out that the increased risk of dying was only true for people who actually thought stress was harmful. The people who, based on the second question, didn't believe stress was harmful, had no increased risk of dying. In fact, they had a lower risk of death than anyone in the study, even people with low reported stress!

The *perception* of stress, in other words, determined how bad stress was for you. And based on their data, the researchers estimated that *the belief that stress was bad* was the fifteenth largest cause of death in the world.

This is bad news for people like Josh, because the best way to untangle the Josh and Emma paradox is by seeing it through the same lens that McGonigal would—as two sides of the same stress coin. Josh and Emma are both dealing with a lot of change and uncertainty, on a daily basis; when it comes to being on the receiving end of stress, Josh and Emma are essentially the same. Yet they're certainly having vastly different results, and that's because the difference between them isn't in the demands and uncertainty of the external world. The difference between Emma and Josh lies in the same place that the longer-lived people of the study do. It lies *inside*. It's in how they *respond* to stress.

Josh Versus Emma

Josh's response is what researchers call the classic *stress response*. It's the fight-or-flight mechanism that you've no doubt heard of.

We developed it through evolution to help us survive in times of danger—it's the "saber-tooth tiger" story of cascading hormones and instantaneous and subconscious body changes that prepare us to fight or run away so we can survive to reproduce another day.

The problem is that while there are no more saber-tooth tigers, there are still plenty of triggers for our built-in response, including things that aren't physically dangerous. When Josh hears news that jobs in his software industry are being outsourced to other countries, for example, his brain interprets that as uncertainty, and that can activate the stress response. That would be fine if it happened only once in a while, say the odd career shift or an emergency of some kind. But in the face of chronic uncertainty, Josh is feeling this way a *lot*. And that creates changes in his body as a cascade of hormones like cortisol and adrenaline crank him up to face danger. In the long run, it's taking a toll. His body is running a chemical cocktail all the time that he should be using only for emergencies. As a result, he's getting sick more. His cognitive skills are compromised. He has trouble making decisions. He's becoming anxious and depressed.

Emma, however, is having a different response. Sure, she's having the odd fight-or-flight reaction, but for the most part, the world around her isn't triggering the same response in her body. Instead, Emma is having what we could call a *relaxation* response. Instead of the racing heart, stress chemicals, and narrowed focus that Josh is undergoing, Emma is responding differently. She's not seeing saber-tooth tigers that aren't really there. She's not panicking. She's able to react to changing circumstances differently, and she's able to do it in a relatively calm way that lets her think more clearly and make better decisions—a process that in turn helps dial down uncertainty even further. She's built a resilience to stress that helps her thrive in the face of change.

What's Your Response?

This resonates deeply with me. I spent my whole life facing change in one of two ways. Early—as a lifeguard, then an attorney—I'd focused my energy on guarding *against* change. Change, I told myself, was bad. Change meant unpredictability. It meant *someone went down.* I was Josh, and eventually, like Josh, my efforts to control everything and save everyone really cost me.

After I pivoted from attorney to CEO and trainer, I decided to take a different approach. I would become an instrument of change. If I couldn't stop change from coming, I reasoned, I could at least head it off at the pass and teach others how to do the same. Unsatisfied in your career? No problem. I can teach you to pivot to something fulfilling. Business not thriving? Running out of runway? No problem. I can teach you how to pivot to something profitable using a carefully planned and executed plan B.

Neither of those approaches is bad. In fact, they're both indispensable. Who doesn't want to be aware of change on the horizon? And who doesn't want to shift from unfulfilled to fulfilled, or from hemorrhaging cash to being profitable? The ability to see change coming and to adjust accordingly is fundamental not just to happiness, but to *survival.*

What I learned, however, is that there's a third way—the Emma way. As the pace of change picks up, and change becomes not just the unexpected rip tide that moves through your life, but a near-constant current, the first two strategies no longer serve you. When change is chronic, you can't be on guard *all the time* without burning out. And you can't construct a careful plan B every single moment of every day or pivot your business every time the wind shifts. Neither of my approaches was working. Time and time again, I was Josh, and it wasn't working.

Success in the face of rapid, constant change requires something else. We still need to try to guard against some changes, and we still need to make big-picture pivots. But in a world where we're facing change all the time, we can't just swim against the current or switch streams. We need to build *resilience* to change—to become change proof.

Unfortunately, that's not a philosophy that's been widely embraced. Instead, we've long told ourselves a story about being chronically on guard. A body of scientific and anecdotal evidence that tells us, in essence, that all that stress is *bad*. For years, the default approach to stress has essentially been to reduce it. And since our brain equates uncertainty with stress, and stress is bad, we set out to reduce uncertainty, period.

These days, that's swimming against a very, very strong current. In a world of chronic change and infinite pivots, there *is* no eliminating uncertainty. There is no planning for every contingency. Instead, we need a new approach. The Emma method, you might call it. Or as I say, we need to stop fighting change and learn to leverage it.

•   •   •

The lesson thus far is this: it's your *response* to stress that matters, far more than the stress itself. We know that Emma and Josh are responding differently at a physical level to stress in their lives. But how? What is Emma doing that's making the difference?

Emma has built a resilience to change. She's learned to embrace uncertainty, and along the way even found a way to leverage it in her business and life. What Emma has learned is that if we can't change the world, it stands to reason that we need to change ourselves. And so we're left with a choice. We can try to tolerate change—to survive it. Or we can transform change and learn to excel in it.

And that, as it turns out, is a completely reasonable and effective thing to do. And it begins with your power to *choose*.

> You can change your response, but you can't change events, so it's your response to stress that matters, far more than the stress itself.

Your Resilience Level

Before we dig in to resilience and what it means for you and for your organization, I want you to do something else. I want you to put down the book and head to your phone or your computer. Go to AdamMarkel.com/ResilienceRank.com and you'll find a Resilient Leader Assessment, which is a multiple-choice test. Don't have any school-age flashbacks; there aren't any right answers.

Wait, actually there are. There are answers that are more right than others. But in this case "right" doesn't mean "correct." The only correct answers are the ones that are the most honest. Be rigorous with yourself. Resist the temptation to "look good" to the test. If you do have the impulse to do that, then that's more information for you, isn't it?

The only one who's going to see the results is you. You're a student and teacher. That's how we learn. So please, for your resilience journey, be brave with yourself. The final result is not actually final. It's truly just a litmus test to see where you are on the resilience continuum. And by the way, it will take you only about three minutes to complete!

We're going to explore the PMES (physical, mental, emotional and spiritual) realms of human resilience. You'll be able to experience each instrument in this quartet and also discover how resilient you are right now. If that doesn't make any sense to you now, don't worry, we'll clear it up in the next movement of our resilience symphony.

So please head to AdamMarkel.com and treat yourself to a little more information on what makes you resilient. Whatever your score is, think about what that means for you, right now, and think about how you feel about that. And then, realize that no matter how you did and how that makes you feel, this is only the beginning.

CHANGE-PROOF POINTS

▶ There's no "test" for resilience other than life itself, but there are specific ways to analyze your ability to respond to change and stress.

▶ Self-evaluation can be uncomfortable because sometimes you don't want to know what you don't know, but it's the first way to actually use change to become resilient.

CHAPTER 5

The Markers of Resilience

We must accept finite disappointment,
but never lose infinite hope.
—MARTIN LUTHER KING, JR.

The companies and businesses that survive have leaders who model the kind of resilience that makes them change proof. They are undaunted by events and so by extension are the companies that they lead.

I often wonder why some people are more resilient than others. What particular set of circumstances makes them able to withstand the slings and arrows that life rains down upon them with dignity, humor, and grace? Are they born with it? Like blue eyes? Or near-sightedness? Are they more genetically predisposed to be resilient? And say, for instance, that a person wasn't born to be change proof, is that it for them? No chance, game over, you lost the resilience lottery, thank you for playing? The truth is, nobody knows for sure if resilience is something you are born with or something you just learn. Like most things when nature and nurture are involved, it's a little bit of both.

Here's what we do know. We know resilience when we see it. We know resilience leaders when we meet them. Take Monty Williams, for example. You may not know that name offhand, but he's a recent example of someone who embodies our kind of resilient leadership. Monty Williams was a journeyman NBA player where he bounced from team to team until he landed with the San Antonio Spurs organization, who helped him transition from playing to coaching. Today, he's the NBA head coach for the Phoenix Suns. By all accounts a wildly successful life. It was, until everything in Monty Williams's world changed forever.

Back in 2016, when he was a coach with the Oklahoma City Thunder, his wife, Ingrid, mother of his five children, was killed when a woman with meth in her system and a dog in her lap crossed the median on a highway in downtown Oklahoma City, going over 90 miles an hour colliding with the Williams family van. The dog owner, Susannah Donaldson, died on impact along with her pet. The three children who were in the vehicle with Ingrid survived, but she succumbed to her injuries the next day.

In less than a week, Monty Williams was delivering the eulogy at Ingrid's funeral in front of his five children and almost a thousand members of the NBA community. With almost superhuman control Monty spoke for just over seven minutes without referring to his notes or losing his composure. I don't know how he did it.

The next day, on the ESPN program *First Take*, noted skeptic, Skip Bayless said, "I could not have done what this man did yesterday. At the funeral of his 44-year-old wife with five children in attendance. It brought tears to my eyes when I first saw it. I've watched at least five more times. Because I'm just sort of dumbfounded by it."

If you have a free moment, I highly recommend you take seven minutes to watch a lesson in dignity and grace under pressure. It's one of those examples where you don't know why Monty Williams is resilient, but you just know that he is.

By rights, he could have railed at the unfairness of an absent God or at the callous negligence of Susannah Donaldson when she got behind the wheel high out of her mind. But Monty Williams didn't do that. In calm measured tones, he spoke about forgiveness and about the need to move on. He was, in his own inimitable way, saying you have to love your life. No matter what. Even at his lowest moment, he was living out his resilience. Because that's what Ingrid taught him. For Monty, a man not naturally predisposed to be resilient, he was made so by Ingrid and the faithful example she set for him and for their children.

When it comes to resilience there's almost no one definition that will suffice. We don't know what it is, but we know it when we see it. Right? Isn't that what we think when we think about resilience? We often think of resilience as something a person either has or doesn't have. But we don't really know what it is. It's one of those undefinable things that makes a person who or what they are. In a dark and lonely valley, Monty Williams could have chosen despair. But he didn't. He chose to be resilient.

The part that interests me the most is the fact that nearly the entire NBA was at his wife's funeral. Monty had a choice: he could, rightly, fall apart at the seams or he could model resilient leadership. He knew that even something as tragic as the death of his wife was an opportunity to explain, to teach, and to model what kind of person Ingrid taught him to be. I believe that the entire NBA, a multibillion-dollar organization, was better because he did that.

Personally, when I think about resilience I think about people who aren't undaunted by events but no matter what happens, they maintain some fundamental core of what makes them who they are. Resilient people aren't thermometers, which can only respond to the changing variables of temperature; rather, they're thermostats, setting the temperature around them the way that Monty Williams did in a crowded church on a cold February day. He set the temperature of that room. When he was finished, the audience leapt to its feet as one. Not to applaud his performance, but I think it was because they were acknowledging the choice he made that day. Like most resilient people, Monty Williams chose to be moved to grow. How did he do that? And how can we do the same thing for our organizations?

The American Psychological Association defines *resilience* as "the process of adapting well in the face of adversity, trauma, tragedy, threats or even significant sources of threat."

Dennis Charney of the Icahn School of Medicine at Mount Sinai New York and Steven Southwick at the Yale School of Medicine performed an analysis of resilience by talking to people who had experienced traumatic events like war, sexual abuse, acts of terror, or natural disasters and asked them simply how they dealt with the awful things that happened to them.

What they found was that some folks who had experienced tragedy eventually began to suffer from depression and post traumatic stress disorder (PTSD), others had mild symptoms of trauma that went away after a period of time, and still others had no symptoms of psychological distress or depression.

Their research identified the main factors marked for resilience:

- Attention to health and good cardiovascular fitness
- Capacity to rapidly recover from stress
- A history of mastering challenges
- High coping self-efficacy—our belief in our own ability to succeed
- Disciplined focus on skill development
- Cognitive flexibility—the ability to reframe adversity in a positive light
- Positive emotion and optimism
- Loving caretakers and sturdy role models
- The ability to regulate emotions
- Strong social support
- Altruism—service

- Commitment to a valued cause or purpose
- Capacity to extract meaning from adverse situations
- Support from religion and spirituality

Based on what I've observed, Monty Williams likely would have some if not all the preceding markers for resilience, perhaps almost all of them. If he were here now, I'd bet he'd agree that while having them didn't guarantee a lifetime free from pain and loss, they definitely helped him find his way out of pain and loss. You hear it when he says of his late wife, "We didn't lose her. When you lose something, you can't find it. I know exactly where my wife is."

We're going to be unpacking each of these markers. We'll be addressing them from a holistic perspective. That means that they'll be applicable markers for you and your performance, but if you're a leader it will also help you diagnose and help your teams and organizations. For now, let's just say this: stress follows change and uncertainty as certainly as night follows the day.

Resilient people are the ones who don't just bounce back, we're after more than that. It's not just about getting back to where you were, it's about getting further than you were. It's about letting change change you. That's what's happening in our bodies as we practice resilience. In fact, I'm not going to use the word *practice* anymore. We simply don't have the time to practice resilience.

Imagine Allan Iverson's voice, "We're talking about practice. Not a game. Not a game. Practice." We don't practice resilience. We perform it. There's an infinity between practicing and performing. If performance at the highest levels is our goal, then it has to start now. As we used to say on Jones Beach, "You feel me?" From now on, that's how I'm going to speak to you. If this book is about performing resilience, then we have to know *how* to do it.

CHANGE-PROOF POINT

▶ None of the 14 markers of resilience are genetic predispositions; they're practical, actionable steps you can take to build resilience before you know you need it.

CHAPTER 6

The Myth of Balance

Limits exist only in the souls of
those who do not dream.
—PHILIPPE PETIT

Just after 7 a.m. on a cloudy, humid morning on August 7, 1974, a lithe young Frenchman, holding a long balance pole, performed the most bizarre act in New York's long history. He stepped onto a steel cable strung between the North and South Towers of the World Trade Center, and using a pole for balance, walked to the middle of the wire. He was 1,350 feet in the air. For nearly an hour, while a huge crowd gathered below, he went back and forth eight times and even laid down in a demonstration of the triumph of human balance. Or insanity.

I remember being at home in Queens when I heard on the radio about the crazy man who walked a wire between the two highest points in Manhattan. 1,350 feet! It just didn't seem possible. To be that high up, contending with swirling winds and swaying skyscrapers, where every millimeter of movement is the margin between life and death. I marveled at the amount of focus it must have taken to not plunge to an abrupt death. Even thinking about that height and the drop today gives me a cold feeling in the pit of my stomach.

Day after day, when I was at the height of my legal career, I had this same feeling. Because I was a David in a city full of Goliath law firms, all I could really depend on was my tenacity. This is how I would win money for clients and myself: my adversaries would say, "This guy is sending me legal papers every single Saturday." The post office in Manhattan was open until midnight. So I would send things out at 11:55 p.m., just to show the other side that I was willing to do whatever it takes. I may not have been a thousand feet in the sky, but it took every bit of myself to stay on the wire I had strung across my life. I was fighting to be the best father and husband I could be, while still ambitiously pursuing my career. I wanted both. Desperately.

In 1974, Philippe Petit was on that cable for less than an hour while the police pleaded with him to come inside, a helicopter tried to lift him to safety and the crowd held their breath (let's be honest) waiting for him to fall. Then it started to rain. Not a lot, but enough that the wire was going to be impassable in a few moments. Still without fear, a Frenchman to the end, Petit simply shrugged and stepped off the wire into the arms of the NYPD. Thus ended one of those strange New York moments where a kind of bizarre magic entered the world in the most unlikely place.

For 45 minutes Philippe Petit was the highest man in the known world. Three-quarters of an hour was how long he had to maintain his balance. 45 minutes. That was it.

Now, here I was, many years later, in a Manhattan law office, standing on my own steel cable between the two towers of *life* and *work*. And I felt every minute of every month that passed.

Just like addicts need more and more of their drug of choice just to get back to a baseline of normal, I was addicted to my own drug: stress. I was taking on more and more work, willing myself to go on, damn the torpedoes, full speed ahead. Because of my stress addiction, I was gripping that pole, high above the city and terrified I was going to fall. I couldn't stay up any longer, but I couldn't step off. When I was home, I thought about work. When I was at work, I just wanted to get home.

That's where most of us find ourselves, on our own high wire, trying to stay in that sweet spot between our work and our lives, between our families at our jobs and our families at home. We think we're doing the right thing by seeking balance. But we should be seeking something else.

When we talk about balance, what we're actually talking about is something more holistic: we're talking about harmony. For years, we've been feeding ourselves this idea that to be healthy in our lives and our jobs, we have to find balance. "Balance is the key," we all said.

As Dr. Ivan Misner, founder and chief visionary officer of Business Network International and dubbed by CNN as the "Father of Modern Networking" told me:

> *Forget about balance, you'll never have it. Especially if you're an entrepreneur or businessperson, your life is crazy out of balance. The problem is, we look at the concept of balance like lady justice, where you have the scales of justice and your life must be in this incredible balance where you're spending this amount of time on your business and this amount of time on your family and this amount of time on a spiritual life and health. Everything's got to be completely in balance. That's impossible. I don't even recommend you try to get it. The true answer to the question is harmony. I believe you can have a life of harmony. Harmony is way different than balance. Even the logo for harmony, the yin and the yang, when separated are out of balance. It's only together that you can create a life of harmony.*

I think when we talk about balance, we actually mean something even more meaningful and impactful. It's a power that, if we can harness it, will allow us to deploy our pause, ask, choose tool for maximum resilience. Let's figure out what we really mean.

They've mostly been phased out of modern parks because kids had a tendency to fall off them, but back in the day, we had these things called teeter-totters, or seesaws. One kid either side, up and down, that's how the game is enjoyed.

Now, if two kids are in balance, no one's going anywhere, the kids are crying, and the game is over. The game depends on constant motion. One is up, the other is down, on and on it goes until they both decide to play something else. The name of the game isn't balance, it's harmony. The true pleasure is the dance between the two states. Not some idealized balance point where no one goes anywhere.

When Philippe Petit was balancing high up on the wire between those two doomed buildings, he was in harmony. He was in harmony with the wire, his body, the looming danger, the air swirling around him, and I imagine, with the higher vibrations of the universe.

That's what we can learn from a strange Frenchman's flight of whimsy 40 odd years ago: it's not the balance we're after. It's harmony.

Think of it this way: if pause, ask, choose is the long, flat beam you sat on when you rode the seesaw, then the force of gravity that powers the ride is this harmony. It's the force that makes the whole thing go. By the way, you know the part of the seesaw where the beam meets the metal fulcrum? It's called the pivot.

A few years ago, I had the opportunity to go to England for a spell, and while I was there, I was blessed to be able to row crew with a team for a few days. We would row at 6 a.m. every day. It was absurdly early, but I remember quite clearly the state of the world at the time.

Everything was calm while the sleeping hearts of the country were still in bed. The ground was still cold and damp while we squished down to the River Ouse hauling our boat. The sun was just beginning to clear the trees. Steam was rising off the water.

Together with a group of powerful swimmers, our oars feathered off the surface of the river, completely in sync as the sun got higher and higher beating down on our backs and our hands were ripped raw. We were what I like to call "synaptically synergistic," which really means that our minds, our hearts, and our bodies were working as one. All the cylinders were firing. Every piece was working in concert with all the others. We were many individuals working as one. It was magic.

You know why? Because it was frictionless. That's the place we're trying to get to with our teams. As a leader, you've got to remove friction between egos. You've got to be harmonized with yourself and your team. It doesn't mean all your people have to like each other. I didn't even know the people I was rowing with. I don't even remember their names. But we did work in harmony.

You don't need to love each other. When your team is harmonized, there's no friction, because you're working as one. You're one spirit.

Now, let's pump the brakes a moment. When we use words like *spirit*, that can mean a lot of things to a lot of different people. There are an infinite number of ways to describe it. The more we try to describe a thing, the more it means how little we know about that thing.

That word might not work for you. I know that you may not adhere to any religious tradition or hold a belief in any kind of higher power. For some of you, the word *spirit* is connected to years and years of trauma, pain, and close-mindedness. For others, the notion of an endlessly loving deity dispassionately observing pain and suffering from a distance is an intellectual bridge too far to cross.

That's OK. You don't have to believe in God or religion. Like John Lennon, you're free to imagine a world without them. It's your right to do so.

For you, it might be the creative force that binds the universe together, it might be love itself, or it may be as simple as a still, small voice inside you that helps you be a better person. Like a song you love coming from another room. It could be the quality of light at your favorite time of day. It could be anything.

What I'm not talking about is something like the bearded man on the cloud or a judgmental God. In fact, when I think about God, I don't even think. It's the force I'm connected to when I have those moments of being in perfect harmony with myself. I'm fully integrated into the present moment. That's where I feel that connection.

There's a fantastic book called *Zen and the Art of Archery* by Eugen Herrigel, an Austrian who spent years studying the ancient ways of Zen Buddhism and its connection to shooting an arrow at a target. It's on par with Timothy Gallwey's idea about the mind that thinks through us instead of judging our actions.

> *There are processes beyond the reach of understanding. Do not forget that even in Nature there are correspondences which cannot be understood, and yet are so real that we have grown accustomed to them, just as if they could not be any different. I will give you an example which I have often puzzled over. The spider dances her web without knowing that there are flies who will get caught in it. The fly, dancing nonchalantly on a sunbeam, gets caught in the net without knowing what lies in store. But through both of them "It" dances, and inside and outside are united in this dance.*

Now, maybe things like Zen and archery are completely meaningless, outdated concepts for your understanding of the realm of the spirit. For me, there's a fun, more modern example that might give you an inkling of what I'm talking about. It's a moment from a movie called *From the Sky Down* directed by Davis Guggenheim about the making of one of the greatest rock albums of all time, U2's *Achtung Baby*, and the time the band spent in Berlin after the fall of the Wall. First, a little backstory.

The band, at that particular moment in history, was coming off the meteoric rise to fame, the inevitable backlash, and then the uncertainty of what would come next or even if something would come next. Along with their producers and their team, they convened in Berlin's Hansa Studios, where David Bowie, Iggy Pop, Eartha Kitt, and Depeche Mode had all recorded albums, for a period of time to reinvent the sonic identity of the band.

For weeks and weeks, they spent a German winter banging their heads and hearts against each other trying to find something, anything, transcendent that would set their new direction. But nothing would come.

Now, there was beginning to be real panic in the ranks. Nobody wanted to admit that it was the end, but it certainly was starting to look like the end. So many days and dollars they'd spent. For what? A handful of songs that nobody was in love with. They had to ask themselves the question: What if this was the death of the band?

The moment in the documentary that still stays with me and contains for us our spiritual lesson, comes when the band is jamming on a song that would eventually become the hit single, "Mysterious Ways." The quartet was working through a familiar series of chord progression that they'd been working on in a rough sketch of a verse, chorus, bridge, chorus, narrative. But on this particular day, a new chord progression flew, like an out-of-season hummingbird, into the room and created the transcendent moment the band was looking for. I love music and play guitar for pleasure as well as the amusement of friends and family, but I'm no music theorist, so I won't get into the particular combination of chords and what that means. All you need to know is that it was the chord progression that would eventually become more than a hit; it became a hymn. "One" is a song that embodies the transcendent connection U2 were seeking together.

You must be asking yourself, "Zen. Archery. Dad rock. What in the deuce does this have to do with spiritual resilience?" The band went to an uncertain space, at an uncertain time, to push themselves and each other into uncertain places, to take the risk to fail, to fall flat on their faces, and risk ruining one of the world's greatest bands. They showed up for uncertainty. They kept working. They kept their discipline and their value system.

They were rewarded with a song that swept in like a spirit. They didn't plan it. They weren't conscious of what they were doing. They were just ready to receive whatever would come because they heeded the words of the great Quincy Jones, who said, "You gotta leave space for God to walk through the room."

Man, that's true. It's resilience.

CHANGE-PROOF POINTS

▶ When you replace the word balance with the concept of harmony, you rid yourself of the quest for perfection and can flow with change.

▶ You know uncertainty is guaranteed, so when you seek uncertain situations where failure is not only possible but likely, you build your resilience reserves for the times when uncertainty seeks you.

CHAPTER 7

Harmony

*There is an Indian proverb or axiom that says that
everyone is a house with four rooms, a physical,
a mental, an emotional, and a spiritual. Most of us
tend to live in one room most of the time but, unless
we go into every room every day, even if only to
keep it aired, we are not a complete person.*
—RUMER GODDEN

This morning when I went for my daily swim, I had to be in
harmony with myself. Why? Because otherwise, I'll drown.

Ocean swimming is an intense physical experience. It's
not a lap pool at the local YMCA. Although that is a perfectly
acceptable alternative, for me, my favorite place to swim is the
sea. Because it's so daunting. The sheer force of it boggles the
mind even when I'm in it. As a result, it takes every bit of my
physical ability to navigate the waves and the tides. I have to
really tune in to my body's signals, I have to be in alignment
with my breath on each stroke to maximize my efficiency. I
really have to set a consistent, powerful pace, or I'll burn out in
a hurry.

As my awareness increases out there, I feel the immensity, the
abundance, when I'm connected to the entirety of the universe.

The absence of scarcity relieves my emotions of their reason for being. It relieves my mind of anxiety. Spiritually, it connects me to the infinite, where I'm "at one" with the vastness of awe.

It sounds a bit out there, but I feel as though I'm swimming in God's pool. It relaxes my body because I'm stimulating it by putting it under stress. Exercise mimics the stress response. Active passivity. Calmly active and actively calm. It allows me to transcend problems and challenges of my own making. I burn away that which is no longer serving me. In the ocean, I replenish, renew, and regenerate.

To add to all that, the little secret that most swimmers don't want to admit or talk about: it's scary. That's part of the appeal. In all honesty, in the back of my mind, I still hear the familiar John Williams *Jaws* theme while I'm out there. At any moment, anything could emerge from the deep. It's a heightened state of awareness. It's a healthy respect for life at the edges. I'm aware that somewhere out there, there's something that can hurt me. But that's part of the pleasure. I'm putting my body and my emotions under stress. I'm excited and nervous at the same time. There's a growth edge when I put myself in situations that are outside my control. I don't turn my back on it. I look into it.

Some of us are making change, while others are reacting to the change. So we put ourselves into separate camps. As opposed to seeing ourselves in each other. Seeing the change in others. One side pushing change, the other resisting it. Too fast, too slow. But change is the thing that unites us: the gas and the brakes are necessary to make the car go. The operation of the car needs harmony to get you where you're going, not balance. Balance is static. Harmony is dynamic. An individual is healthy when all the states are in harmony with each other. Not balance. Because balance is impossible. That's what I learned at Jones Beach: the tide goes out, the tide comes in, it is always in motion. This sense of harmony is how we become resilient.

Now that we've established that it's not balance that makes us resilient, it's harmony, how do we achieve it? In this book, we're going to focus on the four building blocks, the four quadrants that encompass our human experience of the world and allow us to build resilience so it's there when we need it most. Make no mistake, it requires all four.

When I'm swimming, to keep up my harmonious action to be at my best, I'm constantly reminded of these four pillars of equilibrium:

1. Don't hurry.
2. Don't worry.
3. Don't condemn.
4. Don't resent.

For our purposes, these break down perfectly in the four sections that make up our harmony. Pretty easy to understand and almost impossible to forget. When we talk about harmony, that's what we mean.

If you can live these four rules in your day-to-day life, you'll be developing resilience at times when you don't even need it. Then when uncertainty and change call and you find yourself in the Suck, this is how you make it out.

When we talk about pause, ask, choose, it still breaks down the same. I'll explain that in a moment.

For now, let's just marinate in the realms of human experience:

- Physical—the body
- Mental—the mind
- Emotional—the heart
- Spiritual—the spirit

This is how we perform resilience.

- We **pause** with our body.
- We **ask** with our minds and hearts.
- We **choose** with our spirit.

Resilience is only possible if those four instruments are playing in harmony with one another.

How do you experience a quartet by Mozart, Brahms, or Hayden? The composer writes the music so that our brains experience the way the instruments harmonize with each other, with different parts taking the lead at different times. But it's not as though while you're hearing, say, a violin solo, the other instruments all of a sudden stop playing. The cello, the viola, and the piano support the violin while it takes its musical journey for however many measures the composer wants them to. Then the violin gives way to the piano, and the sonata continues on.

OK, how does a human being play a sonata with themselves? And how does that build resilience? How can you break yourself down to the four core instruments that make us human so that you're operating at the highest level possible for as long as you possibly can? That's the question we're going to answer on this journey we're taking through the pages of this book as we pause, ask, and choose our way through our bodies, our minds, our hearts, and our spirits.

That's it. It's that simple. But as you know, nothing in life that's true is ever really simple. That's why this book is about learning to shift how we interpret change and stress so we can thrive in a world that's never quite the same from one day to the next.

My thesis is that the best way to deal with change is to embrace it. To accept it, to work with it, and as you'll see from the example in this book, to profit from it—personally and professionally. To thrive, rather than simply survive. Instead of operating at your peak for short bursts, you'll be operating at a high level forever. The trick, of course, is in the how, and that's what you'll learn in the pages that follow.

My experience, and those of the many people I've worked with over the years, has shown me that the most powerful tool in your arsenal—your silver bullet for dealing with change—is your ability to pause, ask, and ultimately choose the life you want to have. It's a skill that is just as important in business as it is in our own lives, and as I'll show you, it's a skill you can learn.

Like most people, I've learned that change is the new normal. We don't get a choice anymore about whether to be resilient. We have to be. We can't predict the future, and we can't plan for every eventuality. Change, whether we like it or not, is no longer optional. But how we face it is.

I want to leave you with a quote from the Tao. It mirrors exactly what Dr. Misner was talking about, and it's a lodestar that will point us the way to the ending:

> She who is centered in the Tao can go where she wishes, without danger. She perceives the universal harmony, even amid great pain, because she has found peace in her heart. Music or the smell of good cooking may make people stop and enjoy. But words that point to the Tao seem monotonous and without flavor. When you look for it, there is nothing to see. When you listen to it, there is nothing to hear. When you use it, it is inexhaustible.

If you're reading this and you feel like you're always exhausted, then that's exactly what we're going to discuss in the next chapter.

CHANGE-PROOF POINT

▶ The quest for balance is static and keeps you seeking some mythical perfect state, but harmony is dynamic and allows you to assimilate events as they come.

CHAPTER 8

The Resilience Bank Account

Our best selves. We know it when we have it: we operate at a high level of energy, we are actively engaged with whatever we are doing, we are open to and feel warmth and compassion toward others, we are creative, and we feel as if the curve balls of life can be turned into home runs.
—MICHAEL MADDAUS, M.D.

Do you remember opening your first bank account? Maybe you had a little wad of birthday bills and checks. You went with your dad, mom, or the adult you trusted the most down to the local branch. The fluorescent lighting. It was bright and dim all at the same time. The velvet quiet. That smell of metal and paper was intoxicating. That giant vault at that bank that looked like something out of an old cowboy movie. That ancient scale in the corner. The low voices talking about mysterious phrases like "above prime," "mortgages," and "compound interest." The pens on beaded leashes. It was like being let into the secret world of adults.

You signed your checks in your best cursive. Put them in an envelope and sealed them with your tongue. With your mom or dad's help, you made your way to the teller gates where you were greeted by a stern but not unkind face that already knew your name. In a small voice, you said, "I want to open a bank account." You were greeted with a little smile. A hand reached out. You put your envelope, all your worldly goods, in the outstretched hand. Then as patiently as you could, you waited.

Craning your neck, you looked up to the teller filing the bills and the checks. Then a paper slid across to you. You scrawled your signature. The hand reached out again. This time holding a distinctive leather checkbook. With great ceremony you took it, feeling that fresh leather, maybe it was bright red or blue, and flipped it open to see a book of checks with your name on them. Above, the small amount of money that, to you, looked like a million dollars. To you, the possibilities seemed limitless. And they were. You made little deposits over time until you actually had real money to buy yourself something you wanted. Your very first bank account.

Let me explain where I'm going with this. Like you, I wasn't traveling in 2020, and Randi and I were confined to our house. Between one of my dozen or more Zoom calls a day, I was able to dig into more of the research on resilience and where the current thinking is on a subject that was growing more and more necessary by the day.

Among the countless studies and articles I consumed, I had the great pleasure of reading a scholarly paper published by the Society of Thoracic Surgeons called "The Resilience Bank Account: Skills for Optimal Performance" written by Dr. Michael Maddaus. From his research Dr. Maddaus coined a phrase that, as an author, I wish I'd thought of to describe the way we need to be thinking about thriving instead of surviving:

The Resilience Bank Account

What a concept! He phrased it perfectly. Your bank account was opened for you a long time before you were born, but you got access to it when you were.

This premise is very useful for us when we seek to perform the resilience that will keep us engaged energetically for the long term. Just as a bank account operates on a very simple basis of deposits and withdrawals, so does the harmony of our bodies, our minds, our hearts, and our spirits.

For many of us, we unconsciously make daily withdrawals while also depending on the randomness of events to fill up our tanks and make our deposits for us. Operating this way and not planning our deposits will take us to the brink of being broke, that is burned out. Once burnout hits and your body is in a state of "overdraft," you're going to be dealing with a challenging aftermath and consequences that may include chronic sleep issues, health problems, and addiction.

The price of burnout is costly. For me, and my work with clients, I use the pause, ask, choose architecture to frame a strategy to replenish my resilience bank account.

- When we pause, it is our chance to catch our breath, quite literally. This is the reset we must have. Like rebooting your computer when it is slogging along under the strain of all the tabs you have open and before it freezes.
- When we ask, we are seizing the chance to discover deeper meaning in the challenge we're facing. This is the reframe. We reframe the moment for our growth by asking questions like, "What's the creative opportunity?" and "What am I not seeing?"
- When we choose, we are consciously ritualizing small, daily practices for our personal recovery to create mental, emotional, physical, and spiritual harmony.

Recently, I was blessed to be able to speak to an athletic phenom, Michael Andrew, who recently broke an American record during his first Olympic time trial, and his coach and father, Peter. Together, they are fulfilling their purpose to succeed in the pool and in life by challenging the dogmas of endless training hours that have dominated competitive swimming for generations.

I first met Michael at a beautiful pool in Encinitas, California. I happened to be swimming a couple lanes over, and it felt as though there was a mercury propeller engine moving water right next to me. I lifted my head and saw a swimmer rocketing across the surface of the water and thought, "That's unusually fast."

After the session, I felt compelled to meet Michael and his father, because my memory of high school and college swim workouts was radically different than what I was witnessing with Michael. The traditional model of swimming practice has been and continues to be based on gruelling sessions that has athletes swimming between 5,000 and 7,000 yards twice a day to create a massive amount of fatigue and ultimately improve performance when the yardage is dramatically reduced before competitions. This is called "tapering."

During our conversation, Peter explained how they do things differently by training at the speed at which Michael will race and then recovering. "We know that the performance formula is stress plus rest equals growth. Not stress plus stress, that leads you into a deep hole. There's got to be recovery. In all sports, recovery is probably the most important training part, because without it, you don't get better." Recovery is the key to long-term resilience and growth because the number one challenge that afflicts Olympic swimmers of every ability is burnout.

Coincidentally, this is exactly the same challenge for business professionals. Being an entrepreneur or business owner, there's a constant pressure to perform. The culture of business, just like athletics, is about the old paradigm of, "How do we squeeze the most out of people?" We exhaust our organizations and drive our talent to the brink of burnout because we believe that if people are working hard all the time, then we're getting our money's worth from them.

To show us the way forward, Michael and Peter have reset the paradigm by focusing on recovery routines that function like rituals. Sometimes that includes walking away from the pool. That allows them to be, as Peter describes it, ". . . intentional over time. We're ahead of the game because we've been deliberate, diligent, and disciplined, and because we had a higher goal and something we were focusing on."

Intentionality is the why that gives Peter and Michael the how. Michael says, "People often look for this quick, easy, take-a-pill-so-you-can-go-and-swim-fast type of thing. Nothing works like that. There's got to be this day in, day out, building strength repetition. Because it's that compound effect that grows and produces the results." Peter went on to recommend a book called *The Compound Effect* and that's where we come back to the resilience bank account.

Each step is a way of creating simple interest. A modest return that frankly is better than doing nothing at all. We can pause and reset our fatigue and our growth by disconnecting from the work that seems to follow us throughout the 168 hours of the week. We can do just that. Or we can add the ask that allows us to reframe and search for meaning and creative opportunity that lives inside our constantly evolving world. It's only by adding the third "R" that comes from the choose, which is about ritualizing our recovery, that we get the big benefit. The compound interest and effect of exponential growth over time.

The resilience bank account is a metaphor for us to use. When we pause to reset, ask for the reframe, and choose to ritualize making daily deposits, deep habits take hold and before we know it, we're performing resilience without thinking about it.

Everything you've ever done has either been a deposit or a withdrawal. If you think back on as much of your life as you're able to: How many deposits did you make? Was it more than what you took out? I bet it wasn't.

We're going to return to this later when we talk about why you remember more of the withdrawals than the deposits. And it's not because the ledger is off.

CHANGE-PROOF POINTS

▶ Building small, daily resilience habits is a simple, easy way of depositing resilience before you need to spend it.

▶ What daily resilience habits do you currently perform?

CHAPTER 9

Resilient Organizations

It's not the strongest of the species that survives,
nor the most intelligent that survives. It is the
one that is the most adaptable to change.
—CHARLES DARWIN

Most of us, when we think about Darwin, think of survival of the fittest.

Since you were drawn to this book, chances are you're searching for your own resilience. Moreover, if you're searching for your own resilience, then you're probably looking for how your organization can be resilient too.

It's a truism that resilient leaders have resilient organizations. The crew survives if the captain of the ship knows how to navigate through stormy seas. Turns out that the sea itself can teach our organizations how to be resiliently change proof.

For my part, I was born and raised in a little "suburb" of New York City: Queens. It's probably true that I am a city boy at my core, but at heart I'm a child of water. Normally, I prefer the ocean tides, but wherever I am, if there's a body of water, then I'm going to get in it for my daily swim or to surf or play. For me, salt water is my holy water.

It's why I love living in Southern California. Swimming in the seemingly infinite Pacific helps me feel a deep connection to the natural world. The roiling water, the insistent push and pull of the waves, and the fact that anything can emerge from the dangerous dark all provide me with a better, clearer sense of my place in the universe.

As the health of the water of Earth goes, so goes our planet's overall health. When I'm in the ocean, I'm keenly aware of the fact that, yes, our planet and our physical bodies are both at least 75 percent water. When I get into the water, I know right away how healthy I am. It can't be helped. I feel that harmonic connection with my body and the planet. If I'm out of harmony in any facet of my life, if I'm unhealthy in any way, whether it's physically, mentally, emotionally, or spiritually, the ocean, like a very competent doctor, is going to make me aware of that fact in an instant.

Let's go back in time for a moment: April 20, 2010. The Gulf of Mexico, 41 miles off the coast of Louisiana. In a brutal combination of bad luck, human error, and years of deregulation, a capped British Petroleum oil well exploded, destroying a rig, and killing 11 people while injuring 17 others. Barrel after barrel of black crude oil, by the millions, poured into the Gulf for months while the US government tried everything to stop it.

I remember the nausea I felt at the sight of that disgusting, brown oil fouling the beautiful, pure blue salt water. Like countless others, I was horrified to witness such a complex, fragile ecosystem wrecked by human negligence. Maybe it was a freak accident, a one-in-a-million chance, but surely it could have been prevented. Even if it couldn't, how was the Gulf going to recover?

Later that year, after the US government was finally able to plug the well, they had to help the Gulf region recover from this catastrophic environmental shock. There was a massive cleanup effort to somehow get millions of barrels of oil out of the water and a financial rescue of the Gulf's tourism industry. Everything in those early days was about recovery.

Once they were able to do that, they had to ask some really hard questions. How did it happen? Whom do we hold accountable? And how can we make sure that something like this never happens again? If we can't, how can we help them recover faster and better?

In 2013, the US government established a committee to study all the effects of the Deepwater Horizon explosion. It's a surprisingly self-reflective document with some key conclusions we all use in our own lives. The whole document is a fascinating look at how an organization as large and seemingly amorphous as the federal government does their own version of pause, ask, choose. What I want to *drill* down on, in particular, is the second chapter called, "Resilience and Ecosystem Services," as it has a few very important lessons about how the same things that make an ecosystem resilient can be the same for us and for our organizations and teams.

It may seem like an out-there concept, but the way the committee breaks down ecological resilience, I believe can work for you as an individual. But particularly if you're a leader, they can give you some guideposts to measure your organization's overall resilience so you can make sure you're prepared for the next regime shift in your business or industry.

These were their conclusions.

Ecosystem Resilience Is About Recovery

Recovery is the Rosetta Stone for this book. If we don't recover, we can't be resilient. It's as simple as that. But we often delay recovery, waiting until it's forced upon us. When that happens, it's too late.

I'm going to say it over and over and over again like a mantra.

Resilience Is Based on Recovering Before It Becomes Necessary.

The committee defined resilience like this, "Resilience is defined as the ability of a system subject to disturbance to retain its essential structure, function and feedback and return to its pre-disturbance state." Long-term stresses make it difficult to respond to shocks to the system.

Just like within yourself you've got chronic stress, within your organization, you've got the very same thing. It's your job as a leader to diagnose these stresses before the shock comes.

Regular rest and recovery means that when disruptions come to you and your people, you'll be able to weather the storms.

Diversity

Diversity is the watchword of these times. We're more aware of it than at any time in our history. There are some things we've gotten wrong with some cosmetic fixes to structural problems, but in the main, we're more aware of it. And that's a good thing.

In an ecological setting, a system that has an abundance of bio-diversity is a healthy system and one that can weather shocks to the overall system. Our organizations can and should be like this.

You have to have people in your organization that think differently, look different, and have different life experiences from you and each other. When hiring, we unconsciously make the mistake of looking for people who look like us, have our life experience, and exist on our particular frequency. This is not diversity. This is like cloning yourself and expecting all these iterations of you to run the company the way you expect.

But that's the thing about expectations. Resilience isn't about meeting expectations. It's about exceeding your expectations. That's what diversity does for us. Diversity is the key to the planet's resilience because it constantly evolves and changes the status quo. That's nature's way.

Nature is never done. It doesn't settle.

Manage Feedback and Slowly Changing Variables

Managing feedback loops means that you, as the manager of the ecosystem of your business, need to know where and how to manage your resources so you're constantly responding to events.

In the case of the Gulf of Mexico, if the fisheries were just mindlessly spreadsheeting their supply and harvesting the same number of the population every year, then they wouldn't be mindful of the ecosystem that they're managing.

Feedback has to respond to the environmental conditions. It's the same with our organizations. People are not data points, much as we'd like them to be. We're already experiencing the limitations of technology and disruption. The future is going to be defined by resilient organizations that are led by people who understand themselves on a deep awareness level and have the courage to see their employees and partners in the same way. It's as simple as a coach adapting her system to fit her players as opposed to getting her players to adapt to her system.

People survive and thrive. Systems don't.

Modularity and Connectivity

Modularity in a system is when all the components can be separated from one another and recombined in a variety of ways. In a business this can be beneficial because it allows you and your organization to be flexible.

As a marine system, the Gulf of Mexico is a highly interconnected system, so when the BP oil spill happened, the shock was spread throughout the system. Modularity might have contained the damage.

Yet, it's a curious thing that the interconnectivity of the Gulf of Mexico's ecosystem allowed it to recover and thrive in spite of the human catastrophe. Every facet of the system bore the brunt of the spill so the system could come back stronger than before. Again, it's about bouncing forward, not bouncing back.

Our organizations can be like that too. If we allow for our departments to interface with each other so they all have some modicum of awareness of how the whole system works, then your organization will be resilient.

You can't stop the change that's coming, but empowering the connections between your employees means you can thrive in the chaos of change.

Adaptive Management and Learning

Ship's captains can't predict the weather, but in some ways they can be more sensitive to changing conditions to make it seem as though they can. This is a leadership skill that's been lost in the data-driven technocracy that's dominated corporate culture for a generation. Short-term thinking means that managers are forced to think about surviving quarter by quarter instead of thinking about the long-term health of their organization.

The Deepwater Horizon Committee wasn't really interested in better business practices but they may have found some gems for us to harvest. Like this one:

> *Adaptive management has proven difficult to implement in practice, in part because it involves risk taking that can put managers in a difficult position of justifying failures even when it provides valuable information, as well as because it requires resources for ongoing monitoring and evaluation.*

Doesn't this sound familiar?

We learn more about ourselves when we consciously examine our failures than our successes. Every time a toddler falls down, their developing brains and bodies are collecting valuable data about how to walk. When we as parents try to keep them from this, to keep them from hurting themselves, we rob them of precious information that they need.

It's the same with ourselves and our teams. We need to cultivate small, creative ways to fail so that when the big changes come, we've already practiced leveraging uncertainty. Adaptability is rooted in failure. Don't be afraid of it.

Improving Governance and Increasing Social Capital

The Deepwater Horizon Committee's final conclusion is the most important one: ecological resilience is based on the degree to which local communities in the Gulf region could, with targeted support by the federal government, best weather the catastrophe themselves. Rather than FEMA coming in and big-footing everyone, they determined that a community's resilience had to come from within and not from without.

In our organizations, it's our institutional knowledge base that builds trust and confidence within the whole network. That's what builds social capital.

CHANGE-PROOF POINT

▶ Change-proof resilience is about how you, as a leader, get yourself in a place where you're developing your own resilience and then modeling it for your team.

CHAPTER 10

Left Brain Resilience

Stress will break people altogether if they are in the beginning too weak to stand distress, or else, if they are already strong enough to take the stress in the first place, that same stress, if they come through it, will strengthen them, temper them, and make them stronger.

—ABRAHAM MASLOW

Let's move to the left side of our brains and dig into the data about resilience. In addition to you, nearly 2,000 business leaders and executives from companies like P&G, Citibank, and Equitable have filled out the Resilient Leader Assessment from Chapter 4.

Look at Figure 10.1 and you'll see almost two-thirds of all respondents scored in that middle Yellow Zone. Where you're mostly resilient but you've got room for improvement. Yellow lights mean caution and here it's no different.

The high achievers, the Hermione Grangers of change-proof resilience, occupy the Green Zone, which is a pretty high altitude for leaders and executives. However, there are only 6 percent of them in that rare air. Green means go. Keep going, keep doing what you're doing.

FIGURE 10.1 Average Aggregate Resilient Leader Results*

Qn	Master			Zone
1	I take time to quiet my mind on a regular basis.		63.9	Yellow
2	When I come upon a challenge, I take time to reflect, think positively, and find a creative solution.	Mental 66	70.8	Yellow
3	I work in the evenings and on weekends.		56.7	Red
4	I overcome setbacks or difficult situations quickly.		72.7	Yellow
5	I regularly get at least seven to eight hours of sleep and wake up feeling refreshed.		62.3	Yellow
6	I work out at least three times a week.		61.0	Yellow
7	For meals, I'll settle for convenience versus looking for healthy options.	Physical 58	63.3	Yellow
8	I am definitely one of those people that checks my phone A LOT during the day.		45.0	Red
9	When I'm feeling down, I know what makes me feel better and I do it.		66.7	Yellow
10	I often feel like I have little or no control over what happens to me.		69.3	Yellow
11	When I reflect on difficult times in my life, I focus on the lessons I've learned.	Emotional 69	73.9	Yellow
12	I believe in and trust my own talents and solutions.		67.5	Yellow
13	I'm engaged in a livelihood that is in line with my core values and beliefs.		85.0	Green
14	There are significant gaps between what I say is most important in my life and how I actually allocate my time and energy.	Spiritual 66	55.8	Red
15	I don't invest enough time and energy in making a positive difference to others or to the world.		59.0	Red
16	I wake up in the morning excited for the day and with a sense of purpose.		63.2	Yellow

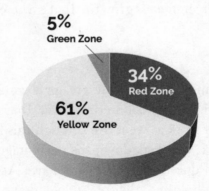

5%
Green Zone

34%
Red Zone

61%
Yellow Zone

RESILIENCE SCORE	RESILIENCE ZONE
0–59	Red
60–84	Yellow
85–100	Green

*This data represents the average scores of 2,500+ leadership respondents across a mix of industries and types of organizations.

The Red Zone includes over a third of all respondents who are in that area where chronic stress and change have rendered them vulnerable to acute events. A blinking red light means something is wrong and you need to stop what you're doing.

What's really important for us is the average score. It's one of the reasons why I chose to write this book: change-proof resilience is the one skill we have to remember how to perform so we can maximize (not just survive) events as they happen.

The average score was 64.2 out of a possible 100. Let's call it 64. Which, as you can see, is at the bottom end of the Yellow Zone and dangerously close to the Red Danger Zone.

On average, we're all hovering above the possibility of burnout. According to OSHA's statistics, the cost of burnout to the world economy is 500 billion dollars. That's a staggering figure.

So even though things might be precarious, there's reason to hope. A 64 on the Resilience Scale means that small, incremental changes will lead to exponential growth. In springtime, that's how nature comes back to life and light.

In our case, green means growth. That's where we want to be.

• • •

There are two findings that bear greater examination because they're both curious and counterintuitive. They're also keys to our change proof work as we move through this book.

In Figure 10.1, we break down the percentages as they apply to the individual questions in the Resilience Assessment. Like the book you're holding, they're broken down into our four realms of human experience: the body, the mind, the heart, and the spirit. Four questions each to bring out the best and the worst of your assessment of your own resilience.

The first thing you'll notice is that none of the averages are in the Green Zone. So fine, we're not excelling as much as we'd like. Yet, that's why we're here together. We want to begin to perform resilience again. Like bike riding when we were kids, you never truly forget how to be resilient. You just need to pick it up, dust it off, and hop back on so you can be change proof in your life and in your business.

The next thing you'll likely notice is the entire Physical Resilience section is completely red. Statistically, it's far, far below the other three with the lowest value coming on the question—"I am definitely one of those people that checks my phone a *lot* during the day." That one question is bringing up the rear by a significant margin. We all know we're addicted to our phones. Our bodies are fused with machines in a way that would have tickled the science-fiction writers in the 1960s but only make us less and less happy every day that passes.

I don't have any data for this point, but I believe that there's an inverse relationship between our mood and the amount of times we check our phones during the day. And yet phones are a ubiquitous part of our lives and they're not going away. So what I want you to do is go on an intermittent "phone fast" for a single hour each day. Thirty minutes when you wake and 30 minutes before bed. That's it. If you can protect those two blocks of time from the intrusion of technology, I guarantee you'll be in the Yellow Zone (or maybe the Green Zone) before long. I began an experiment about a year ago using myself as the only subject. The premise was simple: if I muted the alerts on my cell phone during the beginning and ending hours of the day and switched the screen to gray scale instead of seeing colors, would I feel calmer? The answer didn't take long to take and the evidence is evident. I feel more freedom and ease in my mind even during stressful moments of the typical day.

Now, let's turn to other curious findings. Look at the Mental quadrant. There's only one red area, so generally it's very good, but the red is associated with the question "I work in the evenings and on weekends." Of the 16 questions, this one is in the bottom four.

Let me remind you that this Resilience Assessment has been filled out largely by business leaders like yourself. Like you, they're afraid of losing their edge, so they're working themselves to the bone, riding that edge of burnout, which, as we've said, is a dangerous place to be. The other thing you're doing as a leader is modeling the kind of behavior that will lead to burnout for the members of your organization as well.

We've got these phones in our pocket and in our hands, so in a way, we're always at work. We think that's the way to success. But it's not. It's the way to burnout.

If you're working day and night, first one to arrive and last to leave, then chances are, your employees are seeing that and thinking, "That's how I have to be." You don't. That's why you're here.

The next curious finding is in the Emotional quadrant. In fact, it's the entire quadrant itself. On this assessment, the leaders who are filling it out are scoring amazingly well regarding their self-assessment of their emotions.

I don't believe things are as rosy as all that. If you look closely at the four questions, you'll see that they address the question of self-belief. Which makes sense, doesn't it?

If you're a leader, you get to where you are because you have a strong sense of self and an almost unshakable belief in that sense of self. That's a strong combination and something we want in our leaders.

But it reminds me of a conversation I had with a former Air Force pilot who recounted a time when he was standing with his commanding officer on the tarmac, about to fly a practice sortie (mission) of his own, when a plane full of his comrades went down nearby. The Air Force pilot was a young man at the time, in his early twenties, and he was understandably quite shaken by what he'd witnessed and he wanted to run to help his friends to see if there was any way he could help.

Instead, his commanding officer grabbed him by the collar and said, "Do your job. Walk your plane. Do. Your. Job." Which, in an organization like the military makes a certain kind of sense, because the pilot was about to go up in the sky and any kind of emotional distress could lead to his demise as well. The lesson he got from his commanding officer was simple: Bottle it up. Compartmentalize your feelings. Grit it out.

That's not the change-proof way of leadership. We have to do our jobs. Of course, we do. But we have to be emotionally present and aware so we can do our jobs effectively and efficiently for a long time. "Bottle it up" may get you through the next mission, but what about the next one? And the next?

It works really well in the short term, but we know from the incidence of PTSD, suicide, and other post-military service challenges that it's lethal in the long term.

CHANGE-PROOF POINT

▶ To be resiliently change proof you must be consciously aware of your emotions as well as those of your people. You may not like it or feel ready, but their emotions are your responsibility.

PART III

Change-Proof Hardware

CHAPTER 11

Recovery Versus Burnout

*Houses were shut tight, and cloth wedged around
doors and windows, but the dust came in so thinly
that it could not be seen in the air, and it settled
like pollen on the chairs and tables, on the dishes.*
—JOHN STEINBECK

A friend of mine is a writer, but he comes from a family of farmers in South Dakota. Recently, he told me a story about the last years of his grandfather's life. This man had been a farmer his entire life. He'd been working the ground that he got from his father, who came over from Germany after World War I and carved out a life for himself and his small family. The same soil had been in the same family for almost a hundred years.

But as the years had gone on, my friend's grandfather didn't pass the land over to his son-in-law and grandson. He stubbornly refused to heed their gentle admonitions about the ways he was farming the land. He failed to remove the many boulders that had lived in the earth since the Ice Age, tamping them down deep enough for him to plant crops. He was like the kid who sweeps the dust under the rug instead of into the bin. In sum, because he was stubborn, he stopped doing what he knew worked, and he failed to innovate to the new methods (that harnessed the power of modern technology and the wisdom of the soil), and then he died.

My friend was talking to his uncle at the funeral, who told of whole drainage ditches filling up with dead topsoil, finishing with this kicker, "What your grandfather did to that soil, what he failed to do, it's going to take a hundred years for the soil to return to its natural state." A hundred years.

OK then, let's go back almost a hundred years and imagine it's late 1929. You're not a farmer in the Dakotas but in the Oklahoma Panhandle. You still plow the land your family had even before the Oklahoma Land Rush that gave the state's new residents their nickname, "Sooners," 30 years before. Your family farm has been passed down for generations, providing each with the means to a comfortable, happy life. You have just enough every year but not so much as to grow idle. That's the life you got from your parents and it's the one you'll give to your kids.

Little did you know that too many of the out-of-territory farmers were interested only in making a quick buck off of stolen land purchased for pennies on the dollar. Without the institutional knowledge of the ground that they were tilling, they used mechanized farm techniques assuming that technology guaranteed huge yields. And for 30 years, it has. They've grown rich off the land, sending money and grain back East and building generational wealth in the soil of middle America.

But they didn't know what they were doing to the soil, the earth, the land. They were planting crops in the wrong soil and then keeping them there, season after season, stripping the earth of its nutrients and power. They didn't rotate the crops. They exhausted the land. They burned out the soil. Without realizing it, they created conditions concomitant to catastrophe.

Then the spring of 1930 didn't bring the rain they'd had for the last decade. That continued into the summer and the fall and into the next year, resulting in a drought that changed the American prairie forever.

Now not only can you not get anything to grow, but the neighboring farms are just drying up and flying away into the sky. It's impossible to keep your land alive while everything around it is dying. Next thing you know, your family farm is just choking dust. It's everywhere, all the time, and your once happy, comfortable existence is now a dusty wasteland. You leave your family's farm, the one that's been passed down for generations, empty, abandoned, as you pack your earthly belongings and your family and head west to California, where if you're lucky, you might get a job picking vegetables for somebody else.

In 1930, no one thing caused the drought. It was a natural disaster. You can't really plan for them. Acts of God don't come with a herald or a warning. Usually, the droughts wreak a little short-term damage, but that can be managed within a season or two. When the system is healthy, it can rebound to its original state pretty easily. Acute events can be tolerated in the absence of chronic problems.

But in 1930, because of what the Sooners did to the earth, the drought was catastrophic. Because of the chronic damage to the top layer of soil, nothing would find purchase and grow. Burned out, devoid of any kind of vital force, the soil in Northern Oklahoma, Western Kansas, and parts of Nebraska just kind of gave up and blew away into the air, into the atmosphere, causing the sun-blocking dust storms that give the era its name.

What's the lesson? We might well be on the edge of another Dust Bowl in the farmland today, but in the territory of our bodies we've been heading toward one for too long. If we want to be change proof, then we need to heed the signs.

For 30 years, farmers in Oklahoma failed to heed the warning signs from the land they were tilling. The environment was chronically sick in a way that couldn't be fixed overnight. Our bodies are no different. There's a reason why some Indigenous cultures revere the connection between the land and the body. The health of one is emblematic of the other. It's no accident that as our bodies become more and more unhealthy, we're also witnessing the body of the earth go through the exact same thing. They're inextricably bound up together.

In many ways, both culturally and personally, we haven't been truly aware of why our body functions the way that it does, leading to chronic health conditions that make it truly difficult to recover from truly catastrophic events. An unhealthy body is always teetering on the edge of disaster. Change will come, the only question is how will we be able to respond?

Our bodies, the land, our families, and our business, they're all connected.

> Like the earth that we inhabit, if we want our bodies to be change proof, then we need to heed the warning signs of chronic stress.

• • •

Let's go back to the beach. You're caught in the rip current. You know you're in real trouble and help isn't on the way. You're fighting like hell to swim back to shore, but you've exhausted almost all of your energy stores; your legs, arms, and lungs are about to give out. You look up and you're farther out to sea than when you started. In a literal sense, your body can give no more. It doesn't matter how long you swim, how hard you fight, or how much effort you put into swimming against that rip current, you will be swept away.

Sounds like how we've been living for years, trying to be all things to all people, to our families, to our Zoom colleagues, and to ourselves, and oh by the way, we're not leaving our houses. We're rushing around the same square footage from day to day as the world around us slips farther and farther away. We've felt as though we're doing three jobs for the price of one, the clock is continually running, and we have zero idea when this will all end. Meanwhile, we keep struggling. Because it's all we've been taught.

"Keep fighting."

"Never give up."

"The secret is more effort."

In short, we've become a wasted, used-up husk of our best selves. We're so busy trying to just get through today that when tomorrow gets here we've got nothing left. We're a car running on fumes or as Jackson Browne would say, "we're running on empty." We're burned out.

The term *burnout* was first used in print in 1952 in the autobiography of a Swedish runner named Gunder Hägg. According to Gunder, the local press in Sweden had taken to using the term to rationalize why he'd had a recent series of subpar results.

Indeed, most of our understanding of the concept of burnout comes from the world of elite sports, where athletes compete at the highest levels, oftentimes from a very early age. We can measure burnout because we can distinctly see the moment when an athlete's results take a downward trajectory. If there are no underlying physical symptoms of injury, then we can safely assume that the athlete is burning out.

What are the symptoms of burnout? They're different for every athlete and person, but a comprehensive study by Hernik Gustafson, Daniel J. Madigan, and Erik Lundkvist called "Burnout in Athletes" (2016) found that most athletes are resilient when it comes to stress and fatigue from an event or the grind of a long season. They rest, they recover, and they come back more motivated than ever.

However, to those suffering from burnout, the motivation not only doesn't come back, but symptoms like depression develop along with feelings of helplessness and a withdrawal from the circle of family and friends.

They came up with what burnout looks like:

- **Emotional and physical exhaustion.** This is a feeling of fatigue well beyond the usual empty-tank feeling one might get from a grueling competition or long training session.
- **A reduced sense of accomplishment.** This is that feeling one might see in a person who can no longer derive enjoyment from something that used to give them a reason for being.
- **Activity devaluation.** This is characterized by a cynical attitude toward the thing that makes them who they are. It's that feeling of "nothing matters" in response to training or competing. I imagine some of you feel that way about your job, your career, or your business, especially given how you've been tested.

It's important to note that these aren't merely for athletes. That's just the easiest, most efficient way to measure burnout. Actually, these definitions can be interchangeable when it comes to our business and our career. It's true in our mental states. It's also true of our relationships. It's true of our bodies. Even our spirits can burn out. Burnout is the enemy of resilience. The key indicator of burnout is an overwhelming fatigue that threatens to overrun the body, the mind, the heart, and the spirit.

The bit of the study that gave me pause was this:

> *The burnout experience is individual and the symptoms remain unnoticed for the individual for a long period of time. This makes the early detection of burnout difficult; especially because the negative attitude towards burned out athletes found in sports might prevent athletes from revealing their symptoms.*

It's a scary thing to realize that these symptoms can lie dormant in us and, if left unchecked, can blossom into full-blown burnout before we can do anything about it.

We've all been there: something used to fill us with passion, we're burning to do it, to do it all and all at once, and then one day it's something we do out of a sense of duty. I've worked with countless professionals in that exact place, some of whom are running the company that they always wanted to run. Our ambitions can make us successful, but they can also bring us down. Check out Shakespeare's *Macbeth* if you don't believe me. To paraphrase Mark Twain, the difference between "this is something I have to do" versus "this is something I want to do" is like the difference between a lightning bug and lightning.

OK. You're burned out. What do you do? The first step is admitting you're burned out.

Back when I was a lifeguard at Jones Beach, we were running a comparatively large swath of ocean front territory with thousands of people in and out of the water. We had to be at our best every moment of every day.

But that's not possible, is it? A group of young, fit, wildly attractive people in New York during the summertime in the early 1980s weren't exactly going to spend their free time living like monks and nuns. No, we were going to have fun and do a little partying to enjoy the perks of being the guardians of the Coppertone galaxy. That meant that some days we would come to work and frankly, we would not be at our best. We wouldn't be even close to our best.

What are you going to do? You can't be hungover up on the stand, trying to keep an eye on thousands of people, looking for sharks, and clocking the movement of the currents. That's a recipe for disaster.

So we had a system whereby the drowsy crew member, let's say it was me, went down the stand and grabbed 40 winks so they could be fresh for their next shift. We had each other's back so we could pause, recover, and come back stronger.

But here's the key difference—we had to ask. If I was feeling terrible from the night before, I didn't just wait for someone to recognize that I wasn't operating at peak performance. That's how things get missed. Important things. Like swimming in an ocean that has no sentimentality about human life. That's why our system was based on honesty. To ourselves and to our crew. It had to be.

So if I was still a little banged up from the night before, I'd come in first thing and say to whoever was crew chief that day, "Hey, I got a little out over my skis last night, I'm a little tender around the gills this morning." They'd immediately let me catch a recovery break. Someone might even bring me a slice for a quick snack. They knew I'd do the same for them. That's how we took care of one another. We were honest about what we needed.

That's what it takes. The pause, and the recovery, for us as lifeguards meant we had to be honest. No hiding. No pretense. No false bravado that says, "I'm strong. I got this. I'm just going to fight through the pain." That's how people die on the beach. The stakes were that high.

For us, just that little step, that little tweak made it possible for us to really have each other's backs.

CHANGE-PROOF POINT

▶ If you want to be change proof—you can pause. You can recover. But the first step is you have to be honest with yourself. Even if you're a leader, you have to say, "I'm burned out. I need to change." That's when people can really help you.

CHAPTER 12

Recover Before It's Too Late

Dogs do speak, but only to those
who know how to listen.
—ORHAN PAMUK

This entire section could just be this simple six-word sentence: Sled dogs pause before they're tired. If you take away one thing, let it be that simple fact. But as we'll come to find out, they don't pause themselves. They can't. It's not in their nature, so it has to be done for them. That's what we need to do for our physical selves.

Within each of us is a dog that wants to do everything, be everywhere, and work without ceasing. To master ourselves, we have to pause before we're really tired. The resilience pause is about recovery. And recovery should not be like *Brigadoon* (a mythical Scottish village that appears for one day every hundred years).

As humans we're animals, that's how our bodies evolved. As such, our physical resilience has basically been the same for hundreds of thousands of years because our physiological makeup is nearly identical to the very first *Homo sapiens*. But those early humans knew how to get the most out of their body, in spite of the fact that life back then was nasty, brutish, and short.

As we evolved, for much of that time, our body's cycle was much more instinctual. We ate when we were hungry. Drank when we were thirsty. Slept when we were tired. A simple cycle for simple brains.

But then as our brains developed and got bigger, we began to be able to think beyond our next meal, sip of water, or rest period. Our brains got bigger and bigger, and then one day we woke up and it's 2020. We had built cars and planes to take us all over the planet, and now we carry devices in our pockets that have a million times the computing power of the same computers that landed us on the moon. To the aliens likely watching us, it must have looked just like if your pet dog built a rocket that took her to the back of the butcher shop. We're miracles.

OK. Fair enough, we did it, we accomplished a miracle and in the blink of an eye (evolutionarily) evolved past our baser instincts. But what did it get us? Are we happier? Do we have more energy? Are we using our bodies the way we need to perform at our best for our entire lives?

If we're being ruthlessly honest with ourselves, then we know that mentally we've evolved in a miraculous way, but our bodies are completely unhealthy. We eat when we're starving. And then we don't stop. Then we feel guilty and fast for as long as we can. We don't see food as fuel. We eat because our emotions feel bad. Try explaining that to one of your prehuman ancestors. We forget to drink water because we're slugging coffee and diet soda. We've forgotten that we need glass after glass of water to cleanse our systems so we can actually focus on harmonizing with ourselves and the world around us. We go to bed only when we're so tired that we won't be consumed by the crushing anxiety that's been sitting on our shoulders all day. We toss and turn and wake up more tired than when our head hits the pillow.

Little wonder then we wind up in hospitals taking medicines that usually make us feel worse than whatever it was we were trying to deny feeling in the first place. It's a vicious cycle that we're all familiar with.

That's why we need to take our pause from dogs. My kids are going to destroy me for that unintended pun.

Let me introduce you to a dog named Duncan. He was my lifeguard. No one, and I mean no one, went down on his watch. I'm going to talk more about Duncan a bit later, but for now, I want to highlight this fuzzy golden retriever's lesson for us about how to pause.

Through sheer dumb luck, Duncan came to us after his big brother, Mr. Wilson, had been with us for a year. Wilson really was big, but Duncan grew fast and they were immediately best friends. They even slept together.

For us, Duncan became the loving caretaker of the house and his big brother. See, Wilson would come down with these ear infections that he was prone to getting. Whenever he did, Wilson would just keep everything tight, close to the vest, never letting us know he was in pain. He was that kind of dog. He'd just cruise around, doing his thing. So Duncan would have to stop him, get him in one spot, and lick Wilson's ear. It sounds gross, but some dogs have to be paused. That was Duncan's signal to us that his brother needed our attention. We'd get him to the vet, and good old Wilson would be right as rain. Duncan was responsible for his recovery.

True to his nature, Duncan also took responsibility for me. As I mentioned earlier, I'm a Pisces so I'm constantly in the water, swimming and regenerating my spirit. Duncan, when he saw me swimming out, well, he didn't like me in the water. Wilson would do the same thing every time: He'd swim out 15 yards. And then back. That one lap. That was it. Like an old man at the YMCA pool.

Duncan had no use for it. If you threw a stick anywhere in the world, Duncan might retrieve it. But not in the water. He hated the stuff. From the beginning, Duncan was a land dog down to his paws.

So much so that when I'd take the two brothers to the beach with me, we'd have a quick walk to get a good sweat and then I'd go for my swim. I'd wade out past the breakers trying to ignore Duncan's imploring barks, begging me to come back to the safety of the shore. He just couldn't understand why I wasn't afraid of the water. Like he was.

Then one day, the barking stopped. I turned and swam on my back. Duncan wasn't on the shore. He was swimming out to me. Even though this fuzzy gold dog was terrified of the water, and even though he'd completely misunderstood why I was there, he'd decided that no one was going down on his watch. In Duncan's case though, he was crying, making sounds like a baby because he hated the water and hated what it (he believed) was doing to me. Even his deeply held fear of the water didn't give Duncan pause. He just hopped into the water to run a rescue. To this day, I still can't believe he did this.

This went on for years, the exact same way. I would take Wilson and Duncan to the beach, we'd do our walk, Wilson would do his 15 yards, and I would wade in to get my exercise. Like clockwork, Duncan would be whining and crying alongside me.

And you know what the strange part was? Duncan was a really good swimmer. Doing his little doggie paddle, he was surprisingly strong through the chest; he had no trouble at all keeping up with me. That was the hard part, his dog anxiety was so palpable that I had to swim faster just to keep a little distance between us. No matter how many calming words I said to him, he wouldn't rest, wouldn't stop until he got me back on safe ground. But once we were, he was choking and coughing up seawater. His worry for my safety was making him sick.

A born lifeguard, Duncan didn't know how to turn himself off, he didn't know how to pause. Because he decided that his anxiety, his dog's heart, was not going to let anything bad happen to anyone. In the same way that Duncan was able to pause Wilson, he wasn't able to pause himself.

Dogs and humans aren't really that different. We've bred them to be resilient. But we have to show them how.

In 2020, the *New York Times* did a series of articles and essays on resilience. One of the writers was a musher, Blair Braverman, a female adventurer, who raced in the epically challenging Iditarod in 2019. She's the author of the book *Welcome to the Goddamn Ice Cube* about the challenges of being a woman in the male-dominated field of competitive dog racing.

She's also a fantastic writer and in the *New York Times*, she nailed down the why of the pause before we get to the how. She talks about the wisdom of the animals who pull her sled and how they can anticipate many of the dangers they'll face together on the almost 1,000 miles of Alaska terrain during the Iditarod. Ice, predators, weather—the dogs have a sense for them.

At the same time, the musher has to anticipate the dogs' needs before they're aware of them. Here's what Blair says about the dogs' pause. "One of the most surprising things about distance mushing is the need to front-load rest." That sounds an awful lot like a pause, doesn't it?

> *You're four hours into a four-day race and the dogs are charging down the trail, leaning into their momentum, barely getting started—and then, despite their enthusiasm, it's time to stop. Make straw beds in the snow, take off your dogs' bootee, build a fire, heat up some meat stew (for the team, but hey, you can have some too) and rest for a few hours. The dogs might not even sit down; they're howling, antsy to keep going. It doesn't matter. You rest. Four hours later, you rest again.*

It's counterintuitive for us. We're conditioned to red-line until we burn out. Even if things are going well. Especially if they're going well. We ride that wave like a gambler on a hot streak. We do that to ourselves and those of us who are leaders tend to do it to our people. We say, "She's doing so well. Give her more cases, more responsibility." That's where we often fail our people.

We've got to take the lesson from our sled dogs, who may not like it but they've got to rest at the beginning so they've got something left later. "It's far easier to prevent fatigue than to recover from it later. But resting early, anticipating your dog's needs, does something even more important than that: It builds trust." That's what we're trying to do with ourselves and for the people who work for us. We have to use the pause to build trust so that they'll be able to perform resilience when they need it. That's why sled dogs pause before they're tired.

Blair Braverman puts it so beautifully when she writes: "You can't make a sled dog run 100 miles. But if she knows you've got her back, she'll run because she wants to, because she burns to, and she'll bring you along for the ride." What this means for people, for us, is that we can't just plan to take care of ourselves later. We shouldn't expect to catch up on sleep when we really crash, or to reach out to loved ones after we're struck by loneliness. We should ask for support before we need it. We should support others before they ask. Like Captain Bob showed us, we must get each other's backs. Because if you don't know how far you're going, you need to act like you're going forever.

That's so right, Blair. Resilience is forever. And forever is what we are after.

CHANGE-PROOF POINT

▶ For leaders and their teams, it's vital to build rest and recovery into your schedule so your organizational talent is available for the long journey.

CHAPTER 13

Even Michael Jordan Paused

I want to wake up every day and do whatever
comes in my mind, and not feel pressure or
obligations to do anything else in my life.
—MICHAEL JORDAN

At this moment, I'll bet you're saying to yourself, "Adam, you daft fool, I can't pause! Pause? My business is being disrupted, I have to grind every single day just to stay in the same spot. If I "pause," then my business, job, career, team, and so on will cease to exist."

OK. That's fair. I've heard that before. But you want to be change proof. You want the kind of resilience that's there when you need it for as long as you're around. You want that for yourself and your business too. You want to be built to last. That's what being resilient is all about.

"Can't I do it without the pause?" What if I told you the most competitive athlete of all time, a man who hated losing more than he liked winning, who lived to crush the heart, will, and spirit of his opponents, took a pause that lasted almost two full seasons?

I'm a Knicks fan, born, bred, and buttered. I come from a family of Knicks fans. I don't even remember choosing them. They just were for me and I was for them. That's because if you come from New York, the Knicks are essentially a public trust. They're owned by the Dolan family, but New Yorkers (arguably the smartest basketball fans in the world) know that the team really belongs to them.

Which is why it hurts so much when they lose. Which they've done for most of my life in ways both inventive and banal. We've seen defeat snatched from the jaws of victory more times than I can remember.

Chances are, if you see the words "Knicks fan," they're preceded by the words "long-suffering." We've had years of hope, post-season runs that brought us to the gates of heaven, only to have them locked in front of us. Real New Yorkers know what I mean. Then the years where we're just terrible and there's no hope at all, except for the hottest draft pick or free agent that might be just around the corner. But they never are. And yet Madison Square Garden is always full. And always rocking.

My father, who raised me to have the same Knicks sickness he had, actually wrote a letter to the legendary head coach Red Holzman, who coached the team to their only championships in its history. For years, during the 1970s, my father complained about the style of play the Knicks had at that time. This was back in the days when you could just type a letter to the head coach of the most visible team in the known world, and there was a good chance he would read it.

My father's complaint with Red's coaching was simple: it was the same pattern every game. The Knicks would come out, bored, listless, and disinterested, and they would play down to their competition throughout the first half. As a result, they'd be down big going into the intermission.

Then the second half would start the same as the first, until about halfway through the third quarter. Then the Knicks would go on a run and claw their way back into the game—which was much harder back then because these were the days before the three-point line. The game would go down to the wire, and the Knicks, our beloved Knickerbockers, would lose in the final moments. They would depress our hopes at the outset, our hopes would soar in the middle section, only to be crushed at the end.

My father diagnosed, correctly, that the team was coming out flat early and then using all their energy to get back in the game so that by the time the end rolled around, they were spent. They burned through their collective resources trying to get to level. Little surprise they had nothing left at the end. On a game-by-game basis, they were burned out. Those who know, recognize the basic three-act dramatic structure we Knicks fans are well-acquainted with: tragedy.

Now flash forward to the early months of 2020 and remember how deeply unsettled we all felt. The year began with a real tragedy: the sudden, violent death of the great and complicated basketball player, Kobe Bryant, his daughter Gianna, and seven others in a helicopter crash. Then within six weeks, Tom Hanks and Rita Wilson had contracted the airborne virus that was just beginning to sweep the globe, all sports were shut down, and we were all locked in our homes for, well, no one knew how long.

As difficult as those early months of 2020 were for all of us, one of the bright lights that broke the gloom of quarantines, lockdowns, and rising infection rates was the reappearance of Michael Jordan in my life. His presence was a comforting balm that seemed to ease the anxiety of the moment. Which, as a Knick fan, is the hardest thing to admit, because in the early nineties my beloved Knicks, led by Pat Riley, were the toughest team in the NBA and the ones who pushed number 23 to some of his highest heights.

The year began with Michael giving such a touching eulogy for the little brother he never wanted but grew to love: Kobe Bryant. The notoriously competitive basketball player gave a speech that was part remembrance, part gentle roast, and full of heart and humor. Michael allowed us to see him and that, in turn, allowed us to remember Kobe and his daughter, and, without realizing it, prepared us for the year that was to come.

Then in mid-April, while we were all stuck at home, bereft of sports and its low stakes distractions, ESPN decided to move up its 10-part Michael Jordan documentary called, fittingly, *The Last Dance*. It was wonderful to see Michael again, young, spry, a physical and spiritual marvel, leaping and jumping, and cementing his legacy as the greatest artist in basketball history. As it was to see the zany but canny trickster, Dennis Rodman; the generous but insecure Scottie Pippen; Steve Kerr, with a shot as sharp as his wit; and the Zen master himself, Phil Jackson, a former Knick during their last championship season. Along the way, we got to see glimpses behind the curtain of the real Michael Jordan, a relentless competitor, caustic with teammates and management, with a nearly indomitable will to dominate everyone and everything.

I was fascinated to see the sequence where Michael, after leading three consecutive championship teams (twice beating my Knicks—I will never fully forgive Charles Smith), was exhausted. Beyond exhausted, because a year earlier he was part of a legendary Dream Team that brought the gold medal back to the United States. He'd been driving himself hard, too hard for too long. He started to wonder if he still had the motivation to be "Michael Jordan" for another season. To make matters worse, Michael was the subject of a series of stories about huge gambling debts to some unsavory associates—the sheen was off Michael's squeaky-clean image. He was burned out. He was the victim of his chronic ambition and needed to just "keep going" no matter what. The very thing that made him successful, the white-hot flame that burned inside him, was starting to consume him.

Then it all came crashing down in August of 1993. The world woke up to the awful news that Michael's beloved and respected father, James, who instilled in him the competitiveness that became the driver of Michael's ambition, was murdered in a seemingly random act of greed and violence. This, we learned in *The Last Dance*, was the tipping point where chronic, unaddressed stress met an unimaginable acute event.

We call them "unimaginable" because we literally can't imagine them ever happening. These are the events for which we think we need to find resilience. "When bad things happen, I bounce right back." That's what we say to ourselves. We know that's not how resilience works. In every respect, to truly be resilient, we have to have it before we need it.

So how did Michael Jordan find the resilience to retire, play baseball, and then return to win three more titles? Because he paused. At the time, that's one thing I could never reconcile. He was so competitive it almost bordered on sociopathic. He used his Hall of Fame induction speech to settle old scores and wounds. He really took two seasons off? In the prime of his career? Even though my Knicks finally got to the NBA Finals, I didn't fully believe it.

But stuck at home because of a global pandemic, watching *The Last Dance* 25 years after Michael's sudden retirement, I finally got it. Michael walked away from the game he loved, the game that gave him life, because he didn't have the proper motivation to be a killer 82 days and nights of the season. He was ruthlessly honest with himself, so the world, of course, was shocked.

I can hear what you're saying right now, "Oh, great for Michael Jordan and his millions of dollars who can retire in his early thirties and indulge any dream he had no matter how crazy." You roll your eyes so far you're looking at the ground behind you. "I'd be like Mike—if I had his money." And, to an extent, you'd be right.

But look at it a moment from the thin heights of Air Jordan and see what he was giving up and how difficult a decision it must have been for him. He was walking away at the top. The one thing he fought to obtain and here he was voluntarily giving it up, making a sacrifice of it so that he could be around for longer. There were a lot of people who were depending on him. A person like Michael Jordan is more a corporation than a person. But he had plenty of money. That wasn't the thing that scared him.

I think the thing that scared him the most was once you step off the top of the mountain, you might never get back. That's often why we don't take the risk to pause and recover. We're afraid that everything we've built will vanish. Or we'll be disrupted out of our industry entirely. We see ourselves at the edge of a cliff, on a treadmill running at top speed, and if we stop we'll tumble off the machine and over the cliff. Oblivion.

Yeah, maybe MJ comes back and wins one or two more titles. Maybe that's it. He knew, intuitively knew that he wasn't going to be great for as long as he possibly could. He took an honest accounting of his resources and chose recovery now. Before he truly needed it.

He went to play baseball. This is what he said, "When I lose the sense of motivation and the sense to prove something as a basketball player, it's time for me to move away from the game." On the surface this seems pretty simple. But when we're honest with ourselves it's only simple on the surface.

Just to be clear here: I'm not suggesting that you, as a business leader, step away from your company for two years while you go and indulge your childhood dreams. If you did that, you'd be replaced and you'd have to find another team to play for because your version of the Chicago Bulls can't wait for you.

Michael Jordan was a company unto himself. There were hundreds of people depending on him playing basketball; in fact, it was the entire NBA that was depending on him to sell their game to the country and to the entire world.

Michael Jordan was the most popular, visible, and untouchable person in the world. And he decided to play baseball. That way he could come back in a season and half and go on a run for the ages that turned him from legend into myth. He gave up short-term certainty for long-term gain. By pausing. What you have to do, as a business leader, is stop and take stock of where you are. You have to take stock of who you are. Be like Mike. Go Knicks.

Ask: The Why Before the How

As a business leader, you know full well what a lonely position you're in. You sit at the big desk and make the big dollars, but you've also got the big responsibility. The key for you is how can you empower your organization by everyone being responsible? You might be wondering: How does a physical pause transition into an ask that works for a business? And how can I, in turn, leverage that into an ask that will lead to tangible resilience? Great question. How do you ask with your company?

Now let's look at how we can learn from an organizational ask. There's an interesting story about Sir Dave Brailsford who took over the British cycling team in 1998. In a short, but dense interview with *Harvard Business Review*, Brailsford laid out a very simple structure for how an organization can ask the right questions that lead to short-term results, but wind up costing them in the long run.

It's two questions that we're asking here: *How*? and *Why*? Which question you choose to emphasize and the order in which you do it will define your organization for its life span. If you don't have harmony between the two, that life span won't be long.

Let's dig in. In the interview, Brailsford mentions that when he came to manage the UK cycling team in 1998, even a bronze medal was a fantasy, let alone a dream of a gold medal. That was Camelot as far as anyone was concerned. From the beginning, his intention was to get the UK cycling team to the top of the podium. But rather than forcing big conceptual changes, he thought and taught in increments. He majored in the minor, and extolled his athletes: "Forget about perfection; focus on progression, and compound the improvements." He focused on the *how* first.

Small improvements and leveraging marginal opportunities came from "Podium Principles" that were based on a Japanese concept we'll get to in a bit.

Strategy

"For strategy we analyzed the demand of each event and spent a lot of time trying to understand what it would take to win." They found that they had to be "compassionate but ruthless" with the athletes who weren't measuring up in terms of optimal performance.

Human Performance

"We weren't even thinking of cycling, but more about behavioral psychology and how to create an environment for optimum performance." This is about culture. We're going to return to this later when we talk about the spiritual resilience of an organization.

Continuous Improvement

Brailsford had training as an MBA, and in nearly every business program, students learn the ways of Kaizen. *Kaizen* is a Japanese word based on two characters: "kai" which means "change" and "zen" which means "good." That means Kaizen is a good detour for a book about change.

This concept was developed in Japan after World War II as the Americans helped build back the manufacturing power of their former enemy, and it's been exported all over the world as companies look for every competitive advantage that they can find. The Kaizen Institute says that the entire concept is rooted in continuous improvement and has certain principles that undergird the marginal gains approach:

- Good processes bring good results.
- Go see for yourself to grasp the current situation.
- Speak with data; manage by facts.
- Take action to contain and correct root causes of problems.
- Work as a team.
- Kaizen is everybody's business.

When it came to continuous marginal improvements, Brailsford noted that in the team truck where the bikes were stored and repaired, dust was becoming a gathering problem. In a fast-paced sport like track cycling, the difference between a gold medal and seventh place can be tenths of seconds, so a team has to be vigilant against even tiny motes of dust and dirt. One of these small improvements was deceptively simple: they painted the floor of the team trucks white. Any imperfections would be immediately spotted and it became much easier to keep clean. Clean truck, clean bikes. Clean bikes, fast bikes.

He went further. In these pandemic times, we're all experts on handwashing, but in 1998, it was considered revolutionary. They hired a surgeon to teach athletes about proper handwashing, so they could get through multiweek events like the Olympics without catching and passing cold viruses. They drilled down into the nutritional space as well as sleep training, long before either were publicly accepted. Everybody is accountable. Everybody is responsible.

Simple solutions based on awareness and asking the right *how* questions led, in Brailsford's estimation, to the most impactful consequence of their new attack: a kind of "contagious enthusiasm" among the members of the team. As he puts it, "Everyone starts looking for ways to improve. There's something inherently rewarding about identifying marginal gains—the bonhomie is similar to a scavenger hunt. People want to identify opportunities and share them with the group. Our team became a very positive place to be." So positive that they won not just one gold medal at the 2008 Summer Olympics, they won seven.

Yet Brailsford soon came up against the limitations of a *how* based approach to team building. Track cycling is a sprint. It's on a shorter track, the races are fast and intense. Little gains make a huge difference in the resilience of a team.

Brailsford tried to transfer the *hows* of the track to the leg-and-lung shattering endurance cycling races. I'll let him tell it:

> *Interestingly when I moved from the track to the Tour de France, we didn't get it right at all; our first races were well below expectation. We took an honest look and realized that we had focused on the peas, not the steak. We tried so hard with the bells and whistles of marginal gains that our focus was too much on the periphery and not on the core. You have to identify the critical success factors and ensure they are in place, and then focus your improvements around them. That was a harsh lesson.*

We see here that one operating philosophy will not suffice. You and your organization need to be in harmony. Events ebb and flow and so do the things that bring us success.

The other caveat was,

> *That the whole marginal gains approach doesn't work if only half the team buys in. In that case, the search for small improvements will cause resentment. If everyone is committed, in my experience it removes the fear of being singled out—there's mutual accountability which is the basis of great teamwork.*

That's why resilience is such a commitment, because the moment you think you've figured out the solution to your problem and you're seeing tangible gains, then another problem arises. The tide is always going out and coming in.

There's no one question you should be asking of yourself and your organization. You can ask the right question but at the wrong time. Put it this way: the *why* is the soil in which you plant, the *how* is how you help that plant become the best plant it can be.

CHANGE-PROOF POINT

▶ If you have your values in place and you're asking why questions early on, then all your how questions will be coming from the right place.

CHAPTER 14

Outperforming Challenges

*You can't be brave if you've only had
wonderful things happen to you.*
—MARY TYLER MOORE

W hat's the phrase from when we were kids? "Sticks and stones may break my bones, but names will never hurt me." You remember that little sing-song rhyme we'd have to deploy against our bullies and their relentless name calling? For a million years, if our earliest ancestors of the *Homo sapiens* variety wanted to eat, then sticks and stones were all they had. That's why they climbed down out of the trees and began to run.

That's the theory at least, according to a groundbreaking study done by Dennis Bramble and Daniel Lieberman in *Nature* (2004) who write, "Everyone says humans are bad runners, because when you think of running you tend to think of sprinting. There's no question we're appalling sprinters, but we're quite good at endurance running."

At first, our ambling forebears didn't have much success out of the trees. They just weren't fast enough over short distances to run down prey. However, they were fast enough to realize that if they couldn't sprint and catch dinner, then they were going to run farther and longer than their prey ever could. Essentially, they were running their food until it got heat stroke and collapsed from the strain on its cardiovascular system.

In effect, these early humans' long-distance running ability across the flat grassland of the savannah of Africa—combined with their prey's inability to regulate their own temperature through their skin—made it possible for them to thrive and eventually made it possible for *Homo sapiens* to exist. At an evolutionary level, we're built for the long term, not the short term. Even at our most basic, our resilience is a marathon not a sprint. It's an important lesson to note. Our bodies are built to be resilient. Our bodies are built for long-term endurance.

The question is, Do we feel that way? When we think of exercise and moving our body, do we feel like we were born to run? Did those prehumans run so we could binge the latest season of the new streaming show everyone's talking about? No, they didn't.

Going back to Dr. Michael Maddaus and the resilience bank account, one of the main ways that we can make deposits is a regular course of aerobic exercise and resistance training. What he contends is not only does the body benefit, but our brains also are impacted by regular aerobic exercise. Check out these benefits:

- Thirty to forty percent reduction in risk of developing Alzheimer's disease, with the risk decreasing with even more exercise
- Significant protection against the normal cognitive decline seen with aging
- Improved memory, learning, motor skills, and executive function

The benefits to our brains don't stop there either; regular exercise causes significant improvement in:

- Cognitive tasks that "depend primarily on the prefrontal cortex attention, concentration, working memory, reasoning, and planning"
- A marked improvement in our moods
- A distinct drop in stress levels that can last up to a day or more

So as the early running bodies evolved, the brain evolved with it, in terms of social coordination, planning, and mental maps.

The harmony of resilience needs regular exercise. Just ask our ancestors about when they chose to climb out of the trees and run their hearts out. If you want to have a resilient body, then you need to move that body. It wants to move, it needs to move, and we know now, that it's wanted that for a million years. That means, if you're able to, you have to choose to move your physical body every single day. Some kind of physical exercise. At least 20 minutes. If you want to be resilient for the long term, this is nonnegotiable.

For the moment, let's talk about insurance. Life insurance.

One day, I was doing what we all do sometimes, I was doing some light googling of my name. It's not something I'm particularly proud of, but as a moderately public person, it's something I need to check in on occasionally. As long as I don't engage with it, it keeps the two wolves of anxiety and vanity at bay.

One day, on my travels on the information superhighway, I came across something that made me do a double take and belly laugh. I happened upon a company, based near Richmond, Virginia, called the Markel Corporation. Their product? Life insurance. That's funny because I grew up in a household that abhorred life insurance. My father taught us that.

My dad was a civil servant working for the New York City Parks Department for 30 years, and he's where I got some of my opinionated nature from. Like a real New Yorker, he had a ton of opinions about the world and he wasn't shy about expressing them. I can still hear our tiny apartment ringing with his voice, and I love that about him to this day.

He taught us from a very early age how to love, how to treat people less fortunate than us, and to never ever discriminate against anyone, for any reason. He gave my brother and me permission to be bold and fully expressive, especially when defending a moral or ethical position. It's no wonder, looking back at it, that my younger brother and I both became lawyers.

One of his core beliefs was about the dangers of money, specifically, life insurance. He always said, "Nobody is going to profit off my death." And that's exactly what he would say to the insurance salespeople who would occasionally show up at our apartment door. Can you imagine that today? Somebody just showing up on your doorstep to sell you life insurance? Well, Dad couldn't imagine that either. He would tell these perfectly nice people that no policy to profit from his demise was going to be sold to us.

While he might have been a little hostile to the salesman at the door, he showed me what self-responsible health consciousness looks like. He spent hours a day outside after teaching a class of preschoolers to paint with their fingers and sing songs. He ate something called "wheat germ" and wouldn't eat vegetables that came out of a can. He insisted that we eat slowly and really chew our food. A few clichés to be sure, but he modelled for us the person of someone committed to living a long and healthy life. True to form, my father took care of himself, and he still does.

On the other hand, my wife's dad, a man affectionately known as "Papa Lou," had plenty of life insurance. Papa Lou got his name because he took care of everybody, his wife, his kids, his friends, or perfect strangers. He was a real caretaker because he considered it selfish to think about himself.

Tragically, the one person he didn't take care of was himself. It got so he and I had to have some difficult conversations about his beliefs and how they were impacting his body. I'd say, "Papa, you need to take care of yourself. Your family loves you. We want you around for as long as you can." Sometimes I'd have to really get on him about his belly and his body and what we and he knew it was doing to his health.

But Papa Lou, he wouldn't hear of it. He took all our entreaties with his usual calm smile. To Papa Lou, exercise was a waste of time because it was only for him. He was a man who didn't do anything if someone else didn't benefit too. He was selfish that way. I miss him every day. You see, it just wasn't in his nature to diet or exercise. I firmly believe that there's not a single book that would have propelled that sweet man to move his body the way it was designed to.

OK, on to Angelo Poli and his secret formula for our resilient body. I'll let him tell you:

> *Raise your hand if you want to have better health, better fitness, lose a few pounds, get in shape. Everybody wants that. What's preventing us from getting there? I'll tell you what the missing ingredient is . . . by and large people are willing to put effort into something. Here's what's missing. They have to see results. They need to see progress. The greatest human motivator is progress.*

Progress. Little victories spread out over time. Just as Dave Brailsford transformed the British cycling team into something world class by making uncharacteristically minor changes, we can transform our bodies by aggregating small improvements over time. Incremental change may not sound sexy, but oh does progress propel more progress. For Angelo, progress is the key to long-term commitment to our body's resilience. When he works with his clients, it's important that they see tangible results over time.

However, haven't we all been there before? The holiday season ends, December 31 rolls over to January 1, and beset by guilt and a few extra pounds, we commit, really commit this time, to a program of diet and exercise. Maybe we got a new book as a holiday gift, so we start working out and eating better. For a few weeks or even months, the gains come fast and strong, and we see tangible results every time we look in the mirror. It feels good, better than good, and it feels like it's working.

But then as the winter gives way to spring, we begin to hit the dreaded plateau. The big and fast gains that we were seeing every day all of a sudden start to disappear. Our confidence starts to wane, maybe the calendar catches up with us, and the next thing we know we're eating a whole pizza while our family is asleep upstairs. Or maybe that's just me.

As the kids on the playground courts say, this is where Angelo "eats" because he makes a key distinction that unlocks lifelong body resilience. "We have to eat to live," he told me. "We have busy lives. It's always going to be a battle and it's a battle worth winning. It's never over. You've never won it. It's never, 'I conquered this. I can move on to something else.' That is a constant . . . The difference between values and goals, the difference between character and willpower."

If we're truly engaging in long-term commitment and resilience, then goals are the building blocks that make up values. If you set a goal and say, "By the time my next birthday rolls around I'm going to be this weight." That's great. Goals are a fantastic motivator. But they have a shelf life. Goals expire. Because you work hard until that next birthday and then what? You slide back. Because that's what we all do.

Then Angelo told me a story so this all makes sense. He asked me to imagine:

> You walk by a plate of cookies fresh out of the oven. Will-power tells you "I'm not going to eat those cookies. I'm on a meal plan. I'm going to avoid that." It's a pain that you have to endure every day. You wince a little bit. There

are decisions that you make in life. It's like a muscle. It fatigues you to use that willpower over and over, but there are other decisions that are almost identical that have no pain whatsoever. You sit down at a coffee table at a restaurant and the guy who left right before you put a $20 tip down for the waiter or waitress. You know for a fact that a waiter or waitress did not see them put the $20 tip down. Would you take that $20?

I answered, "Never in a million years." Angelo went further:

Does it take any effort to make that decision? Do you have to wince and go, "That's not my money?" You don't. That's your character. It's in your character. You're holding yourself to that standard. You adopt that as your value, as your character. Now, it's not painful. We can take that and apply those two principles. People ask me all the time, "How do I know when I'm at a place where this is sustainable?" They're looking for, What weight am I? What exercise routine? How athletic do I have to be before I've reached that point? To your point, with everything we've talked about, it's a mindset. It's not where you get your body to or where your health is now. It's whether or not you have adopted the lifestyle that's gotten you there as your value system, part of your character. If you have, there is no backsliding. It's only forward progress.

Again, there it is: Goals help, but only in the short term. Values, if they land inside of us, can last forever. When it comes to real resilience, this is going to be a running theme: if we truly desire resilience, then we have to choose values that make sense for us and for our bodies.

My dad sees his body as a vehicle that can take him where he wants to be if he cares for it properly. Though we never discussed it quite in these terms, I believe Papa Lou put caring for his body a distant second to caring for those he loved. More than anything, I wish he was around to see us now.

These days, our eldest daughter, Chelsea, has taken the baton of family health czar. She reminds her mom and I all the time about maintaining rituals for resilience. And it's ironic that she challenges me the way I used to challenge Papa when it comes to eating well and making time to recover from stress.

Postscript: just as I was finishing that last sentence, our youngest daughter walked in and put a green drink down in front of me—perfecto!

> Rituals, specifically physical ones, if we do them every day, no matter what, become part of our character. We don't even need to think about them, they just are.

• • •

A big part of my journey from *Pivot* to *Change-Proof* was discovering that resilience is the force that not only fuels the countless pivots we're going to have in our lives, but it's the force that binds us all together when the world is falling apart at the seams.

One of the people that I've gotten to know and am lucky and blessed to call a friend is Rodney Flowers. I'm so excited to introduce you to him here because he knows a lot about the limits of our human body and how we can outperform all different kinds of challenges.

Why? Because he went from the physical prime of his youth, on the cusp of the kind of athletic success that most of us could only dream of, when he lost his body. And he almost didn't get it back.

It's a running theme in this story of resilience that we don't know how change proof we can really be until we're tested.

As we now know, the testing never comes in the front door. It sneaks in through the windows, seeps in through the cracks in the foundation, or just crashes in through the roof. It's the way breakup songs are the best love songs and the way Joni Mitchell sang, "You don't know what you've got 'til it's gone."

When Rodney Flowers was 15, he didn't know what his body meant to him. All he knew was his body could run faster, go longer, and jump higher than anyone else his age. Back in 1993, Rodney was a football player. A damn good one. He was a sophomore in high school, beginning to catch the attention of scouts and about to embark on a season that would hopefully end in a state championship. He was just coming into the peak of his physical powers. If we could experience that once in our lives, I truly believe we'd all be gods.

Anyway, at the beginning of the second half of the very first game on the schedule, Rodney was covering the kickoff, running at a speed that would make a regular person feel the thrill of flight. Then the ball carrier turned right into his lane, and Rodney did what he'd been taught: he lit that kid up.

It was the kind of hit that makes the crowd, his teammates, even the opposing team go crazy. But as soon as he hit the ground, Rodney felt that godlike power leave his body in a rush. He couldn't move anything but his head. Instantly, he knew something was wrong. Nothing stops a football game like actual physical consequences for low-stakes violence. Around him, there wasn't a sound in the quaint high school stadium but his mother's panicked cries.

Later that evening, some doctor did Rodney the biggest favor of his life: he told young Rodney, a scared-out-of-his-wits high school sophomore, that he was going to be a vegetable for the rest of his life. Rodney is walking today because he didn't listen to Doctor Doom and he found the inner resilience that made it possible to make it through all the surgeries and the end of his childhood.

Mentally, he was wrecked, because as Rodney says:

> *I was mad at the world and everybody in it. I was mad at*
> *the Creator of the world. If there was anyone to be mad at,*
> *I was pretty mad. I felt like I had been dealt a bad hand.*
> *I was very active not with just football, with just my body*
> *and doing things around the house with my mom and dad.*
> *That came to a screeching halt and it was devastating. I*
> *was a fit guy. I worked out all the time. I couldn't do those*
> *things anymore. I couldn't do anything anymore for myself.*
> *Imagine that as a fifteen year old.*

Plato once said, "All learning is remembering." I go further and say this, "All learning is pain." By that I mean to say, there's no way to learn without suffering of some kind. Learning is based on moving from the certainty that says, "I know this deep in my bones." Then something happens to you that makes you question that calcium-rich certainty and moves you into uncertainty. You struggle for a while with the doubt and shame that come with any kind of change. Next thing you know, you find yourself mastering that change and moving into a new kind of certainty.

Again, tides coming in and tides going out. The tide coming in thinks it's the only tide that's ever going to be. But it doesn't know that the tide going out is waiting for its turn. When we suffer, we're in true harmonic pain that gathers our body, our mind, our heart, and our soul into a ball and hurls us into an infinite abyss. And we feel that this abyss goes down forever. Like dropping a rock down a well with no bottom.

But Rodney Flowers learned the lesson that defines resilience: nothing lasts forever. Not even forever lasts that long. Rodney told me, "Everyone has something in life, and mine just so happened to be in a wheelchair and paralysis. We all have something we have to deal with. That's the defining moment. What do you do when it shows up?" Rodney picked up and chose to ride the tides that were carrying him. Even if he couldn't use his body to get where he wanted to be in life, he still had his mind, his heart, and his spirit.

Rodney's mother taught him a tough lesson when she said to him, "There's nothing really wrong with you. You don't have your legs, but you still have your mind. If you have your mind, you can accomplish anything you want."

Rodney Flowers is walking today because he was grateful to be alive. That's where he started. The light he carries even today is, "The light is that I'm alive." He understood, at a very deep level, that the quality of what you do in the pause defines the quality of your life. The questions that you ask yourself define the quality of the life you get to live. And the choices that you make remake your life into the life that you need. You might not get the life you want, but that's the life that's outside you. Rodney Flowers knew that the one you need is the one inside your body. It's just waiting to get out.

We're not finished with the body, but the body is not enough to get us the resilience we need to become change proof for the rest of our lives. Let's let the indomitable Rodney Flowers take us out of the body and into the realm of the mind:

> *Let me add to the recipe because there is another question that I ask. That question is, "So what?" That question is applied to the things that show up that prevent us from moving, that keep us in the same place. Mine was paralysis. I thought for a while that because I was paralyzed, no one was going to want to hire me, that I wasn't able to get a job. I wasn't going to have a good life, that no one wanted to be around the guy that's disabled or paralyzed. Those were thoughts that are just stories that I would make up for myself because that's what I believed that my situation created for me. I created that story and I believed that story. In order to stop believing that story, I had to start asking "so what" questions, "So what if you're paralyzed?"*

That really jarred my mind because it's like, "That doesn't mean that I can't do this. It doesn't mean that I can't do that. I am paralyzed. I have a disability, but so what? You still can move forward." That's another part of the question and that led to the "what if" question. I would say, "So what do you have? What does that mean?" In the story that I had, it was basically a lie. It was something that I had to research and come to the conclusion that it really doesn't mean that. For people that are listening that may not be paralyzed physically but have something in the way that prevents you, that fear, that thing that you feel is going to happen as a result. That thing that is there but you feel like you can't get over it or go around it because it's there in the stories that you've created around it. So what if you're black? So what if you had a horrible past? That doesn't dictate your future. You are the creator of your future.

CHANGE-PROOF POINT

▶ You can determine the physical resilience of your organization by taking care of the bodies of your people and the environment in which they work.

CHAPTER 15

<hr>

Get out of Your Head

Nothing is either good or bad
but thinking makes it so.
—**WILLIAM SHAKESPEARE,** *Hamlet*

One of the biggest lessons I had to learn as a leader was the value of redundancy. For your people to know what you want, you're gonna have to keep saying it over and over again. Every time I sent a memo or gave a speech, I was worried that my employees were going to roll their eyes and say, "Here he goes again." I thought, "No one wants to listen to a broken record." I was more concerned with being interesting.

So what I did was constantly refresh and renew my message. What happened, without my realizing it, was that my desire to be interesting was getting in the way of me being clear. Clarity is what we're after. That's what redundant messaging gives us. It gives us the ability to be clear. Once you find out who you are, you have to make sure that everyone who crosses the doorway of your business knows who you are. They shouldn't have to guess. They're not mind readers. Redundancy is the key to your mindset.

How many of you know for certain that if you wake up in the middle of the night, the hamster of your thoughts will jump on the wheel of your mind and whirl from worry to anxiety to panic as you run disaster scenarios through your head? We run through all the bad things that have happened in our past and when we're not doing that, we're thinking of all the bad things that might happen in the future. It's our personal version of "doom scrolling."

For many of us on our resilience journeys, our misfortunes become like landmarks we visit on the cross-country journey that is our lives. When I was a kid, our family would take a yearly trip through New England, stopping in places like Hyannis, Bethel, and Stockbridge. Thanks to my mother's gift for being a travel agent, we stayed in beautiful places and created lifelong memories. We forgot about the endless hours in a hot and crowded car.

And later, as we all got older when we told the story of those same trips, even when we blew out an alternator or something that left us stranded on the side of the road for hours in the middle of the night, we laughed about it. After all, we made it through. We were forged a bit in those moments of trouble together.

Those are the stories we tell. Because they make us who we are. It's the things you never planned for, the times when things went wrong, and the ways in which the trip was just one damn thing after another. The damn things. Those are what we remember and mostly laugh at years later. The damn things don't appear on Trip Advisor or Kayak.

But as I get older, I realize that my entire life is a collection of memories that include some damn things despite my best intentions to the contrary. We're all striving to do good in the world, to be our best in our professional lives and in our personal lives. We have plans on top of plans, all created in good faith. Sometimes those plans go to hell in a flaming handcart.

Many of you have lost your business, or your job, or a loved one to the pandemic of 2020. The business you planned to give to your children. The job you expected to retire from. The partner you were going to grow old with. There's no way to assuage the grief of that loss. All the books in all the libraries of the world will not make it different. Because the painful and unavoidable truth is that it will never be different. It will never be the way you thought it was going to be.

Our work is about finding your way out of the darkness of damn things and into the light. Out of the valley and back up to the heights. To not just survive the damn things that happen around you, but to alchemize them into the stuff of real growth.

The key to mental resilience is realizing that all we can control in life is how we respond to events. We have that choice. We have that power. Mentally we can stop worry and anxiety dead in their tracks.

Change is guaranteed. How we respond to change is not. That is our task. There's a quote from renowned acting teacher Sanford Meisner that goes like this: "That which hinders your task is your task."

You're obsessed with something you want, but there's an obstacle in your way. It's that thing that's in between you and what you want, that is the thing you really need. The thing that's stopping you from accomplishing the things you desire? That's your true desire. You think what you can't control or what you don't know is keeping you from performing at your best. You think, "Once everything settles down, then I'll be better."

But that's not how it works. All over the world, in every culture, those leveraging uncertainty are the people and businesses who don't resist change when it happens. They develop new relationships. They ride the new situations instead of panicking. You don't fight the current, you ride the current. Surfers don't mourn a wave they miss or even when they wipe out (which is often). They just get on the next one.

You can do this by taking the courageous decision to throw out the old mental maps and make new ones. Mental resilience isn't a life free from the twin wolves of worry and anxiety. It's about harnessing our energy in creative ways so we can, like Blair Braverman in the last chapter, domesticate them and let them pull our sled. We make friends with change so we don't have to worry about it.

Now, as we transition from the resilient body to the resilient mind, you might be asking yourself: What is mental resilience? Can our thoughts really be change proof? The answer is short, but the journey to get there is long and winding. Yes, our thoughts can be resilient. We can train our minds to be comfortable being uncomfortable. It also may be the hardest work we do together.

Why? Well, here's why: a 2014 study found that people would rather subject themselves to electroshock than be alone with their thoughts. Let's say that again: people would rather experience physical pain than have to sit in silence with the contents of their own mind.

That's why we're going to talk about what the preeminent cognitive psychologist Albert Ellis calls "irrational beliefs" and how they're hindering the task of our mental resilience. We're going to talk a lot about old Albert. It's irrational beliefs that we can't bear to be alone with. It's not our thoughts. It's a kind of thought. If we can find our way to thinking the right thoughts, then we'll be resilient. Irrational beliefs are the damn things that we're going to pause, ask, and choose to find our resilient mind.

Let's commence with pausing our thoughts. You ready? Great, I am too. Let's do it! Put the book down. And see how long you can pause your thoughts. Don't think of anything at all. Let's see how well you can do. I'll do the same.

How did you do? How long did you last? I didn't last long. I tried, I really did. I went back to my breathing and tried to simply focus on that. I lasted maybe 20 seconds before the thought stampede began.

Here's the thing: the dirty secret is you can't pause your thoughts. Any exercise or book that says you can is selling you some well-meaning snake oil. Trying to stem the tide of your thoughts is as absurd a project as "emptying your mind" in the middle of a rip current. There's no on/off switch for thoughts.

Pausing your thoughts is literally impossible. Especially if you have to be a person with a job, a family, and all the attendant responsibilities of being a human in the world. You're not a monk sitting on a mountain. Even a meditation retreat would last for maybe two weeks.

It's the old saw about not thinking about a pink elephant. You're thinking of a pink elephant right now. So am I. Thoughts are tricky things. They're subject to their environment and forces beyond our comprehension.

Trying to hold your thoughts is like trying to hold quicksilver. Or herd cats. Or be a preschool teacher (like my dad was). Timothy Gallwey, the Zen master of tennis and author of *The Inner Game of Tennis*, writes, "The instant [you] try to make [yourself] relax, true relaxation vanishes." Telling yourself to relax works about as well as when someone tells you the same thing when you're in a particularly tense state. Your instinct is to do the opposite.

Our thoughts? They're ungovernable. That's why we need a tangible process to not attach to them. To let thoughts come and go without letting them dictate our actions in ways that keep us from our intentions.

Resilience is impossible without awareness. You see, we've left the physical world behind now; we're moving inward. In some ways, the work we do in physical resilience will be the easiest work we do. Operating in the material realm means we have tangible, measurable ways to gauge both gain and loss. The physical world is just easier to get our arms around. The mental world is far more expansive but nonetheless infinitely more rewarding. The physical world is finite. The territory of the mind? Well, that's a different fox hunt altogether. It's infinite. It's so infinite, in fact, that we're able to ponder the concept of infinity.

I like to think about infinity this way: Imagine a bird, the tiniest bird you can think of, like a hummingbird. Now imagine that this tiny bird goes to a beach and picks up one single grain of sand in its beak. Then it ascends high into the sky, then higher, somehow breaching the atmosphere, flapping its tiny wings in the vacuum of space and makes for the sun. It travels all that distance, those 92 million miles, and drops that single grain of sand into the sun. Then it turns and flies back to Earth, back to that same beach. It picks up another single grain of sand and flies to the sun. Then back home. It goes on like this until it has taken every grain of sand from that beach and dropped them into the sun. Now try to imagine that this tiny bird not only clears that first beach of sand, but she takes every grain of sand from every beach, every desert on the entire planet, one at a time, making the 180-million-mile round-trip journey every time. When every grain of sand is cleared from the surface of the earth? Infinity is just beginning.

That's the scale of deep time we're dealing with, when we think about the inside of our mind. It's literally infinite. It's likely that we know more about the outer reaches of our galaxy than we do about the contents of our own mind. You can't empty out infinity. Nor can you keep track of it all at every single moment. It's enough to bake your noodle. It does mine.

In my work, when I'm helping clients maximize the potential of their leadership or helping someone speak publicly to a crowd for the very first time, there's a phrase I hear all the time, "I'm in my head." Or they say, "I need to get out of my head." Another one that's common is, "We're overthinking this."

When I'm speaking publicly and I don't feel good about what I'm doing, I know exactly what they mean. Because it means I'm thinking my way through my talk, I'm not being guided from within. I'm lost in the chatter of my own thoughts, so I'm not connecting with the audience at a deep level.

Trying to think your way through a task means you'll be a beat ahead or a beat behind. The laws of mind and body are often at odds. The harder you hammer a nail, the faster it is set. Willpower works in that arena. With thought, the harder you try to think, the more constricted your thoughts become. Thinking actually defeats itself. It's self-sabotage. If you think about the moment, the moment's gone. Try to throw a lasso around that one.

Albert Ellis, Virgil to our Dante as we traverse this mental inferno, purgatory, and paradise, wrote, "People don't just get upset. They contribute to their upsetness. They always have the power to think, and to think about their thinking, and to think about thinking about their thinking, which the dolphin, as far as we know, can't do. Therefore they have a much greater ability to change themselves than any other animal has."

What mental resilience looks like is not avoiding the mind and our thoughts and seeing that world as a negative. Far from it. The mind is a wondrous place. It's where your imagination and creativity come from, it's where your ideas flow. Thoughts are thoughts.

Your thoughts are not good or bad. But they can be self-defeating. At every moment of the day, thoughts are passing through your mind at a speed that would make Superman seem pedestrian. Thoughts have the power to influence our own behavior and it can influence other people.

That's why we need to *pause*. Sit with them. See them as though somebody else is thinking them. That stops the flood of thoughts. Then we need to *ask* ourselves the questions that interrogate and reframe self-defeated beliefs. Finally, we'll *choose* useful thoughts that transform into a new set of proactive beliefs that will lead us to take empowering steps forward on the road to lifelong resilience. New beliefs, new actions, long-term growth. That's the key to becoming mentally change proof.

CHANGE-PROOF POINTS

▶ New actions are impossible without new beliefs.

▶ Your thoughts are the rudder for the ship of your body.

▶ Self-consciousness is the enemy of creative potential. Self-awareness is the ally for every growth edge you and your people can think of.

CHAPTER 16

≈≈≈

Mindset Recalibration

In the fixed mindset, everything is about the outcome. If you fail—or if you're not the best— it's all been wasted. The growth mindset allows people to value what they're doing regardless of the outcome. They're tackling problems, charting new courses, working on important issues. Maybe they haven't found the cure for cancer, but the search was deeply meaningful.
—CAROL S. DWECK

A s a business leader, you're constantly on your growth edge. You have to be. Every day is a new opportunity to grow yourself and your business. For some that's thrilling, while for others it's mentally exhausting.

In fact, being on your mental growth edge is a lot like surfing. If you've ever surfed before, you know what a strange enterprise it is. One of the things I love most about riding the waves is if I think about what I'm doing, really think about it for even a moment, I'll fall off because all of a sudden I'm too aware that what I'm doing is, let's be honest, kind of crazy. I'm standing on a ridiculously thin piece of fiberglass and riding ocean waves. It's the kind of insane thing that only humans would think to attempt.

And yet, I love it. Because I'm not thinking. I'm doing a kind of dance with nature herself. Well, most of the time. Sometimes, I'm falling all over myself, ass over teakettle, and swallowing more salt water than I should.

In the calm moments, however, during a lull in the tides, I'm sitting on my board, buffeted by the powerful ocean, waiting for that next big wave, and my mind will sometimes wander to strange places.

One of the stories that occasionally comes up for me is the story "The King Who Thought He Could Command the Tides." It was first set down in the twelfth century by Henry of Huntingdon, the Pete Hammil of the northern stretch of the Roman Empire in the Dark Ages. It's an old story, possibly apocryphal, and consistently misunderstood, yet to me, it contains for us a lesson in how leaders can reform the mindset of their people.

Here's what people think the story is: There once was an old king, in what is now England, named Canute who believed he could do anything. The might of his reach, determination, and will were nearly godlike. In sum, the human King Canute believed his power was absolute. So much so, that he had his senior counselors take him and his entire throne out to the sea at low tide. I like to imagine that they had to carry him the entire way.

Once there, King Canute did the strangest thing to prove how absolute his power really was: He commanded the tide to stay out. He literally told the ocean what to do. Of course, in a matter of hours, he had to be dragged, spluttering and soaked like a drowned rat, from the sea's clutches. Here, I like to imagine his counselors and advisors hiding their smirks and grins as they helped their nearly drowned ruler to dry ground.

But here's the thing: even though that's how we all remember the story, that's not what happened. If it happened at all, then it's also said that it happened like this: King Canute was the wise and humble ruler of a forgotten former corner of the Roman

Empire. All his advisors and counselors were in his ear telling him how great he was, how powerful and wise he was, and how he was God's chosen representative on Earth who could command the winds and the tides.

No fool was King Canute, so he said, "Oh yeah? Grab my throne." He had them take his throne all the way to the sea and there he sat, and in a loud, theatrically booming voice intoned, "*I command the tide to stay out!*"

I like to imagine that he sat there, smirking and grinning at his advisors and counselors as his feet, and then his robes, and then his entire throne were consumed by the incoming sea's tide. Did he hold back his "I told you so" the entire trip home? Because I would have.

So which version is the truth? Which is the real King Canute? It doesn't matter. Because they both have lessons for us. Both involve leaders who are trying to motivate their advisors and counselors. Like you have, so many times, both iterations of King Canute are in a situation where the mindset of their people needs radical transformation. They're trying to communicate their vision of the world and what that means for the people underneath them in the organizational chart.

But what's even more true, no matter which version you choose to believe, is that no leader can change what's coming. The tide is coming in, no matter what the king or queen or prime minister says is different; it comes in, it goes out, indifferent to human activity. Just like change.

I'd like to believe that King Canute was trying, in his way, to teach a lesson to his people, which was about how they were all going to have to adapt to the changing world in which they found themselves. Whether he did it on purpose or on accident, he had to change their irrational beliefs.

That's what change is. It's like the tide. As a leader, you can try to resist it, fight it, or meticulously prepare for it, or you can get better at adapting to change when it inevitably comes. If we want to be resiliently change proof, the King Canute story is about how to prepare your people for change. If we want to be a change-proof leader, then we have to model the resilience we know our organizations are going to need in the future. It starts at the top.

● ● ●

That's what I think about when I'm surfing. How I'm trying to get on my growth edge and how good it feels when I'm feeling my way through the twists and turns of the waves. And how bad it feels when I'm trying to think my way through them. I know it feels bad because of how much it hurts when I fall off.

Self-consciousness, overthinking and all their attendant misery are offshoots of fear. We're going to deal with that when we start discussing emotional resilience. But for now, let's just note that judgmental thoughts are only beliefs. Irrational beliefs. If King Canute could have found a way to get in between his irrational beliefs and his actions, if he could have found some way of disputing them, he might still be out there in the surf today.

Let's turn from the Dark Ages and move into the world of reason and science and dig into the work of Albert Ellis and what he has to say about irrational beliefs. To Dr. Ellis, these irrational beliefs can be divided up into three "musts" that our minds return to again and again and again in a process that he calls "musturbation," which puts upon the world a set of demands that are virtually impossible to meet.

For Dr. Ellis, the three main irrational beliefs are:

- "I must do well and win the approval of others or else I am no good."
- "Other people must do 'the right thing' or else they are no good and deserve to be punished."
- "Life must be easy, without discomfort or inconvenience"

That's it. Just those three. He names others, but these are the three rivers from which all irrational beliefs flow into the roiling ocean of our mindset.

We have to dispel beliefs if they're not helping us. We have to confront the limiting beliefs of our organizations. If our mindset isn't working or isn't open enough, then it needs transformation. Otherwise, it won't last long. Leaders have to be willing to pivot away from the kinds of irrational beliefs that keep companies stagnant. That's what King Canute was trying to do when he got his ass wet in the Irish Sea.

In 2012, that's also what Glitch did. Remember Glitch? Once upon a venture capitalist, Glitch was a video game designed to foster and encourage collaboration between players. It was meant to be a kinder, more gentle alternative to its more violent and transgressive counterparts. In a way, the makers of Glitch were trying to create a virtual family.

In the beginning, they had huge investment and a deep emotional connection with their stakeholders who were all attached to Glitch's mindset of collaboration, community building, and communication. Everything was bound for success. They were walking on water.

Until they sank. No matter what their mindset was, no matter what their intentions were, the product they created just didn't have the kind of mindset connected with their stakeholders. What they thought was going to work simply wasn't.

However, while they were making Glitch, the leaders created a messaging platform for the game and used it to communicate with one another throughout the creation process. That platform was completely new and it transformed their mindset. So maybe Glitch isn't familiar to you. Maybe you know them by what they make now: a ubiquitous messaging technology used all over the world by nearly every company. It's the preferred choice among millennials and Generation Z for creative communication: Slack.

The makers of Glitch saw the writing on the wall: they saw that though their community was beloved, it was small. And it wasn't growing. So they pivoted, went to their stakeholders, and levelled with them. They didn't hide. They didn't obfuscate. They communicated how their mindset was pivoting. They said we're producing something great, but we're not going to get there. We're pivoting. We've got no guarantee, but we're asking you to hang with us.

That's what happened. Stakeholders stayed with them. The makers of Glitch elegantly, gracefully, easefully pivoted into Slack. They disputed their initial beliefs, and they transformed into something even better than what they had before. They survived and they thrived. They looked at what the tide brought in and used it to their advantage. That's how they stayed resilient.

So how did they dispute the beliefs that got them Glitch and turn those new beliefs into Slack? What is the mechanism by which we can do the same for ourselves, for our own growth mindset? And then once we do, transform our organizations' mindsets into something resilient?

They got their DIBS.

CHANGE-PROOF POINTS

▶ If you want to survive as an organization for the long haul, you have to be able to dispute some of the foundational beliefs that made you who you are.

▶ If what you're doing isn't working, then go back to your initial beliefs. Nine out of ten times that's where your problem lies.

CHAPTER 17

Disputing Irrational Beliefs

. . . you almost always bring on your emotional problems by rigidly adopting one of the basic methods of crooked thinking—musturbation. Therefore, if you understand how you upset yourself by slipping into irrational shoulds, oughts, demands, and commands, unconsciously sneaking them into your thinking, you can just about always stop disturbing yourself about anything.

—ALBERT ELLIS

What we're trying to do when we pause is to consciously observe our thoughts. Within that, we can discover patterns. For Dr. Ellis, unlocking the patterns by pausing was through a technique he calls "disputing irrational beliefs," or DIBS for short.

For him, a 10-minute session once a day is enough to pause your thoughts. And it isn't about thinking about nothing for 10 minutes. Oh no, this is a 10-minute cross-examination of these irrational beliefs. You must perform what Dr. Ellis calls, "vigorous, persistent disputing"—something that served me quite well as a litigator.

Start with this question: *"What self-defeating irrational belief do I want to dispute and surrender?"* I love that word! Surrender. Give it up. Lay down your sword. Time to stop fighting. Before you do, you must name the irrational belief you want to cross-examine and write it down.

Let's say it's, "I absolutely must be competent, adequate, and achieving in all important respects, or else I am an inadequate, worthless person." That was one of Dr. Ellis's doozies. Let's say the makers of Glitch looked at themselves and said, "Our game failed to live up to the expectations that we set for ourselves and for our stakeholders. Time to give up altogether and go sell life insurance." They didn't do that. With active and practiced calm, they looked instead at what they had achieved. From that, they forged a new mindset that gave them a pathway to long-term growth.

Then you ask yourself: *"Can I rationally support this belief?"* Can you rationally support the belief that you must be competent, adequate and achieving in important respects or else you are an inadequate, worthless person? Well, the answer is obviously no.

It's as if you're saying to yourself, "If I can't get everything, then I deserve nothing." There's no way to argue that's true and not be a sociopath. The goal here is to interrogate irrational beliefs with our minds, with our reason. Did King Canute rationally support his toadying counselors' irrational belief that he was an all-powerful ruler on the level with the gods? No. What did he do?

He took the next step: *"What evidence exists of the falseness of this belief?"* Now, this is a fun one, because when you really start cross-examining these irrational beliefs, you find that there is no end to the falseness. There's probably no end to the evidence that falling short of your own mindset makes you less than nothing.

Like King Canute, sometimes we have to take drastic action to actually show our people how they're in the grip of irrational beliefs. That means we have to occasionally model these outmoded beliefs. They're all around us. But they're outside of us, so our beliefs can act like a bouncer, keeping us from the exciting club outside our craniums. This list is nearly infinite.

Then you ask: *"Does any evidence exist of the truth of this belief?"* No evidence exists to prove that your utmost, top-of-the-line competent achievement is going to make you see yourself as worthy. Because it's like trying to fill a bucket with a hole in it. It's never going to get full.

Now we turn the screws further as he asks the witness: *"What are the worst things that could actually happen to me if I don't get what I think I must (or do get what I think I must not get)?"* Surely you must see by this point that this is some tortured nonsense. But it's the lengths that our fearful ego will go to wind us around our own axle. It's like the cigarette lighter of your car demanding to drive the vehicle.

Last one now: *"What good things could I make happen if I don't get what I think I must (or do get what I think I must not get)?"* I mean, come on. We can do all kinds of good if we don't get what we want. Because the thing is, we already know. Hundreds of years of fairy tales have taught us the difference between what we say we want and what in our hearts we truly desire. We want short-term success when what we really desire is a long-term legacy that we give to our children and our grandchildren. We want to know people will be at our funeral. It's the only reason why we have them. Isn't it? The only way we get there is if we start performing resilience.

Look at it this way—tomorrow is promised to no one. The world doesn't owe you a single thing. Now, what're you going to do about it? You need to be like Dale Carnegie, who wrote, "It isn't what you have, or who you are, or where you are, or what you are doing that makes you happy or unhappy. It is what you think about."

• • •

In my early life, I was a competitive swimmer. I was a sprinter. Specifically, the 50-yard swim. A swimming sprint is a game of nerves because the difference between winning and losing is sometimes hundredths of a second. The margin, the delta, the space, is a fraction of a breath. In the fast-paced, chlorine churn of competitive swimming, the smallest adjustment, fine-tuning, or recalibration can mean everything. For instance, I learned that in the short two-length sprint, I could race my heart out without taking a breath. That one recalibration gave me a competitive advantage.

If we want to travel in the way of resilience for the rest of whatever life we're lucky to have, we have to be able to recalibrate our mindset from something that's scrawled in quick-drying cement to something that's written on water. That's the difference between a fixed mindset and growth mindset. And thanks to mindset master Ryan Gottfredson, it's going to be one of our true keys to mental resilience.

If we learn anything from this book, let it be this one thing: change is as constant as the seasons. It's happening right now. There's nothing you can do about it. So what do we do? Well, as Jack Nicholson said in the movie *The Departed*, "Act accordingly." We have to, because as the pace of technology drags us by the heels at exponentially faster rates, the only real certainty is uncertainty. Every day, the world is changing the route by which it's journeying to growth and regeneration.

Resilience is about recalibrating. Just like when we're in the car on a long journey and we have a distant destination in mind. Let's say it's the Grand Canyon. I'm old so I remember the days of the Rand McNally map-book of all 50 states (and territories), where you'd highlight your route ahead of time so you knew exactly how to get where you were going. Nowadays, of course, we just pop that destination into Google Maps and our phone does the work for us with satellites that can track our every move. It's almost impossible to get lost these days. Which, in its way, is kind of a shame, because getting lost is where we find the most creative opportunities of our lives.

When we make a wrong turn, when we don't trust our satellite route, or there's some new information like a blocked road or a traffic jam, the satellite goes to work recalculating a new way to get to our destination. Sometimes, we don't trust it. We crave sameness, familiarity. We know that nothing stays the same, but we're so fixed on our goal and our plan that we try desperately to get back to the original route. We don't trust the recalculation. In fact, we're shocked and thrown into a tailspin.

To pull us out of the spin, *Top Gun*–style, we need Dr. Ryan Gottfredson, mental success, leadership consultant, author, trainer, and one of the most selfless and purpose-driven people I've ever had the pleasure of speaking with. In the middle of the tumultuous summer of 2020, Ryan and I met over Zoom for a chat about mindset reform that clarified for me how to discover your innate mental resilience and make it last so that it's there when you need it most. Dr. Gottfredson spoke to me about one of the thinkers who influenced his mindset reform, Robert Quinn, who wrote that people and organizations reform for one of two reasons: crisis or deep learning. The latter we have within our power. The former? Not so much.

The events of 2020 were a crisis that impacted every single person. Like a rip current, it didn't care who we were, or where we came from, or what our station in life was. It didn't care about us at all. If we're in a resilience mindset, that kind of spiritual indifference is a creative opportunity to, as Dr. Gottfredson says, ". . . upgrade our entire operating system."

In mindset reform, resilience is about transforming ourselves before transformation is taken out of our hands, letting other people and events have control over when, how, and why we transform. It's about being proactive rather than reactive. It's easier to play offense than defense. The offense has a plan and a play. The defense has to react to that, just like the white pieces and black pieces in chess. Whom would you rather be?

I can hear you out there saying, "Adam, this is all fine, in the abstract. It's fine for other people to transform. But I didn't ask for any of this. There was nothing wrong with my life. Now I'm forced into all this discomfort and uncertainty. How am I supposed to feel good, when all I feel is uncomfortable and uncertain?"

Understood. But when it comes to how to cultivate mindset reform, we do not have a choice. We have to improvise. Dr. Gottfredson told me:

> *What we're talking about here is the difference between a fixed mindset and a growth mindset. How we see failure shapes how resilient we're going to be because somebody who sees failure as something bad, they're going to have a hard time being resilient. Those that have a growth mindset and see failure as an opportunity to learn and grow, they're going to be much more resilient.*

So do we have to be like Rocky Balboa and constantly wade into punch after punch, blow after blow, getting knocked to the canvas again and again? Because that's how a lot of folks out there define physical resilience. Even Rocky only has to do that for at most 12 three-minute rounds, less than 40 minutes to define resilient greatness. We have to do it day after day, night after night, season after season. Long-term resilience is more mental than physical.

Dr. Gottfredson told me about a keenly operative research study to determine the functional difference between a fixed mindset and a growth mindset. A group of people were given the same task that was a pop quiz of sorts with eight simple questions and four hard questions. The eight were meant to be gotten right and the four were meant to be gotten wrong. The researchers were looking to see what would happen when people encountered failure after successive successful rounds.

"What they found is that those with a fixed mindset went from being rather pleased with themselves to quickly becoming depressed," Dr. Gottfredson went on. "They stopped applying themselves. They underemphasize their successes and overemphasize their failures." A fixed mindset means you are subject to the current and the tides and the flow of events. You've given up control of your mindset to outside forces. The study tells us that this isn't the way of resilience.

Those with the growth mindset, Dr. Gottfredson continued, ". . . didn't get depressed at all. They started to engage in positive self-talk thinking, 'I was hoping this would be a challenge.' They continued to apply themselves. They were much more accurate in knowing how many they got right versus how many they got wrong." The growth mindset group saw the whole thing as a challenge, whereas the fixed mindset group was challenged by the whole thing. That's about as good a definition of mindset resilience as we're going to get in this life.

A growth mindset is going to set you on a track for long-term resilience. And it's something that's achievable in this life. You can change your mindset. It's not easy, but it's not terribly difficult either. According to Dr. Gottfredson, "Our mindset was formed in two ways. One is essentially based on our upbringing and two is our culture." That means we can't just wait for change. Our mindset reform has to be intentional. You have to work at it. You have to demonstrate your mindset to yourself. Self-awareness comes through rigorous self-examination. If you depend on waiting for things to happen to change your mindset then it will never come. It's like what they say, "Prevent defense prevents you from winning."

Dr. Gottfredson told me a very simple exercise that he got from the best-selling book, *The Five-Minute Journal*, which invites you to do something easy you can do just twice a day. All you do is answer three questions in the morning and two at night. That's it.

We're going to come back to my own version of this when we get to the Code of Conduct, but for now, these questions are about three things for which you're grateful. Then at night, you revisit these three questions from the perspective of, "How did the day go? How did I do?"

As we've learned, we know that words have power. Just the exercise of answering five questions, only five, has the power to alter our mindset from something that's fixed in concrete or written on water.

Now, through a global crisis, we've been challenged with the task of deep learning so that our growth mindset makes us open-minded. So no matter what, no matter what life throws in our path, we're constantly recalculating our route, staying with our daily routines, which functions as our GPS, so that we're not afraid of getting lost. We're actually looking for those creative opportunities where the real magic happens. When we seek change, on our own terms, we begin to change, and that change no longer changes us.

We're back at the sea, with King Canute, the way I imagine him, the sea rolling in, his advisors and ministers all panicked, and there he is, surfing on his throne, riding the tides until they bring him back home.

CHANGE-PROOF POINT

▶ Surfers don't fall off a wave and go home. They get back on the board and keep looking for the next wave.

CHAPTER 18

A Little Failure
Goes a Long Way

*Our minds have the incredible capacity to
both alter the strength of connections among
neurons, essentially rewiring them, and create
entirely new pathways. (It makes a computer,
which cannot create new hardware when its
system crashes, seem fixed and helpless).*

—SUSANNAH CAHALAN

If you're looking at your teams or your organization, how do
you change the mind of the collection of people that make the
product you're selling? You have to create space, because space
becomes creative and we choose that space with our minds. The
questions that leaders have to ask of themselves and their organizations is, "How do we choose mentally? Can we change our
minds?"

In spite of all the upheaval around us, I'm really grateful to be
alive right now, because our world is pivoting in such fascinating
ways. As we continue our scientific quest for truth and knowledge
of life's mysteries, we're questioning all kinds of assumptions,
receiving knowledge, and undoing years of scientific dogma.

One of the most important is the idea that as we advance in age, our brains, rather than becoming stagnant and fixed, are actually capable of amazing growth and possibility. The concept of neuroplasticity is the almost radical notion that our brains can change and they can change late in our life span.

Until now, the theory was that the critical period of brain development happened early in childhood but once it was over, that was it. Now we know that's just not true. Change is possible no matter what your age is.

My mom and dad are in their eighties now, although my mom might not want me putting that out there (sorry, Mom!). Let's be clear, they don't change on a dime. Their pivots aren't as extreme or life-altering. But they're still changing. They're still evolving.

They've taught me and my brother to be open to the world around us. To keep questioning our beliefs, our patterns, and our intentions. They've taught us that with an open mind and an open heart anything can change.

As I mentioned earlier, my dad worked in the New York City Parks Department for almost his entire working life. That's what he did, but it's not who he was. For almost my entire childhood, he would work through the normal workday, which would let him be with us after school and so we could all have our epic family dinners together.

Then as we did the dishes and our homework, he would repair into his small den where he would write well into the night. I can still hear the meditative clack-clack-clack of his old typewriter as I drifted off to sleep while he wrote book after book. Nearly every night he did this. No matter what happened in the day or how stressed he was or what was weighing on him. He just made it a habit.

Then as soon as he could retire from his day job, he didn't have to wonder what he was going to do or what he was going to become. There wasn't a deck chair with his name on it. He had a decent pension and the time to do whatever he wanted, so he just became what he always was: a full-time writer. In spite of how many rejection slips he got, he kept going. And he got himself published. He's still writing well into his eighties. And he's a model for our kind of mental resilience.

That's why I want to introduce you to a pioneer who's somehow still out in front of the world of neuroplasticity. His name is Dawson Church. We've taught together at the Transformation Leadership Council. He's got three books, *Mind to Matter*, *The Genie in Your Genes*, and *Bliss Brain*. He's one of the founding directors of the Veterans Stress Project, and he's a pioneer in the field of *Emotional Freedom Techniques* that's been used and blessed by the Veterans Administration to help treat returning soldiers who are suffering from PTSD. This is something Dawson told me he knows a thing or two about: "I'm a happy person and that to me is an amazing thing to say because when I was a kid, I was incredibly unhappy. I was depressed. I was anxious. I had PTSD from a whole bunch of miserable things that happened in my childhood."

If you met Dawson today you'd never guess that his life used to look like that. This man almost embodies mindfulness and the energy that comes from constant, rigorous, and compassionate awareness. He's so dialed into the science of how our brains change. He loves nothing more than challenging the belief that our minds are fixed at a point in our childhood.

Dawson told me about a study that looked at people who went to Harvard in the 1950s and measured them 50 years apart. Dawson explained:

> They found that over time not only did people change, but they changed so much on average that if you looked at the personality profile of that person who was at Harvard in the 1950s and look at them again 50 years later, you couldn't even tell who was who. They changed so much. We

can change. Our brains can change. Our habits can change.
Our beliefs can change. We have a remarkable ability to
change our bodies, genes and neutrons using our mind.

The mind, Dawson contends, is not all that dissimilar from
the body. If you go to the gym and start exercising your biceps
and triceps, and your shoulders, back, and chest, you're going to
look and feel different. You'll maybe have to buy bigger shirts or
pants to accommodate your newfound gains. If you get an injury
or you plateau and give up (the way we often do), then your body
won't keep those gains. You'll go from hard to soft, thick to thin
faster and easier than you did the opposite.

This isn't up for debate. So why don't we treat our mind the
same way? Why don't we choose to use it the way it was meant
to be used?

Full disclosure here: I used to be a crummy meditator. Just
one of the world's worst at sitting still with my thoughts. Not
that long ago, I would have taken the electroshock. But in the
years since I met Dawson who gave me some great tips to really
start focusing on meditation, I've trained myself to do it every
day (even if only for 5 to 10 minutes); to have very simple, compassionate intentions, to be gentle with myself and have no
expectations other than creating a new habit.

And lo and behold, I got better at meditation. If you work
out every day, your body will respond. Yet we do so much work
on our bodies and just expect our minds to come along for the
ride. It's like the old Paul Reiser comedy bit where he talked
about how he never actually cleaned his feet in the shower. He
just trusted the soap to sort of run all the way down.

I'm not a scientist, and neuroscience is deep water for me,
but intuitively it makes sense to me that we have these grooves
carved into our brains because of an excess of worrying and planning. Turns out, Dawson explained, this is how the brain works,
"When we're doing something, when we're writing a poem,

when we're talking to our friends, when we're composing an email, when we're withdrawing money from the bank, anything we're doing, any task that engages us in what's called the task-positive network." Pretty simple, right? When we're engaged in something, our brain is along for the ride and, frankly, pretty jazzed at the prospect.

Dawson went on to tell me that when we're not active, the task-positive network shuts down, and that region of the brain or that collection of neurons isn't firing. When this happens then something else comes online: the default mode network. This is what our mind thinks of as "the Suck" because, "It uses any surplus capacity. If you think of it like a computer, it grabs all your working memory. It grabs all the available resources, all the glucose, all the energy and it uses that."

The default mode network does two things: It worries. It plans for the future. It worries about the future, and it thinks back about the bad stuff from the past. "This bad thing happened in my childhood. I was betrayed by my colleague at work. Suzie took my research and passed it off as her own." An endless parade of bad stuff of the past and bad stuff that might happen in the future.

This is where we find ourselves when we begin meditating. We're not firing up the task network because, well, we're just sitting there. The default mode simply cannot handle sitting and being mindful. We don't see it as a task. This, Dawson says, is like a neon invitation for the default mode to spark to life and say, "I shouldn't be meditating now. Do you know how many emails are unanswered in your tray? Someone that might be mad. That'll be like that situation that happened a few years ago while you neglected somebody."

If through meditation and mindfulness you can shut down the default network, you can begin to experience the feelings that some describe as "inner peace" for a long time.

Mindfulness is the key. But there are many different ways to get to mindfulness, that yes, include sitting still and quiet with your thoughts without judgment. There's no version of our lives where we don't meditate. It has to be a regular habit. Even for 10 minutes every morning. You don't have to be an expert. You just have to do it.

It's what writers call "ass in chair." My father didn't wait for the muses to visit him. He just did the work. Day after day after day. I realize now that writing for him was a kind of meditation. It was a place his mind could go and renew and regenerate itself.

In a study called "Neuroplasticity and Clinical Practice: Building Brain Power for Health" (2016), the author, Joyce Shaffer, contends that dementia is detected in one out of every seven people on the planet. Delaying the onset of dementia by even a year can be accomplished through neuroplasticity, and in so doing, Shaffer writes, ". . . reduce the global burden of Alzheimer's disease by as much as 9,200,000 cases in 2050."

When it comes to mental resilience, we need to have an approach that works for us as individuals, but to also recognize that we're a part of a global community. The more mentally resilient each of us is, in our own unique way, the more that resilience can spread as quickly and pervasively as a virus.

Dawson Church has written books and conducted studies on PTSD, and he's found that meditation is something that moves our mental resilience from a resource to a trait.

> *A trait is a personality characteristic. If someone's patient, for example, they embody it because they have enough neural wiring built. It's people who turn temporary states of feeling better to permanent traits like resilience. These people are resilient. You can throw all kinds of things at them. They're resilient because they've built enough neural wiring in those emotion regulation circuits and also the happiness surface of the brain to where it's not dependent on the outside circumstances, not on the outside world. Anything can happen out there, but they have resilient brains. You move*

resilience into something you literally own. That's the neu-
rological personality characteristic of resilience. That's what
you want to be because no one can take it away from you.

That's just so inspiring. Just hearing that made me want to do a little dance around my desk. Because it's so true! Isn't it? That is what we want to be. We know it on a cellular level. We want that so badly for ourselves, but we're so afraid someone's going to take it away from us. We're afraid to journey to get to the treasure, because when the moment comes, that Indiana Jones moment when you have to take the golden treasure, what we're really afraid of is that someone is going to take it away from us. It's, "If I never reach for it, reach out my hand to touch it, then if it gets taken, it was never mine in the first place. And I won't die."

But Dawson Church is here to tell us that we do have it and the only person who can take it from us is us. That's it. That's the whole thing. It's the difference between something that you do and something that you are. When we really think about ourselves and the harmonic ideal that we're striving for as it pertains to resilience, we're really just a collection of our habits. We are what we do. When we perform resilience every day, then we find that we are habitually resilient.

Through years of practicing resilience performance, when challenges come, I go quiet on the inside. My heart rate goes down. My blood pressure goes down. My breathing slows almost to the point where I could take a nap in a hurricane. I almost find myself yawning in the middle of some great thing happening. I learned that out on the hot sand of Jones Beach.

Now, through many years of mindfulness training, there's no competition for resources in my brain allowing me to be alert, awake, and aware. When things start to go sideways, I just feel healthier. Dawson Church says that's because of immunoglobu-lins. Though they sound like a character out of *Game of Thrones*, in reality, they're these funny little Knights of the Watch that protect us from invading bacteria. Dawson explains it this way, "The higher your level of immunoglobulins, the more resilient you are physiologically." Resilience isn't just an idea in our brains. Our brains are chemically wired for it.

To explain, Dawson referred to a study he'd done at a meditation retreat, "We found that over the course of that week, that people's anxiety and depression dropped dramatically by over 30 percent and their cortisol (the main stress hormone) dropped by an average of 37 percent in one week, which is a massive drop."

Dawson explained why, "It was fine for our ancestors to have this hair trigger response. We needed to escape from the woolly mammoth charging down on us or the Neanderthal running at us with a spear. The Neanderthals, the woolly mammoths, and the saber tooth tigers are extinct."

Our brains are thinking that's what we need to do, so what do we do instead? Dawson gave me a funny example that I don't think he'd mind if I shared, "My daughter lives in Austin, but she's staying with us. She announced one day that she had a pimple. She's six foot two and gorgeous, has a fantastic job and a husband. She has everything going for her except that she was obsessed by this pimple. I looked at her closely and I couldn't even see the pimple."

"The pimple," Dawson told me with a smile, "was all she could see when she looked at her face in the mirror. That's what the brain does because that's what kept us safe from the Neanderthals. That's profoundly unhelpful to us nowadays. We have to learn to rewire our brains."

We're going to come back to a particular meditation that Dawson does in the next chapter, but for now, we just need to know that the things that scare us (our own thoughts) are the very things that will make us resilient in our minds, for our whole lives. If you don't believe me, consider this: over time, Dawson's studied 40,000 meditators.

In this way, I think of my father as one of these brave 40,000, who have the courage to show up, every day, to choose their thoughts, honor them, challenge them, and just sit with them as they pass through, like a greeter at Walmart: happy to see everyone who passes by and has a smile and a kind word.

For my part, at night, there's part of me that still hears the clack-clack-clack of my father's typewriter, and I think that somehow, some way, he was tapping out a message to me and he trusted that I wouldn't get it until far into the future.

I got it, Dad. I hear you. Thank you for choosing your thoughts.

> ## CHANGE-PROOF POINTS
>
> ▶ Meditation and mindfulness keep your primitive, hardwired default mode network from activating your anxiety stores.
>
> ▶ Even five minutes a day of meditation and focus on the breath can be a levee against the floodwaters of anxiety and stress.

Fall, then figure out what to do on the way down.
—DEL CLOSE

Whether you're an individual looking to build your own resilience or you're a leader looking to build resilience in your organization, you're going to have to create uncertainty for yourself. You're going to have to create uncertain situations that test you. If you don't create uncertainty for yourself, the world will create it for you. The former is preferable to the latter. To get to that point, you've got to do things that you don't do well.

It's part of performing resilience. It's like Lebron James says, "You've got to get comfortable being uncomfortable." This is just another way of saying a line from one of my favorite sports movies, *Moneyball*, which goes like this, "Adapt or die."

I miss going to the movies. Of all the things we've mourned the loss of in these times, it's quite far down on the list, but until it was taken away from us, I really didn't consider the role that a night at the cinema played in keeping me and Randi sane. It seems silly to say this in the light of all that's happened, but it was almost like, well, it was like church for us.

Something about the ritual of it: Leaving the kids with a babysitter. A date night! The drive to the theater, full of anticipation, the workday over, Randi and I just chatted about nothing at all on the way. We'd find a parking spot. Like teenagers, we'd walk hand in hand into the lobby. I loved getting hit with that contact high of the smell of popcorn, whatever it is they're calling "butter" and the candy that's somehow always kind of melting. We'd get our tickets that had the title of the movie we'd been looking forward to for months. We'd get our popcorn and candy. We'd make our way in and pick out a couple of prime seats. I miss the feeling of the seats, the almost velvet quiet that used to be in the theater. No music, no games, no preshow shenanigans. It was like setting my brain in a jacuzzi. Just relaxing. Then the house lights would go down, the previews would start, and we'd be taken out of our lives for a couple of hours.

I loved watching the actors on that 50-foot screen creating characters and telling stories with their thoughts and their emotions. I've always been kind of attracted to acting. Practicing law and public speaking is a kind of performance. These days, in our work training corporate speakers to give TED Talks, a lot of the principles we use are influenced by actors and acting training.

Actors, like public speakers, walk into a situation where they know the words they're going to say, but no matter how much they practice those words, no matter how much they commit them to memory the night before in front of the mirror, when they have to meet the moment when they have to deliver, the moment often looks nothing like what they thought it would.

Actors can teach us about how to become change proof, because they have to deal with uncertainty all the time. So much so, that in many cases they learn to create their own uncertainty. The question that I keep coming back to in how we perform resilience: How do we create our own uncertainty?

We can learn a few lessons from an actor I had the pleasure of chatting with late in 2020. His name is Reed Diamond, and for me, he's a model of the kind of resilience we're going to need in the next decade. Reed's been a working actor for over 35 years. You don't last that long in show business without being change proof. He's a New Yorker and he's the kind of actor who, though you may not know his name right away, you would know his face. He's been in everything. He's what they call a "that guy" as in, "I know! He's that guy from that thing."

Reed has an important role in the film I just mentioned, *Moneyball*, where he played the role of Mark Shapiro, the Cleveland GM who inadvertently introduces Billy Beane to Peter Brand. They then go on to change baseball forever and amen.

Reed got to improvise with the star of the movie, Brad Pitt. Improvisation is the acting version of tightrope walker Philippe Petit, operating high above Lower Manhattan without a net. It's not as physically risky, obviously, but the emotional risks are probably as great. Improvisational theater is the kind where there's no rehearsal, no script, no set, and no props unfolding in real time in front of an audience. When it's done right and well by whip-smart folks who have minds like mercury, it's maybe the best human art form. When it's not? It's basically the worst human art form. So there's a lot of wiggle room there.

Reed told me that the main commandment of improv is the concept of "yes, and," which was created, I believe, by Del Close, the father of the Chicago improv scene. Reed said, "In a scene, [it's] the main philosophy of 'never deny' and 'yes, and.' If you say, 'That's a lovely blue hat.' If I go, 'Yes. It was given to me by the King of France.' I've agreed with you. It's an agreement to take it further."

If you deny a scene, then when you say, 'That's a lovely blue hat,' and I respond, 'I'm not wearing a hat,'—the scene dies right there. The scene has to build upon a delicate dance of agreement, even if two characters might be mortal enemies or divorcing spouses, the performers are seeking those little signposts of agreement about what the thing is."

Reed really got a life lesson from improvising with Brad Pitt. The script was written by Aaron Sorkin and Steve Zaillian, but Reed recounted that on the morning of the scene, Brad Pitt showed up with his own version of the scene. Normally, that would be a massive red flag that the day was going to be rough, but in this case, the movie star had reworked the scene so that his scene partner got the bulk of the lines.

That almost never happens. From there, though, Reed said things got even better. "I was given carte blanche. We improvised that scene over and over again. We went to crazy places." While the camera was on Brad Pitt, they improvised for six hours. Then after a quick lunch break where the movie star ate on the set with everybody else like a normal person, they got Reed's side of the scene in two hours. Reed said that Brad Pitt operated like a true leader, because "He made me feel completely invested in it. Why that movie is so great is because people stopped acting and they were having real experiences."

Reed's lesson from that day can be ours as well, for us in our lives and for those among you who are also leading teams and organizations. If there's a movie star in your film, they're the leader on set and in this case, Brad was modeling true "yes, and" behavior because he was seeking uncertainty, he was seeking change to happen in the moment. He wasn't afraid of letting somebody else drive the scene or the moment. He wasn't unloading his anxiety, worry, and fear onto his team. So everyone else felt invested, because they saw him comfortable enough to risk.

That's what we have to do for ourselves and for our teams. Leveraging uncertainty is about cultivating a very specific amount of change and uncertainty, like the inoculation inside a vaccine. You get a tiny amount of the thing so the thing doesn't make you sick.

Reed broke down the discipline like this:

> *If you and I come together and we're feeding off each other, then one plus one equals a million because we're going to elicit out of each other something we didn't plan. I'm always looking to create a mistake. I'm looking for things to go a little sideways. Not intellectually and talking about it, but what you and I come up with is much more interesting than anything we could have planned. That's art.*
>
> *If it's true in art, then it's true in your life and in your business. Train yourself to be comfortable being uncomfortable. That's the secret to mental resilience. It allows you to dance with change rather than fighting it. Inoculate yourself with enough uncertainty that you become immune to the virus of fear that uncertainty produces.*
>
> *Now, the leaders among you might be asking yourselves, "That's fine for people, but I have employees, a board of directors, and shareholders to whom I have to answer. I can't improvise. I need to have a plan. I have to adhere to that plan. Or else I'll get disrupted out of business and they'll replace me."*
>
> *In some companies and businesses that's true. But not at 3M. In my feverish research of everything resilience, I happened upon an article in the Harvard Business Review. It was called "Creating Breakthrough at 3M" and it was written by three executives from 3M who were instrumental in teaching a legacy company how to improvise*

and say the crucial "yes, and" to where that improvisatory development leads.

They started from the presumption that product developers fail to innovate effectively over a long period of time. This happens, according to them, for two main reasons. First, companies have every reason in the known world to think short term. Development is about the future. Companies don't often survive the quarter let alone some hypothetical future. This leads to the "one step at a time" approach, which prizes small wins and small improvements to existing products and ideas. That keeps CNBC happy and if it keeps them happy, then that's something you can sell to shareholders. Simply put, risks get you fired.

The first reason is easy to understand, but the second is more insidious: developers literally don't know how to innovate. There's nowhere to start and even if you do, there's no help for the ones who are already on their way. It's like if you didn't have a chicken or an egg. "Traditionally, the company's management has fostered innovation by taking a get-out-of-the-way attitude toward product developers who, in turn, have worked according to the aphorism, 'It's better to seek forgiveness than permission.'"

For decades this model churned out revolutionary product after groundbreaking innovation, all insanely profitable, but the gains eventually began, as they always do, to wane. Over time, the developers were just developing products 3M already had. So management sent down a shocking edict: 30 percent of sales would be the result of products that had never been thought of. So in effect, 3M decided to "yes, and" a full third of their business. That means 30 percent of their company would have to jump out of a plane and invent a better parachute on the way down.

They developed the "lead user process," which essentially meant that they began outsourcing their creative process to the lead users who were going to be, sorry to be repetitive, actually "using" their products. I'm fascinated by the idea that a Fortune 500 company would, essentially, start improvising by seeking opportunities where the risk was failure. Improvisation is based on risk. Onstage, the risk is usually only to the ego of the actor. But when a company risks failure and commits to it, long-term resilience becomes a part of the company's value system. It's a huge risk, but it's their risk. That means it's not something they have to find elsewhere, it's in the brick and mortar of the place. I don't need to have a business degree or have Oliver Stone's Wall Street committed to memory to know that that's more valuable than whatever next quarter's stock price is going to be.

Improvisation isn't just for actors and people who like borrowing money from their parents. It can work for everyone. When challenges come (and we know that they will), we have to choose to look for the creative opportunity within rip current. If you can regularly inject yourself with a dose of improvisation, then you'll be able to leverage your uncertainty into a cure for the mediocrity that accompanies the status quo, and help your company seek the kind of failure you need to become resilient, change proof. All you have to do is say, "yes, and."

CHANGE-PROOF POINT

▶ When you " 'yes, and' to your failures," then you create a new reality for yourself and for your people.

PART IV

Change-Proof
Software

CHAPTER 19

Happiness Doesn't Deliver Resilience

Happiness is really just about four things: perceived control, perceived progress, connectedness (number and depth of your relationships), and vision/meaning (being part of something bigger than yourself).
—TONY HSIEH

There's a poem by Edwin Arlington Robinson about a man named Richard Cory, who is the envy of the entire town in which he lives.

Whenever Richard Cory went down town,
We people on the pavement looked at him:
He was a gentleman from sole to crown,
Clean favored, and imperially slim.
And he was always quietly arrayed,
And he was always human when he talked;
But still he fluttered pulses when he sai',
"Good-morni'g," and he glittered when he walked.
And he was rich—yes, richer than a king—
And admirably schooled in every grace:

In fine, we thought that he was everything
To make us wish that we were in his place.
So on we worked, and waited for the light,
And went without the meat, and cursed the bread;
And Richard Cory, one calm summer night,
Went home and put a bullet through his head.

To me, that last line hits like a gut punch every single time I read it. Because it's about how the contents of the human heart are as infinite and murky as the mind. We truly don't know how anyone is feeling. Even in the age of endless social media feeds, scrolling every thought, meme, or meal we could possibly consume in a single life span. That's every day. We know what everyone thinks. But we have no idea how they feel.

People all over the world, no matter their origin, religion, or station desire the pursuit of happiness. People like Tony Hsieh. I was a fan of his going back almost 20 years. One year, I gave as a present to my entire company a copy of Tony's book *Delivering Happiness*, and I've held it in my heart ever since I first read the passion and fire he had for people and business and the holistic experience for what we do together in the marketplace. His value system was about creating a one-to-one relationship with each consumer. He was almost like the poet laureate of modern capitalism.

In many ways, Tony was the best of us. He was empathic and analytical in equal measure. He could see the data and the people for their inner truth. Rather than seeing them in binary, oppositional ways, he saw them as extensions of each other. He was beloved by creatives in every field. Someone once said of him that he was the rare human being who was almost innately incapable of seeing any event as an obstacle. Tony Hsieh saw creative opportunity in every single kind of uncertainty. That's just how he was wired.

In 2008, Tony was profiled by *Forbes* and he said, "Chase the vision. The money and profits will come." He understood the harmonic nature of where people and business intersect. He lived in that place.

In an article published after his death, the same *Forbes* magazine said that Tony's experiment with a no-management structure was a failure because "one out of seven employees took a buyout." OK, but that's only 14 out of a hundred. So 86 percent wanted to be a part of the culture Tony was creating. We'd all take those numbers. And it tells us something about why we feel the way we do when this is how a major publication chooses to eulogize a revolutionary entrepreneur. He made hundreds of millions before he was in his mid-twenties. He went on to found Zappos, a revolutionary online shoe store that eventually sold to Amazon for over a billion dollars.

Tony Hsieh lived a different life than the rest of us. And yet, he didn't. He didn't retreat to a state-of-the-art security system disguised as a house, he invested in the downtrodden downtown area of Las Vegas, creating a hub for culture, the arts, and technology where he lived in his own Airstream trailer.

He was worth almost a billion dollars. He could go anywhere, do anything, be with anyone, and enjoy the absolute limit of human pleasure and possibility. And yet, as the days of 2020 began to isolate each of us from one another, Tony's friends started to worry about him. He was a man known to love the company of others; in fact, he needed it, thrived on it. He needed human connection. Did he sometimes have to pay for it? Probably. But that didn't change the content of the man's heart. But quarantines and lockdowns made human contact nearly impossible. In our own way, it's happened to each of us. Our emotional support networks are necessary for our survival. We're social creatures, even the introverts among us. Tony needed people. As 2020 wore on, Tony thought he was managing to keep himself going.

His friends knew better. They knew he was abusing his body with alcohol and drugs. He was getting further and further away from the people who would hold him truly accountable for his actions. He was in "the Suck" and he couldn't fight his way out.

Then in late November of 2020, Tony locked himself in the pool shed of a seaside house and on purpose or accident, no one will ever know, died in a small fire of smoke inhalation. A tiny fire is all it took to create enough smoke to snuff out one of the great hearts of the business community. The smoke took his life, but we know it was despair that really ended it. Left unchecked, despair can be lethal. Even for someone as rich and connected as Tony. For goodness sake, he wrote a book called *Delivering Happiness*. And this was his fate. Tony had everything you're trying to get. He had everything you dream of in your best dreams. He was free from want, from need, and from petty concerns the rest of us worry about every night as our head hits the pillow.

Tony walked among us and he was golden. He modelled aspects of the ideal. And yet, like Richard Cory in the poem, Tony went home and, in his own way, put a bullet in his head. Tony's heart was broken. His heart wasn't resilient. And we may never really know why.

That's what this chapter is about. You may not know the feelings of others, but darn it, you're going to know about your own feelings. It's about how to create for yourself a resilient heart by once again pausing, asking, and choosing the way of resilient emotions. When you do that, you'll be able to resist the kind of dark despair that swallowed a shining, joyful light like Tony's.

Because the world broke him. Every day, in a thousand ways, it breaks all of us. But some of us, as Ernest Hemingway once wrote, "Some of us are strong in the broken places."

CHANGE-PROOF POINTS

▶ Money can't buy you happiness, but happiness won't buy you more happiness, either.

▶ The change-proof mindset says, "My emotions and my feelings have the power to change my reality on a moment-by-moment basis."

CHAPTER 20

Are You Emotionally Agile?

Nothing can be changed until it is faced.
—JAMES BALDWIN

Remember Mitt Romney's statement during one of the 2012 presidential debates? "Corporations are people too."

Old Mittens took a lot of heat for that gaffe. However, what he was expressing was a fundamental truth to the nature of resilience. Thanks to massive financial deregulation and the Citizens United decision handed down by the Supreme Court, corporations and businesses are free to operate in a vague legal fiction that treats them with the same legal rights as a person. In the eyes of the law, corporations literally *are* people.

Now, let's take it further. An organization is made up of people. A collection of hearts and minds. A collection of values. They congeal, coordinate, and collaborate to become more than the sum of their parts. As the great capitalist philosopher, Napoleon Hill, wrote, "No two minds ever come together without, thereby, creating a third, invisible, intangible force which may be likened to a third mind."

Your organization is a collection of emotions. It's not one thing. You may want it to be yours, but you can't. Your organization has its own desire. Sometimes, leading is just getting out of the way. You have to cultivate the emotional resilience of your people.

For our work, pausing emotionally is about getting to the roots of our feelings. To be on our growth edge, we can't be riding the emotional roller coaster. We can't get too high and we can't get too low. That is our choice to make. It's our work.

I grew up in a little suburb of New York City. You may have heard of it. It's called Queens. It's one of the five boroughs that make up one of the epicenters of the Western Hemisphere. Though I haven't lived there in years, it's who I am. No matter where I go, no matter where I live, I'll die a New Yorker. Like a bagel—no matter where you have one, it's just not quite as good as they are in New York City. Maybe it's the water.

Anyway, fortunately or unfortunately (depending on your point of view) I came of age during the 1970s, which if you're old enough to remember was a traumatic time in New York. It was the era when the federal government let the greatest city in the world go bankrupt ("Ford to City: Drop Dead"). As a result, nearly every social safety net was stripped away.

It was the era of garbage strikes that led to explosions in the rat population. Dirty streets, lined with trash and danger lurking around every single corner. It was the era of *The French Connection*, *Taxi Driver*, and *The Warriors*. There were parts of Queens and the rest of the city that looked like they'd been hit by a bomb. It was a desolate, husked, burned-out relic of its former self.

It seemed like there was anger, despair, and trauma sitting on the city like a dusty haze. Poverty and crime were not only on the rise, they were breaking the trend lines. Back then, if you wandered outside your little sphere of influence on the wrong bus, subway, or cab into a different neighborhood, you were taking your life in your hands. As tough as 2020 was for all of us, it honestly pales in comparison to a walk along the Hudson River from Battery Park to Harlem in 1975.

But there were reasons things were like that. Not excuses. Reasons. There were deep, systemic reasons why people were angry. Many parts of the city were still recovering from the race riots of the late 1960s, and a combination of racist and regressive government policies left a lot of good people feeling like they were bad ones. In actual fact, it was the systems that were driving people into poverty and despair. It was, as John Steinbeck described it:

> *New York is an ugly city, a dirty city. Its climate is a scandal, its politics are used to frighten children, its traffic is madness, its competition is murderous. But there is one thing about it—once you have lived in New York and it has become your home, no place else is good enough.*

New York of the 1970s truly was a prison that many people, despite their best instincts, wanted to break into. Because it still personified success. You could make it there, but if you did you'd have to fight for your life.

This is the era of New York that gave us John Carpenter's *Escape from New York* where the once-proud metropolis has been abandoned and turned into a dystopian island prison. It was a place, one could say, full of rage. And if a place is full of rage, then it's built on trauma. I learned that from Ralph De La Rosa, who wrote a book that may be the most "New York" book title I've ever heard of: *Don't Tell Me to Relax*. Even now, I can feel the Dustin Hoffman in *Midnight Cowboy*, "I'm walkin' here" energy wafting off that title's words. Because you do not, under any circumstances, tell someone from New York to relax.

Ralph is a survivor of PTSD, depression, and heroin addiction, and he's a veteran of the clinical foster care system in New York City and Harlem. He's seen firsthand the legacy that poverty, racism, and oppression have wrought on that particular corner of America. In a lot of ways, Ralph is kind of an expert on trauma. He knows firsthand what it means to bounce back from events, but his work is about the emotional resilience that allows us to bounce forward.

Emotionally, we want to use the challenges that seem to be blocking us as a springboard for a resilient heart that's forever and not just a fad. As Ralph put it, "No matter how down we are, the human spirit has this natural organic capacity to overcome when in the presence of the right conditions."

Resilience is baked into our DNA. At a genetic level, we have the capacity for resilience. Even if our circumstances are wildly different, we all have the same access to resilience. It's just about whether we can become aware enough to use it. However, to find that emotional resilience that will make us change proof for the long term, we have to go all the way down to the roots.

New York was decimated in the 1970s but then in the decade and a half that followed it was rebuilt into what it is today: a gleaming, gated community for the super wealthy. They changed the surface of everything without addressing the systemic issues. In effect, it's sort of a fancy lie built on pain. For Ralph, cities like New York are a tangible expression of a civilized society built on deeply traumatic events.

It's like the Greek myth of the Danaides, 50 brides who were ordered by their father to be killed by their husbands on their wedding night. For their punishment they were sent to the underworld where they were each given a bucket and ordered to fill a golden basin. Once the basin was full, they would be released. But the golden basin was dotted with holes. So no matter how fast they moved, no matter how much water they carried from the nearby stream, the golden basins would never be full.

Ralph puts it this way,

We start by tying together some of the threads of the trauma lens, trauma theory, and what's going on in society here as well. Power, greed, clinging to wealth, shoring up far too many resources when others have far too little. It's about

safety at the psychological level. We all have this need to
feel secure in some way. It's gotten so out of hand where
people are shoring up the resources in this overwrought
way, thinking it's going to shield them from pain.

Go back to the beach, to the rip current. It doesn't care how much money you have. There's a rip current in our hearts.

A lot of very wealthy and successful people live in fear. Their fear is a different fear than something like not being able to feed their kids. It's a fear of vanishing or becoming irrelevant. Of the rip current taking their wealth and privilege away forever. They think, "I'm still not there. It's not enough. I'm not loved as much as I should be. I don't love myself as much as I feel like I should. I feel others don't respect me as much as I think they should."

Money, as we learned with Tony Hsieh and Richard Cory, one very real, the other a fabrication, does not buy you happiness. We've been programmed by our modern economic systems, by the media, by religion, to be consumers. In the old days, we used to create. Now we consume. And we're probably more unhappy than we've ever been.

It's like the person who can finally afford to buy multiple houses in multiple locations. No matter how many that person buys, they never get beyond that first rush of excitement and opportunity. It's just a bundle of problems. They're aggravated with the architect, they're getting gouged by subcontractors, the designer isn't implementing ideas properly, the $10,000 credenza doesn't fit where it was supposed to. The list is endless. Where do we find peace? Where do we find unconditional acceptance and love for ourselves and where we are in our lives?

Ralph says the vaccine for the virus of "It's never enough" is generosity. I love what he says about it:

When we're generous, when we're giving, when we have
that openness of heart. It's quite paradoxical. When we're

generous it puts us in touch with how much we have, and that we do have enough. The connection involved in giving is worth more than anything we could hold in our two hands. There's this bait and switch that happens when we hoard. It leads to this increased sense of insecurity because it's failed to address the hole in our hearts that so many of us carry from childhood into adult life.

It's so true, isn't it? In order to feel that sense of enoughness, we need to heal that hole in our hearts. To save our emotional life and protect it for the long term, we need to do it every single day.

For most of us, our ability to discern, to sort through our emotions in a typical day, is like piloting a boat through treacherous waters. Emotional resilience is something we can develop, says Ralph. "We are born with a natural capacity for it." How do we know that? We just have to pause and feel it.

OK, so we need a tool for that. What can we use? What can we use for those moments when our mood is cratering, our attitude is plummeting, and our emotions are in Davy Jones's locker. What do we do? What's something that can snap us back to the surface without getting the bends?

As a business leader, you're going to have times in the day when you need to calm yourself in a fast, efficient way. You need a ritual. You need to shut the door and pause.

There's a meditation that's perfect for this that Dawson Church shared with me. It's a crucial part of how we can check in with our natural resilience when everything around is spiraling out of control. Settle in, because this is a good one:

Begin by feeling the breath, flowing in and out naturally through your heart, your own natural rhythm of breathing. You breathe 28,000 times a day. Feel that breath flowing in and out of your heart. Tap very lightly on this acupuncture meridian on the side of your hand, which is a potent point for releasing stress. As you tap there, imagine all the stress flowing out of your body like a fluid. Stress is leaving your body as you tap on this acupressure point. Tap on a couple of more acupressure points as well. Tap on the side of your eye, feeling the breath, flowing in, flowing out. Tap under the pupil of your eye, feeling your breath. Tapping on your nose, on your governing meridian. Tapping under your lower lip, on your central meridian. Tapping on your kidney meridian, which is to the side of your breastbone, imagining all the stress leaving your body. The last tapping point is to tap again on the side of your hand. Feel the breath flowing naturally in and out.

Stop tapping. Relax your hands. If your eyes are still open, close them. Imagine your breath flowing in and out through your heart. Slow your breathing down to six seconds per in-breath and six seconds per out-breath. Relax your tongue on the floor of your mouth and picture a big empty space between your eyes, breathing in through your heart for six seconds. Breathing out through your heart for six seconds. Feeling the energy in your heart area and sending a beam of that heart energy to a person or place that makes you feel wonderful. Envision that person or place and fold it in your heart's energy beam. Tongue relaxed on the floor of your mouth. Big empty space between your eyes, breathing six seconds in, six seconds out.

Hard energy beam going from your heart to this person or place that makes you feel wonderful. Expand your heart energy beam 360 degrees all around you to connect with every single atom in the universe. Feel the compassion energy from your heart touching every single atom in the universe. Tongue relaxed on the floor of your mouth. Big empty space between your eyes. Breathing in through the heart for six seconds. Breathing out through your heart for six seconds. Feeling your heart energy radiating out to touch every single atom in the universe with compassion. Focus that hard energy beam again tightly on only that one person or place that makes you feel wonderful. Detach your heart energy from every other place and focus it all on that one person or place. As you wrap them in the energy of your heart, very gently disengage your heart energy and bring it back to your own body, inside your own heart.

Send the beam of heart energy to any part of your body that's in pain, that's low in energy, that's sick or struggling. Wrap that part of your body in your heart energy. Tongue relaxed on the floor of your mouth. Big empty space between your eyes. Breathing in through your heart for six seconds. Breathing out through your heart for six seconds. With the next three breaths, prepare to bring your attention back into the here and now, back into your environment. Feel the weight of your body on the surface of which we're sitting. Feel this volume of space inside your hands, inside your feet. The next breath, open your eyes and look around you. With a gentle gaze, notice the biggest green item in your environment. Notice the smallest round object in your work environment and give thanks for the privilege of being in a body, being in a mind, living a life full of love and compassion, wisdom and resilience as you feel your breath give thanks for the privilege of being alive.

That's one simple, effective way to take the edge off your emotions. In the age of rage, Ralph De La Rosa says that it's about the ritual:

It's about the habit itself of every morning, no matter what's going on in my life, no matter how I feel, no matter what's going on in the world, I have a significant moment with myself. Even if that significant moment is complete chaos, I realize that the eighteen to twenty minutes that I'm meditating is very calm.

If we can do this for ourselves every day, we can develop what Ralph calls emotional flexibility and the deepest, most rewarding insights.

CHANGE-PROOF POINTS

▶ To be change proof, you have to go from being consumers to becoming creators.

▶ To do that, you need to spend time with yourself and your feelings every single day. Without fail.

CHAPTER 21

~~~

The 3-4 Method

Can any one of you by worrying add
a single hour to your life?
—MATTHEW 6:27

One of the things I love most about emotionally resilient people is that they're actively calm and when active they're calm. They're aware. They're present. They're the kind of person who when you think of them later you say to yourself, "That person is impressive." It's what we mean when we say gravitas. Even if it's posed. We believe it.

They know that carrying emotion is heavy. Emotions have real weight to them. The emotionally resilient ones just seem to move through the world like they're lighter. Because they're breathing. They're in contact with the movement of air in and out of their body. That allows them to self-disrupt the emotional patterning that the rest of us fall prey to. They don't have the stories that begin, "You're not smart enough." Or, "You're unkind." Or, "Your angry heart drives people away." Or, "Don't quit your day job." We repeat those things to ourselves

Breathe. Take a breath. Feel that energy, moving through your entire body, saying to you, "You get to be in this moment." That's a perfect presence. When you can say to yourself, even if you were caught in a rip current, "I'm still breathing. I get to be here. Fascinating." Performing perfect presence through breath always reminds me of the quote of the great Zen master who was asked, near the moment of his death, to expound some great wisdom. He waited a moment and then he said quietly, "I think I may know one or two things about breathing." That's what a rich subject it is. In many ways, our breath is the rudder that steers our emotional resilience. Every person who has to deal with pressure says the same thing: I focus on my breathing.

There's no great mystery here, folks. Breathe in. Breathe out. Breathe in. Breathe out. There. That's it. That's the book. Go back to your breath. You don't believe me? Ask the fantastic performance coach Grant Parr, who I had the distinct honor of talking to about how breath is the key to optimal performance. He says:

> *It's not just being present, it's with our breath. It's the whole vessel. When you're met with the unknown, the unexpected, you can get right into that breath. You need all of it. You need your breath.*

Grant believes that, when we get into emotional spirals where we feel subject to it, rather than it being subject to us, then the secret is the breath.

The 3-4 Method

This method is based on four thoughts spread out over a single breath, which is separated into three parts:

1. Inhale—the breathing in
2. Holding it for 10 seconds
3. Exhale—the breathing out

My breath pattern has a series of four thoughts associated with it. That way you're consciously thinking of something specific while you are, at the same time, engaged with yourself in your breath. This is a simple way to get present, in your moment, and interrupt the emotional patterning that keeps you from performing resilience.

On the breath in, you think a very simple thought—

1—Do I like feeling this way?

Chances are, the answer is usually "no," but you have a chance to decide that for yourself in a conscious way. If you like feeling anxious that you think your entire financial life is under attack, then by all means, continue on as you were.

Then you hold that breath while you think two consecutive thoughts—

2—Do I want to let it go?

Yes. Of course you do. You want to let it go. If you think about it, for even a second, you want to drop it like a hot coal.

3—Am I willing to let it go?

This is the sticky bit. This one isn't quite so cut and dried. That's why you're still holding your breath. Because this one could go forever. Can you hold your breath forever? No. Not even Tom Cruise can do that.

So think, really think: Are you willing, really willing, to let the feeling go? So often, some part of us says, "Yes! Yes! God willing and the saints be praised! I want to let it go!"

Then like the ancient gods of HP Lovecraft, some other voice answers, "*no.*" This is where we usually hang on to emotions. They're what we know. What we've known our entire lives. Again, it's part of our patterning that we got from our caregivers and our genetics. Nature and nurture both say, "This is mine."

Don't decide yet, just keep that breath in while you simply exhale and say to yourself—

4—When am I willing to let it go?

All you have to do is say, "Right now." That's it. "I decide to let this go." Simple. Of course, the emotion might still linger. Of course it will. It almost always does. There's no magic bullet for the feelings you got before you were conscious of them.

Go back to the beginning. See how long it takes your eye to travel to the beginning of the exercise. That's at least a few moments when you were consciously deciding what to feel while you were breathing.

So if the emotion is still with you, you've taken some of its power. And if you can take some, you can take more and more, until there isn't any "there" there anymore. Once you're breathing, you can decide how you wish to experience the energy of the emotion moving through you. That's the three parts of the breath and four simple thoughts. It's awareness and presence.

One of my favorite athletes today is the great Golden State Warrior guard Stephen Curry. He is one of those basketball players who approaches his craft like a tradesman who takes immaculate care of his tools so that when he needs them, they're available. In this case, the tools are his harmonic self: his body, mind, heart, and spirit. The bulk of his work is done on his physical self. He has to keep his body in shape, but he also has to look at his movements. So he has an objective lens through which he can view his performance from the inside and out.

When great athletes watch film, they can look at their performance dispassionately, removed from the mental pressure of the moment and the emotional experience at game time.

But we so rarely do that with ourselves. We rarely get present with our experience. Which is a darn shame, because it's the only one we get to have. The 3-4 method of breathing is a way to be objective with yourself and watch your own tape in the moment that it's happening.

There was a lawyer who was on the opposite side of a case I had once, a particularly difficult case. Of course, I was working

days and nights as much as I could. And weekends. One Saturday morning I was in the office fashioning and refashioning
every aspect of the case, when my phone rang. I picked it up to
hear a familiar voice on the other end: it was my opponent, the
other side of the legal case. He was just calling to see if I was
in the office on a Saturday. My family was at home, living in
the beautiful mess of a house full of children. And here I was
at work talking to another lawyer who just wanted to check up
on the competition to see who he was dealing with. He was
impressed that I was working so hard. If I'm honest, it felt good
to get that kind of validation. But as I sat there at my desk, the
morning light warm on my face, a cup of coffee steaming by my
elbow, I felt at war with myself. One part of me rejoiced at being
in the arena, mixing it up, like a late-stage Gordon Gecko, the
greatest city in the world at my feet.

But all I wanted was to be home, hauling my kids from lesson to practice to meal to playdate to home to dinner to bath
time to please go to sleep, to blissfully exhausted. I hated the
way I was feeling. I hated being at war with myself, and my
heart started to go to some pretty dark places. I'm not proud of
that. But I did. At that moment, I didn't do the 3-4 method. But
I did something like it.

Then I was reminded of an interview with John Lennon, who
was asked about his lovely ode to his son, Sean, called "Beautiful
Boy" and how it was such a true expression of a father's love for
his child. True to form, John wasn't having it.

> *Gauguin was stuck in Tahiti, painting a big picture for*
> *his daughter. So he's in Tahiti painting a picture for her,*
> *she dies in Denmark, she didn't see him for 20 years, he*
> *has VD and is going out of his mind in Tahiti—he dies*
> *and the painting gets burned anyway, so nobody ever sees*
> *the masterpiece of his f***ing life. And I'm always thinking*
> *about things like that. So I write a song about the child,*

but it would have been better for me to spend the time I wrote the f***ing song actually playing ball with him.

Sitting there, shooting the breeze with another overworked but weirdly competitive lawyer on a beautiful Saturday morning, this is how I felt too. This should have been the thing I wanted. Recognition from a peer! Validation! I had arrived. But I felt like the couple who rents a place on Airbnb based on the photos and then once they've arrived, instantly knowing they've made a terrible mistake. It seemed like everything I'd ever wanted, but it was nowhere I wanted to be.

I was nearing the top of the ladder and I was suddenly afraid of heights. Not of success. But of what the success was going to cost me. And it was going to. In all four realms of experience, I was going to pay. I didn't realize it fully yet, that would come later, when I thought I was having a heart attack, but this is one of the stones laid out that led me to walking away from a high-priced law career in the highest-paced metropolis in the known world.

Just by being momentarily aware of myself and my feelings led me to John Lennon. I didn't realize that realization was the beginning of the emotional resonance I still have today.

CHANGE-PROOF POINTS

▶ The 3-4 method of breathing in, holding for 10 seconds, and breathing out is a simple way to let go of feelings that hinder us from our growth potential.

▶ If you find yourself feeling things you don't want to feel, then use this method to pause, ask, and then choose to let it go.

CHAPTER 22

Follow the Bubbles

What we've been given is precious. It's majestic in
its smallest details and its largest manifestations.
Anyone not humbled by the power of the ocean
should take a good, long look at a fifty-foot wave.
If you don't have respect for water, it's only a
matter of time before the ocean teaches you to
get some. We're all equal before the wave.

—LAIRD HAMILTON

When we talk about emotional resilience, things can get very muddled and confusing. Feelings are tricky things to nail down. They live in our bodies, sort of vague and formless, and we rarely feel we're in control of them. In fact, it's usually the opposite. Most days, we're at the mercy of our emotions. If we "feel good" the day seems to fly by and everything we touch seems to work out for the better. If we "feel bad" then we all know how those days go. We're like Alexander from the children's book by Judith Viorst, and our day goes from terrible to horrible to no good to very bad.

Emotionally, we feel tossed into the deep, deep water where everything is dark and we don't know up from down. It's in those moments that we need to "follow the bubbles" and I learned that from one of the best surfers out there, Dave Kalama, who, if you can believe it, is an even better man. Dave is change proof in all the best ways. Because of the bubbles, you see.

As I mentioned earlier in our story, I love to surf. It's a magical, fruitful place. It's where all the lessons of this book come into the sharpest focus imaginable. Because the growth edge is the place where we're one with the flow of the universe. We're not ahead. We're not behind. We're simply riding the waves as they come. I don't do it to unplug, rather I use it to plug in to the source of all things.

It's also the most dangerous place to be, because one of the first things that lifeguard training teaches is never turn your back on the ocean. That's where you're most vulnerable. Surfing takes that to another level. Once you catch a wave, you're literally turning your back on all of the other waves that are following behind. Dave Kalama knows full well that just because you're on a huge wave, the next one might be even bigger. Nobody respects the ocean more than surfers. No matter how experienced they are in the water and the waves. No matter how many big waves they've plunged down on their board. No matter how many hours and days and months they've been in the ocean. They know full well what it can do, how big, powerful, and remorseless the ocean is to those who dare to tread on its surface.

Dave found out just how remorseless one day on the North Shore of Maui. Usually, the lead surfer is Laird Hamilton, famous wave rider, and someone Dave usually surfs with. I'm going to share with you big chunks of what he said, because not only is Dave a great talker, but it's exactly what we need to hear when we're fashioning our emotional resilience.

> To set the scene, Laird Hamilton was out of town. Laird is the Alpha Dog on any given day and without him there, that allows me to take that position. My confidence

is raised. My role is perhaps inflated. I look at it as an opportunity. I'm going to reset the bar of how things go out here and who I am. My approach might have been too confident. I tried to make a very aggressive move on a good-sized wave that distracted my focus from where it should've been. I was focused more on my touchdown dance, than I was on running with the ball and making sure I got the touchdown. That's exactly what happened. I wasn't paying attention to the water when I should have been. I was focused on the people in the channel and what their cheers and screams might sound like, as opposed to catching and running. I hit a bump, which bucked me up on my board and started a hole literally downward spiral figuratively and literally underwater which started the whole episode.

Now, when I'm surfing, a big wave to me is eight feet. What Dave was dealing with was a 35-to-40-foot wave. And that's not even the peak of the waves at Peahi on Maui's North Shore, also known as "Jaws." Falling off it was just the beginning of Dave's problems that day:

It's funny at that moment I'm sliding down on my back, like a car wreck or something of that nature where time slows down, I have this internal conversation going on with myself. The old surf footage that you see of the guys at Waimea, this is what it felt like. I almost have this little giggle. How can I be having this conversation with myself when things are about to get as ugly as they possibly can? It comes back to a survival mechanism that kicks in, trying to lighten the moment so that you don't become overwhelmed.

Dave realized that we all have this survival mechanism that kicks in when we're in situations, times of emotional chaos, in our business, our jobs, our relationships, or with our children.

When things start to go downward, we freeze, we tense up. We panic. Just as it is when we are in the rip current.

Dave continued:

> *I'm tumbling and I'm spinning. You have so much energy and so much adrenaline, and at that point there's still a lot of oxygen in your blood. Even though it's scary, it's not life-threatening. Literally, almost anybody can handle one of those waves. The first one, you've still got a lot of energy and a lot of oxygen in your blood. It's the second one, the third one, the fourth one that your energy is expended. Your oxygen has been used up and that's when things get extremely serious. While I tell a story that brought a lightness to the mood, by no way in any shape or form did I take the situation lightly. I tried not to let it seize me up. Panicking is absolutely the worst thing you can do in almost any given situation. Regardless of if it's waves, life, anything.*

Now, at this moment, Dave popped to the surface. He took a deep breath and tried to orient himself. One of his friends pulls up on a jet ski to pull him to safety. His friend risked his own life to get to Dave because there are more 35-to-40-foot waves pounding down on both of them. One hit and hit really hard, ripping Dave off the jet ski, the force of the wave driving Dave down deep, deeper than he'd ever been in his life. The pressure in his ears told him something was wrong.

> *I'm in the second wave, I'm deeper than I've ever been. I'm more fatigued because I've experienced the first wave and it's all down, but I still have a bit of energy. I'm trying to keep my wits about me and that the internal conversation is still going on. I remember saying to myself, "If you're ever going to have trouble, this is it. If you're going down, you're going down fighting. Let's get going. Time to go to work." I start swimming for the surface and after about*

three or four strokes, my body goes into these involuntary convulsions, which completely caught me by surprise. I had no idea what was going on. It seemed like an odd place to lose control of my body. In any case, after about three or four of them, they stopped. I took a quick inventory of whether I still had control of my limbs, which I did.

I figured out I don't have time to figure out what happened. The surface is where I need to focus. I start swimming again and my eyes are open and it's completely dark. You couldn't see your hand two inches from your nose. I'm swimming, I'm taking four, five, six, seven, eight strokes. Still, pitch black. All of a sudden, I start to see the tiniest hint of light in the water.

This is where Dave saw the bubbles. And what you do, when you're deep like that, if you can see bubbles, you follow them out of the dark.

That is an indication that you're anywhere from three to six feet from the surface. That gives you a lot of hope because you know where you are, you know you're close to the surface, and there's a chance you can make it. That gives you a lot of confidence, which calms you down. It gives you energy at the same time. I keep going and sure enough, I break the surface.

I took a deep inhale, orientated myself again like the last one and it's an exact carbon copy. There's another giant whitewater bearing down. The difference from the first time is I know that I need to get on that rescue sled, hold on for dear life because it's not an expression anymore. It's literally life and death. That rescue sled is very floaty and I know it will make it to the surface before I can. I get on the rescue sled and I hold on for dear life and brace for impact. I remember one of the thoughts in my head before we got hit by the whitewater was, even if my body's not on this rescue sled anymore, my hands need to be. That's how much I was anticipating holding on that my hand would still be there even if my arms ripped off because I was not going to let go.

It was as serious as it could possibly get. We tumbled and we rolled. I hit the ski, but my hands were holding on for dear life. I stayed with that rescue sled. As I anticipated, the sled and the ski have so much buoyancy. They came to the surface quite quickly when the whitewater released us, which got me to the surface. As I swam out from under the sled, my partner, Brett, swam out on the same side. We broke the surface together. I'm looking at his eyes and he can see that I'm shaking seriously. I look at him and I go, "Thank you. I love you. You saved my life." It was a pretty intense moment.

Most of us, if not all, have not had experiences like this where we experience the nearness of death, but we've likely had moments where we feel a crushing weight on our chests when we wake up in the middle of the night. Night after sleepless night. The fear, the pressure, the endless worry and anxiety that we might lose everything we've worked so hard to build.

Dave came up out of the waves with a renewed sense of energy and purpose:

Looking back on it and at other times in my life when I've had massive failures, those are the moments that are the key to success. Without that kick in the teeth and that reality check, I don't take things seriously or not to the level I did. Without taking them as seriously as I was after that incident, I don't become as educated. I don't become as skilled. I don't become as well-rounded in so many other areas. It all grew from that experience that without it, I don't become as successful or as capable of a waterman as I am without that failure.

Dave became an early adopter of something called the personal flotation device (PFD). Failure took him to the edge of the veil that divides life and death and in that space he decided to advocate for something that went against the macho posturing of the sport. It's something he wears all the time now so that if he's ever in that space again, he's protected. Now many other surfers are wearing them too.

But Dave also created rituals for emotional resilience:

> *Every time I get in the water, I say a little prayer that's very based on appreciation and thanks. Looking for a little help and guidance because you never know what can happen when you get in the water. I would say throughout my life that has probably been the most consistent ritual of anything I've ever had. I don't do anything that would draw attention or make you think I'm praying when I get in the water and I'm on my way out, I check in with myself and whatever term you want to give God, spirits, the ocean, wherever you check in with. I do that and show my appreciation for what's going on, where I am, what I have and ask for a little help out there, "Keep me and everybody else safe and enjoy."*
>
> *Going through that process of opening my mind again and starting with a clean slate, not bringing my old thoughts and concepts to the table was much more difficult than I ever thought it would be and has proven to be extremely beneficial in so many different aspects of my life because what I realized was, I don't want to take chances.*
>
> *I want to be safe. I want to do the safe thing. In that process, I realize I can't do the same thing. Stop being afraid. Stop being afraid of change. Stop being afraid of new ideas. That wasn't isolated to my board design in the beginning, I know that's a very small thing, but it had a profound effect. I realized I could look at everything I do and all the decisions*

> *I make and it was like, "Am I making those decisions out*
> *of fear and trying to be safe? Am I making those decisions*
> *because they're literally the best decisions taking everything*
> *in?" That has taught me so much about how to approach*
> *things and how to move forward and make better decisions.*

Such sweet, elegant simplicity. That's what I love about surfing and surfers. It's not complicated. The rest of us on the land make it more complicated than it needs to be.

A simple ritual of something that looks like prayer. If we want to be resilient in our day-to-day lives, we've got to start the day with that ritual, the same way Dave does when he paddles out into the mystery of the universe.

There's an old saying among surfers that goes something like this, "You can't surf calm water." We think we want our lives to settle down. We think we want calm, unbroken pond water. But we don't. Do we? We want the rush. We want the adrenaline spike that hits our brains when we're on the edge—uncertain, anxious, but deeply alive.

Yeah. You can fall off. But our kind of emotional resilience is our own personal floatation device. Our own PFD. When the waves toss us and we lose our edge, there's something on our back that can help us rise to the surface. The bubbles are those little things you don't think of at the moment. They brush by us without leaving a mark. But when we look back, at our day, our month, our year, our very lives, it was the bubbles that helped us survive. The kind word. That random expression of gratitude. That text that said, "Hey, I'm thinking of you." It was the smile you got from that person you thought was your nemesis. It was the check that finally arrived. It was the break in the relationship when your partner says, "I'm sorry." It can be a shaft of light. A song or lyric. The book you're holding. A time of day. The bubbles are there to lead us home. We just have to stop panicking and see them.

Your life is filled with changes. Big and small. They can be scary. They can be threatening. They can seem like the world is ending.

Or the changes can be challenged. The thing you're afraid of can be exciting. Maybe the world is ending so another one can be born. Maybe that pivot you were afraid of is the thing that's going to save your entire life. Maybe your big break is coming after lunch today.

The bubbles are all around us. Every morning can be for us, "I'm grateful for the waves I'm going to ride today." Every time I ride the (small) waves, I'm full of gratitude that I get to be a person who gets to do that.

For you, it might not be surfing. But there's something out there for you that puts you in touch with the feeling you have when time floats away and you're right where you're supposed to be. That's how our days can go. There are bubbles every day. We just have to look for them. Then, a little bit every day, when we find ourselves tossed, turned, nowhere to go, down is up and up is down, and our breath is pounding, pounding so hard in our chest and we just want to give up, give in, then what do we do?

Like Dave Kalama, we follow the bubbles.

CHANGE-PROOF POINTS

▶ The bubbles in your lives are the simple moments that pull you out of the deep water of dark feelings and moods.

▶ Make a list of the bubbles you saw today and be grateful for them. I guarantee you'll feel yourself taking a deep, refreshing breath and facing the future with joy and peace.

CHAPTER 23

≈≈≈

Calm Is Contagious

Embrace the Suck
—NAVY SEAL MOTTO

How do we keep our cool when everything around us is spinning out of control? How do we not panic when we find ourselves in a rip current that's hurtling out to sea? Our emotional resilience depends upon doing that. But so often we find it difficult to stay present, in the moment, in our hearts, and in the hearts of our business.

Not all of us are leaders, but each of us, in our ways, is leading something. Maybe it's not a business, team, or organization, but maybe you're a leader in your family, your place of worship, or your peer group. Maybe you're the captain of your softball team, because no one else will do it. At the very least, though, we're always leading ourselves. We are leaders in our own hearts. To be a leader, you have to be resilient, and if you want to be resilient, you have to be calm.

There's a story from sports that I've never forgotten. It's embedded in the lore of the National Football League and it's a lesson in contagious calm from probably the coolest person to ever lace 'em up on Sunday: Joe Montana, the iconic quarterback for the dynastic San Francisco 49ers. I mean, get this, his name was Joe Cool. How cool is that?

Anyway, the story comes from the Super Bowl in 1989 when the heavily favored 49ers went up against the scrappy Cincinnati Bengals. Vegas had San Francisco as 11-point favorites, which sets an expectation that they'd beat Cincinnati pretty handily.

By the fourth quarter, the game was much, much closer than anybody expected. The 49ers had tied the game at 13 early in the quarter and then with less than five minutes to play, the Bengals went ahead by 3. The score was 16–13 and the almighty San Francisco 49ers were under three minutes from facing an upset of historic proportions.

So onto the field comes the 49ers offense—the linemen, the receivers, and the tight end—to wait out one of the many television timeouts that are the hallmark of the Super Bowl. Harris Barton, the talented, young lineman was in the huddle trying to exhort his teammates on to success. Now Harris was known at that time as a relentlessly charismatic player prone to fall prey to his worry, his anxiety, and his fear. In that moment, he was unloading all of that onto his teammates who were on the brink of a catastrophic failure.

Then into the huddle strolls Joe Cool himself, Joe Montana. With the offensive team in front of him, on the edge of breaking down, he gets Harris Barton's attention, saying, "Hey, Harris, look, it's John Candy." He points down to the opposite end zone where, sure enough, the great Canadian comedian, John Candy, was indeed standing on the field with the other VIPs. As one, the offense turned to look at John Candy. Before anyone else had time to comment, the whistle blew and the series that would decide their collective fate was underway.

Joe Montana was as cool as his nickname suggests as he led his team down the field to the winning touchdown. In two minutes, in the moment of the crucible, Montana spread his cool, calm demeanor to the rest of his team and led them to victory.

I want to talk about a true renaissance warrior that I had the opportunity to spend some time with. His name is Commander

Rorke Denver and, in addition to having one of the greatest, coolest names I've ever heard, he's run every phase of training for the US Navy SEALs and led Special Forces missions in the Middle East, Africa, Latin America, and other hot spots around the globe. He's the author of two best-selling books that take you inside the heart of America's warriors, to show us how and why we fight for the people and things that matter.

The mantra of the Navy SEALs is simple, "Embrace the Suck." That's as true a definition of resilience as one could possibly write in three simple words: Embrace. The. Suck. We lifeguards call the deadly rip current, "the Suck," so we're finding synchronicities everywhere. If you're in the rip current and you make the choice to embrace the fact that it's happening rather than fighting it, if you actually embrace "the Suck" then you are going to survive.

For Commander Denver and the rest of the Navy SEALs, mission-critical times call for real resilience that's built on the foundation of preparation. That preparation, for people like him, in their business, is grounded in suffering, pain, and hard times that you and I can't even imagine. And he has a story about SEALs training, probably the hardest training in the whole world, that has a lot to teach us about how to maintain your cool in the face of overwhelming hardship.

So much of the training that Commander Denver participates in is based on the idea that if you fail to meet a certain standard, you are going to deal with some harsh correction. And it's not something that is based on abuse. That's not what they're doing. They're saying that we're going to create increasingly difficult situations so that we can find out who's truly resilient.

But the interesting thing Commander Denver told me was about the times when the class would show up in perfect formation a solid 30 minutes before the required time to be on deck. Six o'clock in the morning and all is well, right? No, it's not all right. Let's set the scene:

Laser-like ranks, fins in front of them, dive mask on top, razor blades for knives and they'll have a little bit of a grin on their face because we walk in and they'd be like, "We did it right," and we'll beat them worse than the day they showed up late. What will happen is inevitably 2 or 3 will be like, "This is unfair. This is a total BS. I'm out of here." They'll quit. For those that stay, we'll be like, "The reason you're going to do right by this job is what you're going to recognize is the acts of violence on the actual battlefield, they are random." While they can feel personal, they're not. It's the way that construct unfolds. If you're not the type of person that can do everything right and have it go horrifically wrong, be fine with that and come back fighting the next day, you're not long for this job. It's not for you. So our training methodology is that you could do everything perfectly right and it can go catastrophically wrong.

So much of our lives is not just about trying to avoid mistakes, but avoiding situations where it's even possible to make a mistake. That's just the truth. We're conditioned to take the easier route to be comfortable.

But it's not about just keeping calm when we're up against it. Part of keeping calm is just doing the thing that's in front of you and not getting your emotions lost in fighting battles about what was fair or unfair. That's a losing proposition. Even when we're correct and we're fighting over what is fair or unfair, we're losing. There's right and there's wrong. That's different. That's worth fighting for.

Staying calm in the face of what we perceive to be unfair will trickle down to the people around us. That's what the SEALSs believe too, because they want a situation where their graduates are on a mission in a dangerous hot spot, they know that the people around them are just as resilient as they are. They don't have to think about it. They can depend on their collective resilience. That creates contagious calm.

The results come from preparation. And your preparation prepares you to forge bonds with the people who've experienced hardships with you. As Commander Denver says,

> It's a remarkable thing when your foundation is knowing that the people you're around at a minimum will never fail you or never quit you. It's very hard to replicate or it's much harder to replicate post my time in the military. I know those guys would do the exact same thing in our post-military life when I'm around them and I can feel that. It's a special thing to be around. I come from a family that my brother and my dad, my mom, and all those people are very much the same way. We have that commitment to each other and so that's special. Those are bonds that are exceptionally hard to replicate in your next life. It's why a lot of the guys and girls that come out of elite units in the military do struggle sometimes in their next life because they don't feel the same level of purpose and commitment of those around them as the whole block of time they spent doing what we did.

Unfortunately, the US Navy SEAL training isn't available to all of us. The world would be a vastly different place if we all had to go through something like that after we graduated from high school. Some kind of training that tests us to our limits. Even the people who quit Basic Underwater Demolition/SEAL (BUD/S) training know something valuable about themselves. So the next time they're in a similar crucible, maybe they make a different choice. The point is, we have to get comfortable being uncomfortable. That's what "Embrace the Suck" means.

Now, how can organizations do the same? If you're a leader, you can't put your team or your company through heavy-duty training. And everyone can see the stereotypical trust fall exercises and corporate training from a thousand feet away, so it's hard to forge those kinds of bonds.

Sometimes embracing the suck is about just taking a moment and saying, "Am I OK with failing at this?" If the answer is "yes," by all means, make that choice. But if, in your heart, you're not OK, then you will just choose to do what it takes. I know, having been in those moments, how it feels when things are falling apart around you, and everything gets calm and clear. And you say to yourself, "I want this." Then no matter what happens, you will be resilient. You will know, on a heart level, what's worth fighting for.

Suffering and pain have a way of making us see the truth of things. To me, that's a peaceful, calm place.

CHANGE-PROOF POINT

▶ If you're calm, then spread that calm like a virus.

CHAPTER 24

Resilience Is a Choice

The realization came over me with full force that a good part of the remainder of my life was going to be spent in finding errors in my own programs.

—MAURICE WILKES,
Memoirs of a Computer Pioneer

As a business leader you know full well that your day often begins before you're even awake. The night before, sleep, when it came, came at the expense of all the worries, thoughts, and problems spinning through your head. Your dreams are full of the data dumping of that process, so when the alarm goes off, you're instantly thinking of those very things because you really never stopped. And then your day is just one thing after another. Until the night. And then you do it all again rushing headlong without consciousness.

So, let's pull back up above the trees. I want you to think for a moment. I want you to feel your way inside your body, your mind, your heart, and your spirit and use your imagination. Really, think: "What's my ideal day?" And not your perfect day, a summer day away from it all, on vacation or at a spa or on an island. Those are perfectly good things to imagine when you want to unplug and unwind. What we are about to go into is a deep awareness of your life as you are living it, so that you can become the change you seek as opposed to seeking ways to avoid change. This exercise is going to be a journey through your entire day, starting with the result you want in the end.

In a moment, you'll close your eyes. All you have to do is breathe. And just feel that. Pick an average day in your life. Any ordinary day that you've walked through. Go through the entire day, beginning with how you wake up. How you get clean and dressed. How you take your coffee, really try to get granular with it. Just see. How work goes. Notice your states of being. Do you feel stressed? Anxious? Calm? Your interactions with your partner or your family. Or your coworkers. A friend. A date. Where you might eat breakfast, lunch, and dinner. What you might eat there. Who are you with? Using your mind, try to go through that entire ideal day and how you feel in it being in charge of your own emotional experience.

OK. Close your eyes. And remember those states of being as you "experience" your day. I'll be here when you get back.

How was that? How did it feel? Being in charge for a change? Were you able to allow yourself to actually be in charge? It's OK. No wrong answers. It was an exercise, not a test.

Now, let's talk about how we get there, to that place of being in charge and flowering resilience in your own garden. I believe that harmonic resilience plays like music between our four realms of human experience. However, it's not something that just happens. It's something we can learn to apply, like a skill, and it's something you can start applying first thing in the morning, a ritual that, if you do it every day, you'll find yourself surfing the emotional waves like Dave Kalama or Laird Hamilton.

In our work, emotional resilience is saying to yourself, "I am experiencing the feeling of being in my own experience." Rather than giving your day away to others to dictate your experience, it's you dictating the programming code of your day.

If I leave the house without my phone, I feel as though I've left without my pants. I've achieved some kind of transhumanism where I've fused with the machine that makes my life go. Indeed, our world today is defined and controlled by computers. Ones and zeros all the way up and all the way down. Lines upon lines of code that make up the architecture of our entire society. Just the amount of code that goes into my website, AdamMarkel.com, is greater than that of the rockets that took humans to the moon in 1969.

In a lot of ways, our lives are designed by the algorithms all around us. The only algorithm we're oftentimes not aware of is the one that lives inside us. It's the secret to that ideal day we're searching for.

Now, I'm no mathematician, but as I understand it, basically, an algorithm is just a list of rules to solve a problem. A recipe for beef bourguignon in a Julia Child cookbook, for instance, is an algorithm. It's a series of steps of taking chaos and making delicious order out of it. In computers, an algorithm tells a computer or program what to do.

To make an algorithm, you have to write a series of codes. The collection of codes adds up to a set of actions for a computer to perform. Unfortunately, we're not computers. There's no set of buttons to press to write the code that will dictate perfect thoughts and actions.

But my morning ritual, one that I do every day, is a 13-step checklist I follow to create the algorithm of the day. It's what I call my Code of Conduct. By doing this each morning, I fine tune my emotional programming to become the conscious creator of my own life experience—and you can do the same.

There's a difference between noticing and attracting. Right now, we are focusing on noticing. It's something I wrote briefly about in my previous book, *Pivot*. I check in with it every morning. I do this so I can program my intentions for what I would like to experience as my day begins and progresses. I have used this Code of Conduct as I start each day for more than 12 years and I'm going to share it with you now.

My code consists of a list of experiences—states of being—that I want to feel on any given day. Within 30 minutes of waking, I sit alone and read the same 13 simple statements out loud. Each statement takes the form of a declaration using the words "*I experience _____ today*." Here's my code:

> *I experience gratitude today.*
> *I experience a positive and harmonious attitude today.*
> *I experience myself adding value to other people's lives today.*
> *I experience creating from a place of relaxed focus today.*
> *I experience myself living by a higher standard today.*
> *I experience living in absolute integrity and kindness today.*
> *I experience being the conscious creator of my own life*
>   *experience today.*
> *I experience creating empowering solutions today.*
> *I experience living with a fearless heart today.*
> *I experience the presence of unconditional love today.*
> *I experience myself being healthy, wealthy, and wise today.*
> *I experience, receive, and manifest miracles today.*
> *I experience forgiveness today.*

I still have the original piece of paper I wrote my first Code of Conduct on. It's yellowed, faded, torn, and taped, and covered in notes, but many years after I created it, I still pick up that worn piece of paper each morning to start my day.

To create your own Code of Conduct, I recommend you sit in a quiet place for just 5 or 10 minutes and ask how you want to experience your life today. How do you want to experience your business, your interactions with others, your finances, and health? Use my list as a place to start, but know you should change and adjust the earlier statements to suit your unique experience. You don't need to start with 13 either. There's no magic number. For me, and my clients, the best results have come from using at least 5 statements each day, but no more than 15.

The practice is powerful in intervals of 10 to 20 minutes. In fact, substantial benefits have come from just a few minutes of this practice, and if there's one single thing you take away from this book, let it be this. It's about making a fundamental choice of how you start out your day, which will lead to fundamental freedom.

Using the Code of Conduct to set the algorithm for your day is about taking emotional responsibility for your experience. How many times do we do that? We give our day away to people all the time, and what they think, feel, and do puts thoughts in our heads, feelings in our hearts, and makes us do things we may not really want to be doing. The important thing about the Code of Conduct is to do it first thing in the morning. If you wait to check in with it until your day goes sideways, then it'll be too late.

People who are emotionally responsible for their own life experiences are resilient people. How could they not be? It's all about how you want to experience yourself being on any given day. Emotional resilience is about existing in that loving space where you're noticing the abundance all around you. When you make the Code of Conduct a resilience ritual, everything you truly want will follow. You'll notice you're walking differently. The air will pass over your skin differently. Your interactions will be different. It'll be subtle, but if you're noticing them, they'll seem huge.

Then at the end of the day, you pull out that piece of paper and check to see how you did. You want to create a bridge between the pure potentiality of your day and what is produced by your day. Ask yourself: What's going on in my world? Then ask: What's going on in myself? If done daily and nightly, this Code of Conduct will allow you to dance between external events and the movement of your inner life.

In addition to the algorithm metaphor, there's yet another way of looking at the Code of Conduct. One of my favorite sounds in the world is when I go to a concert or a musical and the orchestra tunes their instruments together. They're getting their individual instruments tuned to the same frequency so that collectively they can create beautiful music. If you've never listened to the Grateful Dead play live, they turn tuning up into a form of improvisational art.

Think of the Code of Conduct as a way for you to tune the only instrument you have: yourself. You'll start to hear your own inner tuning, and after only a few weeks, you'll start to hear it in other people too. You'll naturally make connections and solve problems because you won't be thinking about them, you'll be feeling them.

Both computer programmers and musicians know how crucial minute adjustments are to the overall composition. If we extend this metaphor, the musician's instrument doesn't tune up and stay in tune. They have to tune it every time they use it, or it will go so out of tune that what they intend to play becomes impossible.

Having this Code of Conduct allows you to check in throughout the day to see how you're doing. Yet, it's vital that you check in with it in the evening. You started the day with an intention, and the nighttime is where you can check and see how you did.

On the day after a game, sports teams watch the video of how the game played out. They can see objectively how well they did compared with what the game plan was. You're checking your own performance. We so rarely do that, right? When we begin our day, we often start with the certainty of plans, but our plans often are changed without our will or consent. Resilience, emotionally, is about leveraging that uncertainty so we're in tune with ourselves, our families, our business, and the world around us. It's as Kierkegaard wrote, "Life must be lived forwards, but it can only be understood backwards."

The Code of Conduct is your key to living your ideal day, not just tomorrow, but all the tomorrows after that so you can gain a greater understanding of the resilience that lives inside you. The key is to use the unknown as your ally and advisor. How can you let the future use you?

Then you can have that ideal day that you imagined. For real.

CHANGE-PROOF POINT

▶ The Code of Conduct, when you do it every morning and every night, will allow you to create the reality that you desire for yourself.

CHAPTER 25

The Myth of Authenticity

They're not going to be listening to what you say. They're going to be listening to hear if you're an honest person.
—**PHILLIP JOHNSON,**
quoted by Kurt Vonnegut

Hide and seek. It's a game played by kids in every culture around the world. It was one of my favorite games to play with my four children. Even now, I get a little stab of heartache when I remember the little giggles and squeals that would drift out of the dark corners of our house as I would seek for them. Like all kids, they could play for hours without tiring of it.

It's no different than peek-a-boo, in that it's part of how kids create and test the boundaries of attachment with their parents and each other. It may be a silly game, but it fulfills a very real developmental purpose in helping little brains grow and little hearts feel safe.

But as we grow older we often don't put silly games like hide and seek behind us. We keep them inside. It's how some of us cope with anxiety and fear. For many of us, the game is the same but no one's giggling. You may not know it, but you're hiding. You're hiding past traumas. You're hiding addictions. You're hiding money, or the lack of it. You're hiding what you truly want. We're hiding from the world, and we're hiding from ourselves. We're hiding our true selves from what the world expects of us. How do we find our true selves when the world is constantly telling us we "should be" something else?

If we are truly to become resilient, then a lot of people would say that we have to be authentic. *Authenticity* is a buzzword that gets thrown around a lot these days. In fact, it gets thrown around so much that it's starting to become meaningless.

In a lot of ways, it's like our balance versus harmony dichotomy. We say balance when we mean harmony, and in this case, we say authenticity when we mean transparency. Transparency is rooted in clarity. Get clear with yourself and then you can get clear with the people in your life and in your organization. You have to be clear about what you want, what you need, and what you're willing to do to get it. If we want to be change proof, we have to get the window cleaner out and share ourselves. How do we do that?

Meet Todd Kane, for most of his life, a man skilled at hiding. Husband, father, veteran, entrepreneur, philanthropist, and author. Todd wore all these masks to great success. He was able to effortlessly decide what mask to wear depending on the situation in which he found himself. As a member of the US Army, he was leading men and women, he was comfortably married with two children, and he was a respected member of his community, but he was not living a truthful, transparent life. He was living a lie. Because Todd Kane was hiding the fact that he's gay.

For him, it was fear that kept him in the shadows, "I wasn't born afraid. I learned to be afraid. That was a big aha for me.

To know that fear is a liar." Todd learned early on that the most devastating lies are the ones we tell ourselves.

He first had this realization in, of all places, the military as a tanker, clothed in camouflage, surrounded by tons of metal. "We looked alike. We walked alike. We talked alike. I was drawn to that because I felt different forever. I could literally step into [it] and be guided by normality." Todd had gotten really good at doing things by the numbers, doing exactly what he was told, and moving up the chain of command, because Todd had learned that feeling different made him feel afraid. As a tanker, he had armor around him that was nearly indestructible.

It was very similar for me when I was a lawyer: I was waking up every morning and feeling a bit like a fraud. I was doing it mostly for the money and how I perceived that money providing safety and security for my family. I didn't love it. I wasn't inspired by it. I was playing my own game of hide and seek when a new client or opportunity came into my life. Every time I would play it, I could feel a little bit of the trust I had in myself drop away into the ocean. That trust, once it's gone, is exponentially harder to get back.

Here's what Todd Kane says you need to do to live transparently.

Trust in Truth

We have to be honest and rigorous with one another. That's real support. That's what we crave. But resilience is impossible without an honest accounting of ourselves. If you desire long-term growth, it requires short-term pain. That's the opportunity cost of leveraging uncertainty. The payment you make toward transparency in the short term will produce long-term creative opportunities that will last you the rest of whatever life you're blessed to have.

Hard-Wired for the Required

Todd Kane says, "Fear is necessary. It's the physiological response to danger. We are very cognitive beings. We have intellect that is far greater than anything else on the planet." In emotional resilience, truth gives us peace. We're hardwired for survival and true survival can only happen if we tell the truth. As Abraham Lincoln said, "A house divided against itself cannot stand." We can't tell a truth out of our mouths that doesn't come from our transparent hearts.

The Harder Right and the Even Harder Wrong

Transparency comes when you make the tough choices. That's a very simple thing to write and a much harder thing to execute. So many of our choices come down to the lesser of two evils.

There are layers to truth. I used to think it was black and white, good and evil. Even as a lawyer, even though I trained myself to find gray areas, the crawl spaces in between this truth and that truth. Inside though, I knew full well that there's a true and there's false.

Todd found this out firsthand when he came out at 33. He explained things this way:

> You're feeling you got this truth and you go, "I didn't have the truth. What does this mean?" It was like, "This is exactly what this means." We don't always know the truth. We don't know what someone is going through. We don't ask. Do you know what else we don't do? We don't articulate our truth. What do I believe?

The harder right and the even harder wrong are emotional problems that can only be solved with our truth. We get that from our final step.

Harness the Power of "I Am"

Todd's journey to transparency has not been an easy one. Even after he came out and declared his truth. That's not the end of the story. He married a man. But that partnership wasn't meant to last. Todd was still working through the layers of his own truth. It wasn't as though he just declared himself, audience applause, cut to black, and rolled the credits. Life must be lived outside that frame. That frame includes a lot of stuff that we need to work through to be transparent.

•   •   •

In my line of work, I'm blessed to be able to travel the world working with companies that are trying to figure out how to be change proof. Recently, I had the opportunity to travel to North Carolina to lend a hand to a hospital group down there. Like many organizations, they were stuck, stagnant, and knowing they needed to change but didn't know how to do it. We've all been there. Where things were going well, but they could be going better. We're idling in a comfortable gear that we've been in for a while.

When I meet people or groups in this phase of things, then I know that something is wrong inside that's been papered over by events and time and the endless rush of daily activity. That's where people and organizations are the most vulnerable. They're sick inside, not terminally, but sick, and if left unchecked, that inner sickness is going to fester and eventually it will be terminal. This is the part of my job that I enjoy the most because I get to open things up so that sunlight can get into dark corners. I know because I've been there before.

Once I got there and started opening things up, I soon learned what the issue was. The CEO of the hospital was on the edge of burnout, which is a nice way of saying she was burned out already. Burnout is one of those states that is like a black hole, where the closer you get to it, the more the gravity and density start to act in a way that actually breaks down the reality of things.

It was very familiar to me. The CEO was driving herself to a crisis. Physically, her body was out of whack. Her mind was stuck in endless worry and anxiety. She couldn't engage emotionally with her people or her family. She stopped valuing what it was she was doing. Classic burnout black hole.

Then she got real with me. She felt as though she was having a heart attack. I knew full well what this was. It was a panic attack disguised as something worse. The CEO did the brave thing. She didn't grin and bear it. She didn't grit it out and keep going. She drove herself to the hospital to get the help she needed.

That was the brave thing. The radical thing she did was tell her organization what had happened. She got transparent with herself and her team. She didn't hide her perceived weakness. Transparency is the place where bravery becomes radical. Any single time we're in the place, we're on the way to being change proof. She came back and said, "If I'm setting this example, then I'm the reason why we're stagnant."

Too many times as leaders we don't want to be transparent about our own struggles. We're afraid that in the kill-or-be-killed world of business, any scent of weakness is going to be seized upon and used against us. Nobody wants to be Wally Pipp. He's the Yankees' first baseman who sat out a game and was replaced by a young up-and-comer named Lou Gehrig. The same Lou Gehrig who didn't miss a game for 2,130 games.

Real leadership is admitting we can't do it all. Real leadership is being radically transparent. Like Todd Kane, the CEO didn't hide, but instead she sought a place where she didn't need to hide.

CHANGE-PROOF POINTS

▶ The leaders of tomorrow are transparent today.

▶ Don't hide from your weaknesses, seek them and you'll find them eventually becoming your strengths.

CHAPTER 26

"We'll Figure It Out"

How you are in anything, is how
you are in everything.
—ANONYMOUS

I love that quote. It tells me everything I need to know about everything. But let's take it further: how you are in your life is how you are in your business.

Who you are is defined by stated and unstated expectations. Let's be honest, if you're a business leader, then you expect your team to be mind-readers. If you're willing to be radically honest and transparent about your expectations of yourself and your team, then you're going to be resilient.

As leaders, if we want to choose emotional resilience that will last a lifetime, then a huge portion of that is our relationships. Our most important relationship is like a compass for what direction we're heading in. The lesson that follows is applicable to our friends, our coworkers, and even perfect strangers.

Resilient relationships are about honest communication. That's necessary in every relationship you could possibly have. Communication is based on seeing the other person as clearly as you want them to see you.

One of the biggest reasons why relationships aren't resilient is because of assumptions. Randi and I have had a running debate for years about this. One day I came home, charged up by an idea I thought was going to change the world, and I said to her, "The issue with relationships is *expectations*. If we get rid of all expectations, then we'll all be in harmony with each other. Right?" Randi looked at me for a minute and then she said, "Are you crazy? How can you possibly have a relationship without expectations? They'd go nowhere."

Chastened, I sulked back to the drawing board. And then it hit me, Randi was completely right. And in my way, so was I. Relationships are not resilient when the expectations are unstated. That's the issue. Unstated assumptions are the termites that will eat the marriage mansions we've built together. We expect our partners to be mind-readers. We expect that people will know exactly what we want.

Resilient relationships nearly always begin in a positive way. With a wedding. Weddings are where we state our expectations for each other. Then over time, we forget about what we said.

I love weddings. I really do. In fact, the older I get, the more I love them. Just the sight of two people, in front of all the people who love and appreciate them, dressed to the nines, so clean and fresh. I love all the traditions and rituals. The vows. The music. The readings. The tears, the laughter, and the stories. It's just so moving to me: the idea that anyone, in spite of the overwhelming odds, knowing how statistically precarious marriage is, would take the risk to commit themselves to one person for an eternity. It's just so extraordinarily hopeful and courageous. Even now, thinking about it, makes the hairs on the back of my neck stand up.

My wife, Randi, and I have been married for 30-plus amazing years. In a culture where every other marriage ends in divorce, to last that long in a single relationship you have to be resilient. Everything that applies to you, your business, or your team, applies doubly to relationships, because that's where you face the most change and the most uncertainty. Sometimes in the course of a single day.

I'm not saying I'm an expert in resilient relationships. I mean, I'd love to be able to tell you that Randi and I have discovered some kind of special secret formula that helps you stay in one relationship for as long as we have. I wish I could tell you exactly what to do, what steps to take with your partner, and boom, you're together for the rest of your lives.

But when it comes to "what it takes" to have a resilient relationship, there is one idea that I want to talk about. It's about rowing in the same direction or being "equally yoked." In the old days, before industrial farming, we used oxen to pull plows and heavy loads. If you want to use more than one ox, you need a yoke, a long wooden bar that encompasses the necks of two oxen.

If you're plowing furrows in a field and you want them to be straight, what do you do? The oxen have to be a similar size and of a similar disposition. Why? So they can pull in the same direction. You can't have one ox twice the size of the other. If you do, the larger animal will take the lead and go where it wants, meaning the smaller will naturally follow. That's not a recipe for straight furrows. No matter what your personal beliefs are, I think this notion has a deeper lesson for what makes resilient relationships.

I could write a whole book about Randi and what she means to me. It would be longer than the entirety of the Harry Potter series. For now, I want to talk about one specific moment that I believe illustrates how our three decades together are based almost entirely on resilience.

In *Pivot* I wrote about the moment when I suffered a panic attack that felt like a heart attack and how that "near-death" experience was the catalyst for quitting a successful and lucrative legal career that pivoted me into the life I have today. But that wasn't the end of the story. True to form, I was given the message embedded in my panic/heart attack and I ignored it.

I had encountered death, or what I feared was the end of my life, and I was given a second chance. Like most human beings, I was too caught up in not disappointing my family and my friends. I was trying to be the best I could be. I was doing my best to be the kind of man and provider I thought I was supposed to be.

With the panic attack, the universe was trying to communicate with me, but I wasn't listening. Until Randi, the smartest, most change-proof person I know, used her resilience to communicate in a way that I could truly hear. She made me listen, by seeing me in a way that I couldn't.

But let's go back to the beginning. I want to say up front: we're no different than you are. Randi and I have the same problems you have. We argue about the dishes or our kids or any number of things. Just like you do.

Randi is lucky in that she comes from a very happy home where she was raised by two parents who loved each other consistently with a high level of communication and respect. So that's what she had, in terms of modeling, when I met her in 1985 at the University of Massachusetts at Amherst.

Randi was a dual child psychology and education major. She was on time and prepared in our Intro Psychology class, and true to form, I would always scoot in just as class was starting. She was always put together, calm, and composed, and I was always sweaty because I was coming from, and I'm not kidding about this, trampoline class. Every time, I'd plop down next to her, and I'd ask to borrow a pen. So she made sure she always had two.

That's the essence of our relationship right there. She was thinking at least one step ahead of me. I later learned, as the semester moved on, that Randi was sure I wanted to ask her out. Positive. We guys think we're being suave and cool. But women always know. Randi knew. The sweat, the pens, the trampoline class. It was obvious to everyone but me. It was obvious to the class. It was obvious to the professor. It was probably obvious to aliens watching us from space. But I never saw it.

So Randi asked *me* out. We spent the entire night talking and listening to records, and we're still talking all these years later. Thanks to Randi, that's the one thing we've never lost: our ability to communicate clearly with each other. Little did I know, we'd need this 20 years later in our relationship. But Randi did.

As I mentioned earlier, I was a practicing attorney for 18 years. My specialty at the beginning was bankruptcy law. That meant I got to see firsthand what was going wrong inside businesses that would lead them to the place where they'd have to file bankruptcy. I was always lucky enough to have clients. Naturally, in the beginning, they weren't always paying clients. I'm a bit of a soft touch when it comes to people in trouble. Randi used to kid me, saying, "You can have all the clients in the world that you want if you don't charge them." One of my clients actually paid with a rug! Randi says now, "Don't get me wrong, it was a nice rug, but rugs don't buy groceries." Always the practical one, my Randi.

Slowly but surely, I got more and more comfortable with billing and managing expectations. My business grew, and Randi was settling into the seasonal rhythm of teaching. Simultaneously, we were building a family. She was building our home and raising our kids, as I was gone as often as I was present.

Randi was flourishing, building her community. We were close to her parents. I was the hard-charging lawyer, building my business a little bit at a time. It was all working. This is how relationship roles are meant to function. Or so we thought.

Early in our marriage though, Randi began to notice that on the days I was lucky to be home from work, which weren't many, I was disappearing for two to three hours at a time. I always came back and was in a great mood. It was strange.

Finally, she asked me outright, "Where do you go for hours at a time?" She told me later, I looked sheepish, almost ashamed when she asked this. So she asked me again, "Be honest: Where do you go?" So I told her the plain truth. I was going swimming.

I wasn't drinking with my pals. I wasn't at the movies. I wasn't gambling at the race track. I was taking care of my body and spirit.

"I thought you'd think I was being selfish," I finally said. Well, that's the moment that put things together for Randi. Once again, she got there before I did. She realized that in our relationship, any relationship, there are three people: there's the new person that's made when two people get married. That's what we say at weddings. Two become one.

But the two who made the one are still there too. That means, before we even had kids we had three people to take care of on our journey together. Randi showed me that I'd gotten myself sideways when I thought I needed to be secretive about taking care of myself and my body. Randi shut that down right quick. Because she had to take care of herself and her personal needs the same way that I did, and if we couldn't honor that for each other, we had no chance of surviving.

Randi taught me that the math of a resilient relationship is actually two become three. It's like rowing a boat. You have to be pulling the same direction at the same speed with the knowledge that you have to take care of each other while you're rowing. They're essentially the same.

But soon I was waking up in the morning and feeling familiar anxiety. I could tell it was weighing on Randi. To her, I was like Michael J. Fox in *Back to the Future* in the photograph with his brother and sister. Bit by bit, I was disappearing. I was showing up for the family, thinking I was whole, but in fact, I was in pieces. Randi could see it well before I could.

I was just broken bits of human. The charming trampoline man she fell in love with, who borrowed her pen because I "forgot" to bring my own, was slipping away. Pretty soon, I was going to disappear completely. And Randi knew it. She didn't want that knowledge. She says now that was the mistake she made: she kept it down.

Then after the events that I discussed in *Pivot*, with my panic attack disguised as a heart attack, it was obvious to Randi that I had to make a change. But we were so leveraged. I had to keep working, grinding, because that's what men think they're supposed to do.

Six months later, I was back at it, working 80 to 90 hours a week, spending 3 to 4 hours in the car, commuting into Manhattan several days a week, sleeping in my office. If anything, I wasn't getting better, I was actually worse than before.

Then one night, the night that changed everything, I was late coming home. That wasn't a surprise. Here's how Randi describes it: "It was pouring outside. It was like Noah and the Great Flood came to Central Jersey. I'll never forget it. You walked in the door. You were dripping wet. You were wearing this wool Brooks Brothers coat and you looked like a drowned cat. More than that, you just looked so sad. The joyful boy of our youth was replaced by this sad, soaking man."

In the entryway of the home we'd built together I looked at her. She looked at me. Neither of us said anything for a minute. Almost 20 years later, Randi says, "I knew the look on your face. You had something you wanted to say. I knew if you got there on your own, then the universe had pushed you to this point." Finally, I whispered, "If I keep doing what I'm doing, you're going to be a widow." Randi took a deep breath. A shaking, uncomfortable breath. And we thought of everything, the expenses, the mortgage, the kids, our parents, and just . . . everything. It all dropped away and faded into the rain.

All Randi saw was the person that she loved. Nothing else was important. Then she did the bravest thing I've ever seen anybody do in the middle of such uncertainty. All she said was, "We'll figure it out."

Now, from a responsibility standpoint, Randi would have been well within her rights to say to me, "We need you to work. Figure *that* out. Do what you have to do." But she didn't do that.

She couldn't. "We'll figure it out." If it feels dramatic, well, it was. Randi says now, "What was I going to say? We had to get this right. We had to remember that to be together we had to take care of each person in the relationship."

And we're still here. Figuring it out. What a woman. Even today, reading these words that she wrote about that night, I know that she's the most *real* person I've ever known. Because of Randi's example, I didn't have to have the midlife crisis. I didn't have to hit the wall the way a lot of people can. I certainly could have. I didn't need to move my feet to quit my job. I had an opportunity to do something different at the moment. Because of Randi, we pivoted from what surely would have been a midlife crisis and instead we created a midlife calling. We pivoted as a family because of Randi's resilience.

Thank you, Randi. I love you.

CHANGE-PROOF POINT

▶ Every relationship, be it love, friendship, or professional, must be based on a shared purpose that has you pulling in the same direction.

CHAPTER 27

Self-Disruption Versus Stagnation

The Toothbrush Test

Circumstances—what are circumstances?
I make circumstances.
—**NAPOLEON BONAPARTE**

You want to be change proof? Then brush your teeth. Yep, turns out your mother and your dentist were both correct when they said that all you had to do in life to be successful was keep your teeth clean.

Ok. Maybe it's not that simple. And yet, it's a simple trick I use with clients who find themselves stagnant, doing the same thing, day after day, getting the same results. I ask them a question: What hand do you use to brush your teeth? Usually they look a little concerned that they're wasting their time with me, so I gently ask them again. What hand do you use to brush your teeth? Most say, "My right hand." The other 10 percent say, "My left hand."

Then I ask them to do something easy: for one month, brush their teeth (at least twice a day, to satisfy both Mom and four out of five dentists!) with the other hand. That's it. Brush your teeth with their nondominant hand. Thirty days. That length of time, we've been told, is the amount of days you need to change a habit.

Like most things, at first, it's going to feel strange and uncomfortable. And something that they've taken for granted for pretty much their entire waking lives is going to be difficult. So what does that do? It's a simple task with complicated implications, because what it tells us is awareness doesn't come without a price. Learning doesn't come easy. Even something as banal as brushing one's teeth. It breaks down like this: *awareness, understanding, reprogramming.*

We all want to learn, we all want to grow, and we all want to live our lives and run our organizations with more awareness. So many times, though, we don't want it to be difficult. We want the benefits without the cost.

That's not how you get to be change proof. That's not how to change proof your organization. Learning costs. It just does. Anyone who tells you differently has a trunk full of snake oil in their wagon.

The first thing the toothbrush test does is create an awareness that we don't have all the answers, we don't have universal expertise. That's awareness.

The other thing it does is it introduces a conscious uncertainty into your daily routine. Because after 30 days, you become ambidextrous. You can brush with your left or your right. And you've dealt with a tiny bit of uncertainty. Gradually, after a few days or a couple of weeks, something that was awkward and unwieldy became easier. That's understanding.

The final stage is thinking of the toothbrush test as an uncertainty vaccine. You introduce a little of the virus into the body's ecology, and next thing you know, your body converts it into a Star Wars–type defense system. A little uncertainty every day will eventually make you immune to the fear of change.

By the end of the 30 days, you've literally rewired your brain to respond to change. That's reprogramming. Awareness. Understanding. Reprogramming.

Sounds familiar, doesn't it? That's because it fits within our pause, ask, choose system. We use our rules of three to consciously seek change and uncertainty. Because change and uncertainty, as we know, are inevitable.

• • •

Like much of my resilience philosophy, the toothbrush test has its roots back on Jones Beach when I was a lifeguard. That's where I learned that the only thing I could count on was that every day was going to be different from the day before. As a crew, we had to be aware that we were dealing with a powerful force of nature: the Atlantic Ocean.

Nature changes every day and every night. When we arrived in the morning, the beach that we left the night before could look completely different. The pounding ocean waves would literally cut the shelf of the beach. East and west. Three or four stands to the east and west. Busy days, weekends, four stands on either side of our headquarters.

We had to respond to the conditions of the changing ocean and her tides as well as the ever-changing numbers of human traffic that would flow onto our beach. The conditions were in constant flux. We didn't take it as it was, we didn't do what we always did. We had to change ourselves and our design every day so we could better respond to events as they transpired.

Our decisions are a product of our thinking. As such, we lifeguards had to design our thinking every morning we arrived on the beach. Designing the beach to prepare for change. We had to make spontaneous changes that led to better decisions no matter what the weather or the crowds threw at us.

Remember Kaizen? More change is good. More change produces more options. You can't live on yesterday's success. As a leader, you have to be impatient with the state of your business. Like nature, it has to change, it has to evolve. The point of leadership is to say, "Things are going to change. We need to design change before change designs us." That's the radical part of change-proof resilience. It requires nerve, it requires courage. It requires less courage and less nerve if you understand that nature's software is based on change. You're just leveraging the greatest known in the universe. That's the unknown. It's the master key to uncertainty.

There's an old saying: "If you are trying to drive to Canada and you realize your car is headed south to Mexico, you're not going to get to Canada by slowing down." To get where you're going, you have to turn the entire car around and head in the direction you intended. Humans have tried slowing their impact on the planet, but that, well, it just hasn't been working.

Our current climate crisis (you rarely see those two words apart from one another) is a motley collection of symptoms, but a large portion of our impact has to do with our farming methods. The industrial way we put our food in the ground and feed that to the meat we eat.

Some of those methods we've already discussed in our resilience story. We can't just slow down. We can't just hit the brakes and slow from 75 mph to 60 mph and expect things to get better. We have to get radical about how we farm. We have to turn the entire process around and innovate.

How? Well, there's a way to reduce carbon emissions and regenerate the land from which we grow our food. It's a way that existed for thousands of years before modern factory farming. It's what the oldest civilizations and indigenous peoples did intuitively right whether they knew it or not. It's called regenerative agriculture.

I don't want to get too deep in the woods here so I'll explain this as simply as I can. It's a method of farming that not only grows healthier food in a healthier way, but also actually makes the soil from which the food comes healthier as well. We can feed the earth as it's feeding us. That, to me, is radically resilient. Rather than sucking every last resource from the ground and moving on to the next fertile plain, what if our methodology and our actions actually improved the conditions of the land? It's possible.

Imagine if we could do the same in our day-to-day lives, where the things we do, our actions, our choices, and our dreams, actually remake us anew, from the inside? It's possible.

Now we move into the fourth realm of our human experience: your resilient spirit. We're going to be using the word *spirit*, but we could also be using the word *soul* because to me, in our work, they're interchangeable. If the word *soul* makes more sense to you, then please just substitute it in your mind as we move forward.

It's harder to quantify, but our spiritual resilience, if we can harness it, is the binding agent that keeps our physical, mental, and emotional resilience from slipping away from us. What is our spirit? How can we define it? Then once we've defined it, how can we remember to pause, ask, and choose so that we're spiritually resilient, so that we can make better decisions in our lives and in our business?

So how do we define the spirit? Albert Einstein wrote, "My religion consists of a humble admiration of the illimitable superior spirit who reveals himself in the slight details we are able to perceive with our frail and feeble mind." That's pretty good.

Here's another one, from the great psychologist William James, "Of all the beautiful truths pertaining to the soul none is more gladdening or fruitful than to know that you can regenerate and make yourself what you will." That's a little bit better.

Finally, here's one of my favorites, from Black Elk:

The first peace, which is the most important, is that which comes within the souls of people when they realize their relationship, their oneness with the universe and all its powers, and when they realize at the center of the universe dwells the Great Spirit, and that its center is really everywhere, it is within each of us.

So much of our work on spiritual resilience is going to be about other people. Here's why: you have to realize that until now we've been discussing resilience in the three realms of your human experience. Your body, your mind, and your heart, they all belong to you. Yes, they're the result of genetics, modeling, parenting, and friends and our love relationships. But they're ultimately yours.

But now we turn to the realm of the spirit. I want to be clear about one fact: your spirit does not belong to you. You are its steward. You've been tasked with keeping safe, intact, and flourishing while it's in its human form.

Our spirits are ancient. Far more than we give them credit for. They were here before you and they'll be here after you. That's why our resilient spirit is vital to our transformation. You can change your body, you can change your mind, and you can change your heart, but your spirit is ephemeral. You just have to appreciate its perfection. We almost never do that.

Our spirit not only survives, but it thrives. Go back to the beginning of this section and read that quote again. Those of you brave resilience warriors who've been through Alcoholics Anonymous 12-step programs will recognize the quote from Reinhold Niebuhr, often called the "Serenity Prayer."

What nobody ever mentions is that specific, well-worn quote is a bit longer. That little bit makes an infinity. Nobody ever mentions where the prayer really intends to go, and to me, it's a shame, because it's the part that makes the whole idea meaningful. The prayer ends with "Forever and ever in the next." It means our work is not just for this moment, this day, this life-time. It's actually for all the moments, and all the days and all the lifetimes your spirit will flow through the universe.

I take comfort in that. It implies the existence of the spirit that lives within us and will live after us. That spirit is already change proof. It's already resilient. It's already what it is, because what it is cannot change. You just have to harness it. Let's talk about how we do that.

> *The difference between a Western settler mindset*
> *of I have rights and an indigenous mindset of*
> *I have an obligation. Instead of thinking that I*
> *am born with rights, I choose to think that I was*
> *born with obligations to serve past, present, and*
> *future generations, and the planet herself.*
> —STAN RUSHWORTH

CHANGE-PROOF POINT

▶ Our spirit does not belong to us: it belongs to the world around us, so we have to see ourselves as a piece of a much larger puzzle.

CHAPTER 28

What Change-Proof Culture Can Do for You

Every CEO is in fact a Chief Cultural Officer. The terrifying thing is it's the CEO's actual behavior, not their speeches or the list of values they have put up on posters, that defines what the culture is. Without these four powers (Hiring, Firing, Promoting, Punishing) any employee at the company is along for the ride in a culture driven by someone more powerful than they are.
—SCOTT BERKUN

I f we've learned anything in our journey together thus far, being change proof is about being consciously aware and present with the movement of the world around us. As a leader, our business is to raise the level of our own awareness so we can notice and connect with the awareness of the people who depend on us.

The most important qualities that a business leader can possess are:

- Self-awareness
- Transparency

- Leading by example
- Leading with the spirit

Every one of those four is a component of what I call our "software," which is the part of our bodies, our minds, and our hearts that connects us to the world around us. You can't have them without it. It's literally impossible.

The culture of a business is a combination of collective values and an undivided collective awareness. As a leader, it's your awareness that defines the values that create the culture of your business. It's that easy.

Every person is unto themselves a kind of business and every business is really only people. They're all pivoting in ways large and small. They're failing and succeeding. The survivors, they wash out. The thrivers, they're able to pivot. For our work, resilience is the yeast that makes the pivot rise. The resilient *Pivot*'ers don't let success go to their head and they never let failure go to their heart.

The intention that I set for myself every day is to be a conscious business leader. For me that means I have to commit to my resilience. It's like a relationship. You don't say your vows, take your photos, have the reception, and then rub your hands together saying, "Well, we're good now. We got this thing figured out."

Any relationship takes commitment. That's what our kind of resilience is. Change-proof resilience is about what I call closing the gap between you and another person. It's about your awareness recognizing their awareness. Being a business leader or owner is tough, even on the best days. To do it well certainly requires you to be resilient and to model that resilience for your team and the people you're blessed to work with.

In my business, I can model that resilience because I've had to be resilient. I have to set that daily intention because I'm keenly aware of how many times I've failed in my life. When I was in school I had difficulty paying attention because of the way my mind works. Nowadays, we'd call that ADD or ADHD (attention deficit disorder or attention deficit hyperactivity disorder), but back then, that was just a misunderstood kid. There was zero awareness of what that meant.

Somehow, I made it through high school and into college. I met Randi at the University of Massachusetts at Amherst. I was a sophomore and she was just a freshman. But she had to ask me out because I lacked some awareness and confidence in myself. I failed at seeing what was right in front of me. But thank God for Randi's awareness and for seeing me.

Then when I graduated college, my law school of choice was Harvard. I wanted to be the best and Harvard was the best. Well, I wasn't their student of choice. Nor was I the student of choice for a slew of other schools. But I made it to law school and through it, passing the bar exam on the first try and building a multimillion-dollar law firm over an 18-year career. But as successful as I was doing that, I became aware that I was also selling myself and my family short in the process.

With Randi's help I pivoted away from hamster wheel of fortune and into what I thought would be my life's work as the CEO of a large training company. That success would last about five years. And then another pivot was required when I was forced to part ways with the organization I helped create. From there, I started the epic company I have to this day with partners I cherish and respect.

My first book was a collaboration with several other authors. It dropped like a lead balloon. Just a few reviews and dismal sales. But not long after, I set to work on book number two: *Pivot*. It hit the *Wall Street Journal*'s Top Ten Bestsellers list. Now, here's the book you're holding that I had the opportunity to write during a time of pandemic change and uncertainty.

The common denominator in all these situations is failure, but also success. I've failed at things repeatedly and that has allowed me to succeed. I don't say all this to brag or boast. My résumé isn't going to help you become change proof. When you lay your life out on the timeline, you can see how the road winds between success and failure, between change and stagnation. The only thing that kept me going was resilience. My own and the resilient spirits of all the people around me.

That's how it works. Resilience isn't about being strong. Though that helps. It's not about surviving setbacks. Though there will be more times where you have to. Maybe soon. Resilience is about being able to fully receive the gifts of one's experiences, whether those experiences are easy or tough, and then move ahead as something greater. At our company we call this bouncing forward.

When you're resilient, you become like a spring, meeting that opposing force not with force, but letting that oppositional energy pass through you, without internalizing it. Then leveraging it forward. Just like in the rip current, the key to making it out isn't fighting the good fight with Mother Nature, but just going with the flow of water, conserving your energy so you can swim when she decides she's done with you.

Spirituality isn't about praying your way out of the current. You can pray, don't get me wrong, but spiritual resilience is about being prepared for the rip current before you even decide to go to the beach. It's the same thing in our organizations. If we wait for a crisis to figure out our values, we'll be out of business. It happens to hundreds of companies every single day.

There's a saying that "Practice makes perfect." But there's another that says, "If you keep doing what you're doing, you're gonna keep getting what you've got." If you keep practicing the same thing, with the same habits, then you'll find yourself again and again in the exact same place. Instead, our mantra must be, "Perfect practice makes perfect." Now, that doesn't mean that anything less than perfection is failure. Far from it.

It's the quest for perfection, what Emmet Fox calls *Divine Discontent*, the restless and endless search for the absolute harmony of our being. Building resilience is a daily practice that takes constant vigilance. There's no other way. The good news is, once you develop that divine dissatisfaction about your life and your business, your capacity for resilience will keep expanding forever. Are you ready for that?

Building culture comes from knowledge. You have to know so you can be honest and unmerciful. If you engage in covert tactics, you cut yourself off from genuine connection with yourself. The one way to know is if you're cut off from the people around you. We're social beings. It's how we evolved—in social groups. In the age of social media, our social circle could include the entire world but our immediate social groups are getting smaller. That's a recipe for emotional and spiritual decay. We pull inward, like a turtle in a shell.

Go with me back to the Code of Conduct. When we discussed these core principles, it was in regard to our emotional resilience. Until now, it was for self-leadership. It was for our own programming.

Once you implement it for yourself, your leaders can use it to create a value system for your business. That value system will have you seeking change, seeking failure, which will result in harmonious innovation.

I experience gratitude today.
I experience living with a positive and harmonious attitude today.
I experience adding value to other people's lives today.
I experience creating with relaxed focus today.
I experience myself living by a higher standard today.
I experience living in absolute integrity and kindness today.
I experience being the conscious creator of my own life experience today.
I experience creating empowering solutions today.
I experience living with a fearless heart today.

I experience the presence of unconditional love today.
I experience myself being healthy, wealthy, and wise today.
I experience, receive, and manifest miracles today.
I experience forgiveness today.

Now, some of these might not apply in a one-to-one way for your business. Fine. Write your own. They'll be a value system for you and your business. You'll have a culture that will last long enough to become a legacy. That's what we're all searching for, isn't it?

> ## CHANGE-PROOF POINT
>
> ▶ Do the Code of Conduct for your organization the same way you perform it for yourself to experience and create a cultural harmony.

CHAPTER 29

Connecting with Others Connects You with You

Just as the wave cannot exist for itself, but is ever a part of the heaving surface of the ocean, so must I never live my life for itself, but always in the experience which is going on around me.
—ALBERT SCHWEITZER

I don't know about you, but I've been sentimental about time since I was 10 years old. I remember, clearly, being nine and moving into my tenth birthday, and to me, it seemed such a huge thing: to be 10 years old, the big double digits and three years away from manhood. Even then, I felt my life altering in some mysterious and even ominous way. Ever since, I've felt melancholy about another year passing, and the mystery that is my unfolding life.

As I've gotten older and I begin the back half of my life, I'm more and more fascinated by mystery, by things that I can't explain, predict, or understand with human language. Like the idea of my 10-year-old self, I can flash back to him in a nanosecond, like I'm right there. Like when I hear a Frank Sinatra tune; all at once, time and space collapse and I'm back at the dinner table with my family listening to Ol' Blue Eyes open his heart for the microphone. I can hear the lyrics from that bittersweet sad song "Deep in a Dream" in my head right now as I type these words:

> *My cigarette burns me, I wake with a start*
> *My hand isn't hurt, but there's pain in my heart*
> *Awake or asleep, every memory I'll keep*
> *Deep in a dream of you.*

And I'm there with my family all of us together in a held moment. We were happy. Everything seemed possible. Until the fighting started and our family began to slowly break apart. We're on the other side of all that now and we've put the pieces back together, but it wasn't easy. Because we remember the moments when we were together.

And yet in other ways, there is only this moment, right now, this moment in time and there are no others. There's no past. No future. Only right now and what's possible in our lives in the present moment. There's real power in that.

We can access the past in a moment, and at the same time, we have to let it go so we can grow—the way the seed lets go of the ground so it can reach for the nourishing, life-giving light. Spiritually, when we let go of something, some old regret or resentment, when we choose to let it go, we recapture the energy of the moment and harness it for the energy that we need to move forward. And yet, it's the soil from which we grow. The ground is full of decay, death, waste, and from all of that, life, like hope, springs eternal.

To grow, our spirit needs to pause. When we allow for that to happen, our spirit, without prompting, without conscious effort, reaches out to connect with other spirits. That's what it desires. As we already know, our spirit does not belong to us, so when we take the shackles off of it, it will seek communion with the spirit in other people.

That connection with others is one of the main signifiers of resilience. Our ability to find, make, and maintain networks of spiritual connection leads to a whole host of creative opportunities and limitless outcomes. Your soul is creative, it wants to bring something new into the world. We need other people to help us find and maximize those opportunities.

That's something I learned talking to the powerfully resilient actor Sandra Joseph, who went from a "scared kid from Detroit" to setback after setback, failure after failure, until she finally landed the female lead of *The Phantom of the Opera*, where she played Christine for more than a thousand shows over 10 years on Broadway.

She cowrote the book *Your Creative Soul*, and she's tapped into her spirit in a way that can teach us how to get present with our resilience. She dealt with years and years of rejection, yet she stayed with it when others could have (and did) quit. How did she grow when others wilted away?

A study determined the five domains of what the researchers called post traumatic growth, but for our purposes they're a guide for us to be change proof and resilient (Tedeschi, Calhoun, 1996):

- An appreciation of life
- Improved interpersonal relationships
- Seeing possibilities in life
- Spiritual connectedness
- Personal strength and empowerment

These are the markers of resilience that help people not only survive but thrive after a traumatic event. How many of these five would you say you have? If you have even one, I'd say you've access to your resilience. But if you don't feel that you have any of the five, that's OK too.

They're inside you. All you have to do is practice and find them. The way you do it is through connecting with other people. It's difficult because in turbulent, uncertain times, our tendency is to pull inward, to protect our vulnerability. That's why we have our spirits. Your spirit desires connection.

So what do you do? Make a list of all the things you have instead of worrying about all the things you don't. Connect with someone you've lost touch with. Find one thing, just one, in your future that you're working toward. Take a walk outside for at least 20 minutes, and while you're out, breathe in and out for one minute. Do the 3-4 method. Think about all the people in your life who did something kind for you. Find something you can do for them.

Having a resilient spirit is about getting inspired by your life and the world around you. I use that word for a reason. To be inspired means to be filled with the breath of the spirit. People used to believe that when a person was inspired, it meant God was literally breathing into them. Actors like Sandra Joseph know that inspiration is the foundation of real presence and that has to be forged through resilience:

> In theater, we're so used to rejection. We go to audition after audition. It can take 50 or 100 "No's" before you get one "Yes." That one "Yes" can be the pivot, can change everything for you. I'm grateful I stuck it out, and I'm incredibly fortunate that my agent got me an opportunity to audition for Phantom. Even that did not happen overnight. I blew the first audition.
>
> My old fears and nerves got in the way and I ended up not expressing myself the way I wanted to. I had a second audition and I blew it again.
>
> We can all do this. We can get in our own way. Even when you know better, you can screw up sometimes by either your fear coming in or self-doubt at the last moment, and you don't show up the way you want to.

Our spirit wants to do the best for us so when we're present, we do our best. It's that feeling of being in "the zone" where you're completely tapped into the universal frequency.

Sandra got the audition she was praying for, and twice, she held on so tightly to her desperation with her body, mind, and heart that her spirit couldn't take the lead. Then she beat herself up over it. Sound familiar?

Sandra couldn't get present then or after, as she recounted to me:

> *It was devastating and I was so ashamed of myself, embarrassed, disappointed, heartbroken. The worst part of it was I knew better. I knew that the most important thing in any audition or performance or connection with a person is your presence. It's that quality of authenticity and the ability to be real. That's what moves an audience, when you see something real up there. We know that those are actors playing roles, but there has to be a ring of truth so that you feel it in your heart. You connect with them. That's Acting 101. That's the most important thing and somehow that went right out the window. I was angry at myself and depressed for a while.*

We're addicted to the chase because we're so wrapped up in ourselves. We don't see the world around us. We're locked in a room in our heads and hearts with that inner voice, and we're a prisoner of whatever we happen to think or feel that day. If it's good, we're good. If it's bad, the day is bad. That's what happens when we're only focused on ourselves. Sandra explained:

> *We're addicted to the chase. We can race through life that way and never see where we are, to stop for a moment and look back at our life. How often do we do that and say, "Look at how blessed I am? Look how fortunate I've been to be breathing and to have made it through what I've made it through?" We're all faced with incredible challenges and suffering throughout our lives. To still be present and connected to the heart and able to look up and see the*

sky can bring us back to the present where we step out of the chase and we get off the treadmill. That's where, in many ways, the richest parts of life are found in those moments.

Our resilient spirit gets us at least looking out the window of that room. It's the part that got Sandra looking up into the sky, to see it, to see its beauty and grandeur. In spite of the rejection she was facing, from the world and her own self, Sandra was able to process her disappointment by embracing where she was by ritualizing her appreciation for everything she had in her life, even the parts and roles that were going to other people. Sandra performed her joy for them. And her joy became real: "These practices can tune us into the frequency of the heart and what is beautiful, good, wholesome, and exciting about life. These practices for me are sustaining and absolutely essential."

Sandra was able to connect to the world because she was able to let go of her attachment to herself. That's what the Buddhists mean when they talk about nonattachment. They don't mean you just blithely float through the world, gleefully unattached to anyone or anything. That's not real. And it's not possible.

Letting go isn't easy, because we have to let go of our idea of what we believe the world absolutely must be. Again, it's the Albert Ellis thing about musturbation and how our patterning keeps us locked into those record grooves. Surrender helps us skip out of the grooves that have become a habit.

Finally, Sandra was called into a third audition. The third and final one. It was this or nothing. Sandra had made a conscious effort to do the spiritual work on herself. Rejection after rejection didn't make it easy. Failing at the opportunities she was given made it almost impossible. She made it a habit. She didn't just luck into resilience. Her spirit opened the doorway to her heart so she could just be present with her abundance.

So as she walked into that final audition, she could say:

You have to be without clinging. That was a huge part of what made me ultimately give the best audition of the three. I wasn't walking trying to prove myself, trying to make a certain outcome happen. It allowed me to be in a space of more ease in that final performance. That's how I ultimately got the part. After all that gratitude and surrender. I always try to make it clear I'm not suggesting that all we need to do is let go and surrender and be grateful, and then we're going to get what we want. It's not a magic formula for making a particular outcome happen. It doesn't work that way. It is a magic formula for getting what we ultimately long for, which is a sense of grace and ease and presence.

Sandra got the part she'd wanted for so long, but her kind of radical resilience is not about fixing yourself so the cosmic bellboy will bring you whatever you ask for in the moment you ask for it. It's about getting present with yourself so you can feel peace. The part that changed her life came after that.

Presence leads to peace, says Sandra, "Truly, the much bigger prize isn't whether or not I had gotten the stupid part. I tasted a moment of authentic presence and that's the real goal. That's what we want. That's why we do the things we do. It's to inhabit our aliveness." Sandra committed to the idea that if she connected to the spirit outside herself then her inner life would find the equilibrium of peace. Our spirit is seeking union with itself. The yoga of love.

Before we said good-bye, Sandra quoted Thomas Merton saying, "If only they could see themselves as they really are. If only we could see each other that way all the time, there would be no more war, no more hatred, no more cruelty, no more greed . . . I suppose the big problem would be that we would fall down and worship each other."

That's how we connect to other people, we get present with our spirit, and then we're resiliently moving through change and uncertainty. Just like Sandra Joseph.

CHANGE-PROOF POINTS

▶ Presence leads to peace.

▶ Get present with the people around you, and you'll experience the peace that will allow you to be change proof.

CHAPTER 30

～～～

Breakthrough Without a Breakdown

Breakthroughs don't get planned,
they are prepared for.
—GOITSEMANG MVULA

One of the most painfully true endings in the history of movies is the end of *Mary Poppins*. I watched it when I was a kid and with each of our four children, and each time I've been struck by the poignancy of Mary having to leave the Banks family for good. They've grown to love this woman who floated into their lives and mended the family's broken heart.

But the wind is changing. And Mary has to go. The Banks family has to let her go. Because that's what life is, the continuous process of consciously letting go. What are we prepared to let go of?

That's what our spirits are trying to teach us—that it should be everything. Absolutely everything. So we can be resilient in the face of change.

We can't do that if we're unconsciously wandering through the journey of our lives. For spiritual resilience, we must be consciously aware so that our awareness surrounds us throughout our lives. That way, when we're performing resilience we're not just managing change, we're using it to our competitive advantage for our better growth edge.

Most of us, in our lives and in our business, are habituated to react to events so we can avoid risk. And yet, at the same time, we're constantly forced to extricate ourselves from dramatic entanglements. How is that? The paradox is we're risk avoiding but unconsciously addicted to drama. That's the crossroads at which so many of us find ourselves. If we want to create pivots for ourselves so we can be change proof, then we have to be able to change our lives without needing a crisis.

I learned this from Lisa Garr, the host of *The Aware Show*, the owner of at least two companies, a mother and a wife. She's literally doing it all. Lisa's resilience lesson for us is about how to find breakthroughs without needing the breakdown.

She worked with a therapist, Gary Salyer, who had her lay out the timeline of her life:

> *He literally mapped it out on the floor and we put these index cards on every decade of my life that I had breakdowns. Then he had me put different color index cards on every decade of my life or parts of my life, like specific ages, where I had breakthroughs. It was totally, clearly mapped out on that floor. Every time I had a massive breakdown that would come first, then I would have the breakthrough. Then another breakdown. Then another breakthrough.*

Unconsciously, Lisa had been addicted to the paradox of needing to bottom out before she could bounce back. That's not resilient, it's reactive. It's as though Lisa was seeking rip currents to get caught in so she could find new levels in her life. It's an exhausting way to live, Lisa says:

> *I looked back and I saw, "Do I want to do this for 30 more years?" I'm 50. "Do I want to create this level of bullshit*

*for 30 more years?" I don't want to do that. I really don't.
All the relationships I'm going to destroy from continu-
ingly creating that pattern, it creates emotional havoc,
relationship havoc, cellular havoc. But it's been what I've
been doing.*

We don't need to get cancer. We don't need the divorce. We
don't need our business to go bankrupt. We don't need to lose
our house. We don't need drama as a springboard for change.
All we need to do is anticipate and prepare for change. OK, so
how do we do that?

Lisa's resilience lodestar is a great quote from Wayne Dyer,
who said, "If you believe it will work out, you'll see the opportunities. If you believe it won't, you'll see the obstacles." For Lisa,
her thoughts are guided by the spirit that says, "Where are the
opportunities?"

The trouble for us is sometimes the obstacles are easier to see
than the opportunities. Spiritually, we have to set ourselves on
a course that says, "No matter what happens, I got this." That
gets us past the fear that keeps us paralyzed, believing that we're
going to get wiped out and devastated.

Lisa is truly change proof because she's got her own ocean
metaphor:

*You can't turn your back to the ocean, because that's when
you get hit and you get blindsided. We've always got to look
forward and say, "What's happening there? Is there something I might not be seeing?" I really think there should be
a position in any corporation, the Did-You-Think-of-This
Person, the What-If Person. "What if this happens? What
if they do it this way? What if someone hacks the system?"
Just to be able to look at things that are potentially going
to happen.*

So what does Lisa do when she can feel the breakdown coming on? She's got a fascinating ritual she does when she's mid-breakdown. It's a gratitude sandwich that's backed up by science. If there's something that is happening that is upsetting, that is a crisis, that is breaking down in its moment, you cannot deny it and say, "This isn't happening, let's just go to love."

The brain is going to say, "You're lying to me. F— you." The minute I see the breakdown and say, "This is happening," I go right into what I'm grateful for. I force myself to name three things that I am grateful for, just right then and there. If it is the fact that I'm walking and then I have a body that can walk, or that I have an amazing, loving child or whatever, I just have three things I'm grateful for.

What that does is stop the chemical cascade in the brain of going toward the fight-or-flight cortisol, stress-release hormonal cascade. That is just a trigger of cascades of chemicals in the brain. It interrupts the pattern of the brain chemicals and of the thought process. You immediately start to go toward dopamine, serotonin solution-oriented brain chemicals. This is a very important piece. The brain automatically starts to look for opportunities because it has a pool of serotonin, and it's now got some dopamine to help itself look for some type of shiny object. It will start to find a solution. There is science that tells us for every one negative thought, your brain needs five positive thoughts to counteract the chemical balance. This is something that actually works.

Instead of beating yourself up or the nearest person around you, you force yourself into five things. I start off with three things I'm grateful for, then the other two just wind up flowing, wind up happening. Then you go into the area of, "What's possible? What are the opportunities? What am I not seeing? I've got this." The positive thoughts will set loose a flood of brain chemicals that make it possible to look for creative opportunities.

Lisa has given us a tremendous gift because instead of our negative thoughts landing us in a ditch that could last for an hour, a week, a month, or a year, we can arrest the process early and actually get creativity from our negativity. We don't have to react to our emotions. We can use our spirits to get proactive with them.

When I was a lifeguard on Jones Beach, we were most concerned about "double drownings," which are some of the most dangerous rescues we would run. Here's what would happen: Somewhere in our water, someone would get into trouble so we'd run a rescue. Making my way out to the person who was flailing and getting sucked under was the easy part. The hard part was once you got to the person, they were in a panic. They were drowning in their heads and hearts.

The trick was to connect with them, let them feel the safety and security to snap them out of their fear. I'd talk to them about positive things in their life or in the view. If I didn't do that, and it happened sometimes that the swimmer was just too locked into whatever they were feeling, then they'd try to grab a hold of whoever was there and there was a real risk they'd drag me down too. Now, how often do we do that to people in our lives? We let our emotions and anxiety drag us down and then we do it to anybody who gets near us.

CHANGE-PROOF POINTS

▶ Think of the five positive thoughts as five lifeguards who will rescue you from the one negative thought. Thanks to Lisa, when you do that, you'll see opportunities instead of obstacles.

▶ Awareness creates resilience so we can break through without breaking down.

CHAPTER 31

Leverage Uncertainty

If the only prayer you said was thank
you, that would be enough.
—MEISTER ECKHART

In the tale of the werewolf, an ordinary man bitten by a wolf becomes transformed into a wild creature once a month when the moon is full. At that time he wreaks havoc on the humans around him, killing men, women, and children. No one is safe from his bloodlust. Nothing can stop the werewolf. Not his human reason, because that's been taken over by the wolf. Not the people he loves, because they're in more danger now that he's a predator and they are prey. During a full moon, when man has become a creature unknown to himself, no gun, sword, or weapon can pierce his skin. He's unstoppable.

Well, almost, because this man-beast hybrid can be stopped by only one thing: a bullet made of pure silver.

What I like about the werewolf story is how it's about the war between a person's reason and their basest instincts. We have that too. We've established that our worry and our anxiety aren't products of evolutionary advantage and progress; they're holdovers from a time when our very physical survival was constantly under threat. They're our animal nature. Useful in some circumstances, less so in nearly every single other one.

Our higher self is our spirit. And that part can only be rescued from the twin wolves of worry and anxiety by a single thing: the silver bullet.

We've talked about a lot of aspects of resilience and how to continue to perform it over the course of your life so you can truly become change proof. We've been through the body, the mind, and the heart, and now that we're in the realm of the spirit we come to the one virtue that ties everything together.

Nothing will stop change from happening. By now we know that change is guaranteed. You can't predict when and where it will happen. What you can control is how you respond to change and find the creative opportunity within.

There's a reason why the central image of this book is the rip current. It's because many of us who are living and existing with constant uncertainty can feel like we're caught in a relentless tide that takes all of our energy to fight—just to maintain what we've been taught is some arbitrary and impossible balance.

The rip current is similar to what happens to the werewolf during the full moon. Something takes over and all of a sudden, out of nowhere, we're swept away by fear and panic. We feel isolated and alone when we're in it. Our body is engaged in a losing battle, our fear has given way to panic, and the voice in our head is just a screaming alarm.

As we've said, if we want to survive the rip current, it takes spiritual resilience that we discover long before we require it. What that spiritual resilience will give us is the inner strength to let go and go with current rather than fight it.

How? One simple idea. More than any other, it's the thing that recurs the most. Experts in every single field extol its virtues. If you did a word cloud of all the public talks I've given, the clients I've had, the mentors I've been blessed to share space with, the thousands of hours of talking and writing, there's one word that would be largest by far—gratitude. The Roman philosopher Cicero put it best when he wrote, "Gratitude is not only the greatest of the virtues, but the parent of all the others." Habitual gratitude is the silver bullet for leveraging every single kind of uncertainty you could possibly face.

Robert Emmons, author of a series of books on gratitude, including *Thanks: How the New Science of Gratitude Can Make You Happier*, studied gratitude in over a thousand subjects who kept a gratitude journal, where they recorded the things in their life that they were grateful for every day for three weeks. Oh, and the subjects ranged in age from 8 to 80. Here's what he found: Gratitude will make you more resilient. Period. In your body, your mind, and your heart. It's your spirit that uses gratitude as the pivot point to leverage uncertainty into creative opportunities that you can use physically, mentally, and emotionally.

Emmons breaks gratitude down into two basic parts:

> *First, it's an affirmation of goodness. We affirm that there are good things in the world, gifts and benefits we've received. This doesn't mean our life is perfect; it doesn't ignore complaints, burdens, and hassles. But when we look at life as a whole, gratitude encourages us to identify some amount of goodness in our life.*

Gratitude flows from our spirit so we can be clear-eyed about our resilience and where the second component of gratitude comes from. It comes outside of us, when we see how other people have blessed us with kindnesses great and small, seen and unseen.

Beyond all the wellness benefits of gratitude, what it does for us is put us in the mindset where we want what we have instead of relentlessly chasing what's outside of us. The mindset of gratitude puts us exactly in line with resilience because we take the world as it comes to us, as it is, instead trying to make it correspond to every "must" that churns through our heads and hearts.

Like Robert Emmons, Ryan Fehr has studied gratitude, but in his case, he's studied how organizations can cultivate gratitude, and by extension, resilience. Fehr explains:

There's this notion that gratitude is a fleeting emotion that you experience every once in a while, and that's kind of it. We believe that gratitude can play a stronger role in organizations. In particular, multiple experiences of gratitude, over time, can lead to a persistent sense of gratitude that affects the way people think about their jobs and their experiences at work.

But you can't do half-measures to try to inject gratitude into your organization's culture. If you do, your employees will spot it a mile off and they'll resent you for it. You've got to cultivate your own gratitude for yourself so when you begin seeding in your business, it will be authentic. Fehr says:

At the treadmill of work, we don't often take a step back to see the positives. Appreciation programs, beneficiary contact and developmental feedback can help people see the great results of their work and develop appreciation for their colleagues and their jobs. But it has to be managed carefully and genuinely. If an organization really wants to move forward a culture of gratitude, it has to be all in.

As we've said many times throughout this book, leveraging gratitude is the choice to be proactive rather than reactive. In our spiritual resilience, gratitude can be looked at in a way we're intimately familiar with. We pause and reflect on our lives. Really reflect on it all. Then we ask ourselves a series of questions around the concept of "What am I grateful for at this moment? Who am I grateful for? How has my life benefited in ways that I wasn't paying attention to?" Finally, we choose to act on that gratitude, writing it down, every day. Eventually, we won't have to write it down, because it'll be an unconscious process.

When we pause, act, and choose our gratitude, we're resilient. We have to seek it, it's the silver bullet that's already inside of us.

CHANGE-PROOF POINT

▶ Find at least one person every day that you can express gratitude to and for, and you will end up being grateful for the place you are in your own journey.

CHAPTER 32

The Mystery of Death

And I get the urge for going when the meadow grass
is turning brown / And summertime is falling down.
—JONI MITCHELL

The one constant in the universe is that everything changes. Everything. Death. Taxes. Change. These things are certain in every season and every generation. Some changes we make. Some changes take place. They both call us to reimagine our resilience.

In a lot of ways, the changes, both good and bad, cause us to say—"Everything happens for a reason." We've all heard it a thousand times, in a thousand different ways, from a thousand people. Other than "OK" and "Coke," it's probably the most common phrase in the world. No matter where we come from we all want to believe it. OK, then let me pour myself a frosty drink and ask, "If everything happens for a reason, then do me a favor, please, and explain the reason."

People like to say to me, "Everything happens for a reason. I can't explain to you why. It's just a reason. Everything will be all right and it will be wonderful once the fullness of God's plan is revealed to you." Bullshit. Pardon my language. But it is. And yet we still need to believe it. On and on we go.

Then it occurred to me recently that the statement, the old saw or platitude, is actually incomplete. Like the serenity prayer. We leave out the spiritual part, the infinite part. Because that scares us, the idea that we're a tiny speck in the vast ocean of deep time. "Everything happens for a reason" should be followed by a comma, which is a pause, a rest, a slight break in the rhythm of time. So it should be followed by a comma that suggests a deeper, everlasting world.

That comma is followed by what the great Paul Harvey would call, "The rest of the story." "Everything happens for a reason, and that reason is there to serve." To serve your path to a higher consciousness, humility, awareness, or gratitude. To serve some purpose outside of yourself, your needs, and your desires. We may not know why things change, but what we do know is to lift our values out of the petty concerns of our body, our mind, and our hearts.

As a leader, you have a single purpose and it's not the one you think it is: you are there to serve. Serve yourself, your family, your company's values, your stakeholders. Service is what we can do for our organizations and our people. If you feel like there are elements in your organization that aren't serving you and the company, then rather than fight back against it, start serving *them*. I guarantee the results will be something you didn't expect.

If you don't believe me, just ask Dr. Ken Druck, thought leader, innovator, and the man with the same name as my father, Ken Markel. Ken wrote a book called *Courageous Aging: Your Best Years Ever Reimagined*. Dr. Ken is a self-described appreciator of the "pivot points" in the course of his distinguished life and career. He's one of the kindest, most authentic, and grounded people I've ever had the opportunity to share space with. Moreover, he's an "alchemist of resilience" because he's keenly, expansively aware of how the world can change in an instant. Because for Dr. Ken, the world split open in 1996 when the phone rang at 10 p.m. near the end of an otherwise ordinary day.

*   *   *

I've told you a lot about my upbringing in Queens, New York. The sound of music and my father writing and my mother keeping everything together, keeping it all moving. That's the comforting mixtape of my youth.

The other side of that tape is less comforting. I remember the sound of my parents fighting. They were married 25 years and for many of those years they were at each other. There were nasty fights, loud sounds, and things no kid should have had to try to figure out.

At the time, I internalized it. That's what kids do. We turn it inward and somehow, some way make that conflict our responsibility. Because we learn that love is conditional. It's the worst thing for a child to learn about the world. It erodes their spirit.

When you act right, you're loved. When you act wrong? You're not. When you get good grades, you're loved. When you get bad grades? You're not. When you do what you're told, you're loved. When you don't, then you feel the desert of your parents' absence. It's an impossible circumstance to thrust on a child. Yet we do it all the time. We do it to our kids and we do it to the people who work for us. We choose the way of fear over the way of love and honest respect.

As those kids get older, it seeps into the child's cellular structure. Into their relationships, their work, their creativity, their parenting—into every single aspect of their waking lives. That's how much parental conflict impacts all four realms of a child's experience. They'll grow up and they'll self-sabotage. Or they'll overachieve at the expense of their relationships. They'll grow up and they'll waste money. Or they'll be terrified they'll lose it all. They'll be addicts. Or they'll be terrified that they might be.

They're going to spend a lifetime grieving, feeling unsafe, and fighting like hell against the rip current. They'll always fight for safe ground. The things to them that seem random, chaotic and altogether impossible to contain, are the result of their parents working out their own trauma on each other.

I know that because I've lived it. I don't want to say that I've "healed" from it. As a leader in my business, I choose to integrate it into my daily life. I have to. My resilience commitment is to treat it as a part of me, a part of my experience. That makes it possible for me to recommit to Randi and to our children. I'm not running away from it. I'm keeping it with me while I run. It's really that simple.

Dr. Ken says this:

> *I absolutely believe that we have an opportunity all the time to reprogram, to recalibrate, to redo, and to address directly some of our fears, our insecurities, our blind spots, our patterns that are not proving helpful. They slow us down, they rob us of time and of joy and of loving relationships. That's our inner work. I'm a work in progress. I need to be working. I need to be doing this work for the rest of my life. That's a strength. It's an opportunity.*

Dr. Ken adds that the secret isn't being so vigilant and aware of ourselves that we're paralyzed by overthinking. To him, it's the calm of acceptance of being what he calls a "work in progress," constantly evolving and changing. We don't have to be, think, or feel our way through anything. In our work, Dr. Ken says that we have to see the "Fullness behind the emptiness. There's healing behind the lostness."

I love that word he used there, *lostness*. It implies a state or condition of being perpetually lost. It's about being resilient in the face of adversity, heartache, and loss. It's about rising when we're falling. It's the paradox we face as individuals and leaders. But that paradox, Dr. Ken says, "makes room for resilience.

That's what resilience is. That's how we achieve it. Sometimes it's by allowing life to be what it is on its own terms. You're not trying to resist it, fight it, deny it or hide it, repress it, outrun it, outnumb it, outwork it. You're going to stand in and face it down.

Dr. Ken knows all this because his daughter Jenna died when she was 21. He and his wife got the call every parent dreads the moment they hear their baby's first cry. Our kids are our most precious thing. Randi and I could lose everything tomorrow and as long as our four children were OK, we wouldn't bat an eye. But Dr. Ken had to face this moment. You want to talk about resilience? This is the kind that's nearly impossible. Or it is without the spirit. That's what we learn from deep loss that cuts a hole in the fabric of the universe and time stops.

In Norway, on an island where a huge group of progressive campers were terrorized by a right-wing gunman, there was a proposal for a memorial that would literally carve a section of the island away, leaving a gap, a wound, forever unbridgeable and unhealed. After objections from the grieving families the plan was scrapped. Maybe it was for the better, I don't really know. I'm not an art critic.

But Dr. Ken knows that it's accurate to what it feels like to have a piece of your heart ripped out of your body. That's why he was asked to speak to families in New York after 9/11 and in Newtown after the awful tragedy of Sandy Hook. He always asks himself what he needed to hear after the death of his darling daughter.

He told me a story of getting a message from a dear friend who was involved in Law of Attraction work. The friend said, "Remember, it's your choice to have a nice day." Dr. Ken got this message after leaving the cemetery after helping a family say good-bye to their daughter who was kidnapped, raped, and murdered. "I said to myself, 'Could I say that to this family? Tell them it's their choice to have a nice day? Are you freaking kidding me?'" Dr. Ken didn't say that, because it would be a lie.

It's not just about the loss of a child; it could be a living loss. We lost touch with a family member over a forgotten grudge. A son or daughter could have addiction issues. It could be a divorce and the dissolution of a partnership. They all require spiritual resilience. This led Dr. Ken to something he calls the "Five Honorings," which we can use as five bedrock principles for our spiritual resilience.

- **Honoring our own survival.**
  It starts with honoring the loss we suffered. Honoring that it happened. And that we are also still here. Alive. Breathing. On the planet. This is self-care. Not a day at the beach or the mall or high tea at the spa. This is about finding good, professional mental and spiritual help. We can't do it on our own. Seek and find competent and kind help that will show you the way back to your resilience path. Don't be a hero. Don't be afraid to ask for help. That's the most radical kind of resilience. To know that you don't have to be resilient on your own. Your spirit needs other spirits. That's just the way we're wired.

- **Do something good in the name of what you lost.**
  For Dr. Ken, this meant starting the Jenna Druck Center to help children who have addictive diseases. His daughter had created a leadership program when she was 16, so Dr. Ken and his wife kept that alive and now 18,000 girls went through that. The important thing is to share your loss and do some good with it. I promise you: people will find you. Trauma gives us the ability to hear frequencies the rest of the world doesn't always hear. It's our job to give a place to those who don't hear so they can learn to listen just like us.

- **Embody some element of their essence.**
  This is a great one because I know full well the traits that I've picked up from my four kids. They got their personalities

from Randi and me, just based on genetics. That's not the end though. We learn from them. Heck, that's why they don't sleep for the first year. They set our boundaries for us so that we can parent them. Babies are nature's best pregnancy manual. When we lose a child or a person in our lives, or even a business, it's important that we take the parts of them that are gone to live on in us.

- **Begin to develop a spiritual relationship with them.**
  This is heartbreaking stuff but acknowledging it is a big part of how we perform spiritual resilience, says Dr. Ken.

  > *We realized we were never going to get a phone call. There is not going to be any visit. We don't get to go through the part of life we had been so excited about: watching a child graduate, watching them have their first loser boyfriend, watching them find a great guy and falling in love with him as a son-in-law. The love that never dies needs to be carried on. We need to feel it and receive it and give it. We don't know for certain what the true nature of life and death are. We can bet our faith.*

- **Write new chapters.**
  This one takes the greatest amount of courage, because we have to be in the world. We can't curl up in despair and hide forever. We can. But we wouldn't be honoring the loss. We have to be resilient on purpose to show the world that it's possible. Even for those people who have seen the dark abyss that sits just under our world. Those of you who know loss know what I'm talking about. There's a bottomless dark under our world that we spend a lot of time ignoring, denying and pretending it isn't really there. It is. Yet, it's our human trick to keep breathing. To keep walking. To keep living. Forward. In spite of the next loss

that's inevitably coming. We are such resilient creatures. So much more so than we give ourselves credit for.

Dr. Ken has faced this loss and found his resilience, and now he's helping people find the courage to age with courage. He's helping people determine their own legacy.

> *Once we've come to terms with life's package deal, once we've made peace with life's terms, the natural thing that flows into us is the desire to pay the good in our lives forward out of gratitude. Instead of kicking and screaming as we go and leaving a legacy of chaos and clutter and unfinished business, we get to leave a legacy of love that's born of our sensitivity, our compassion, our consideration, our love, our generosity of heart, and our strength. Our acceptance that this is the way of life. This is what happens. It's the cycle of life. I'm a part of it. I surrender to it. I'm blessed to have this ride and I go forward into the Great Beyond.*

Things are going to change, that change is going to come when we least expect it, and that change will happen for a reason, a reason that's there to serve our spiritual resilience.

CHANGE-PROOF POINT

▶ There's no quick, easy fix to becoming change proof, because it's a lifelong journey with peaks and valleys, twists and turns, rained-out paths and rocky footing.

Imagining the Future

*I believe that imagination is stronger than
knowledge. That myth is more potent than history.
That dreams are more powerful than facts.
That hope always triumphs over experience.*
—ROBERT FULGHUM

If you found yourself in a rip current tomorrow, how would you survive? Do you know how to do it? Let's model organizational redundancy and refresh.

To survive, you don't fight the current, exhausting your limited resources; instead, you have to stop wasting your effort on an impossible fight and *pause*. Then you have to ask yourself a series of questions to get fully aware of your situation, and you have to see yourself, floating on the surface of the water, recovering your energy. Finally, you have to choose to swim back to shore.

But our kind of resilience isn't about merely surviving within the rip currents that pull at us every day. We thrive by activating the four harmonic realms that exist within us: our bodies, our minds, our hearts, and our spirits. We don't need them to be in balance; we need them to be in harmony, like a quartet playing a Mozart sonata.

In the process of developing resilience—our ability to benefit from life's situations no matter what—we need to *pause to reframe* almost as easily, and sometimes as frequently, as we breathe.

We then *reset by asking* the right questions that all come from the one big question: What's the creative opportunity in this moment? If that's our starting point, then every question we ask after that will point us in the right direction.

Last, we must *regenerate by choosing* to ritualize our recovery from stress—daily rituals that we perform to use change, rather than change grinding us on the twin wheels of stress and anxiety.

In the rip current, no matter how panicked you might be, no matter how much you want to undo the situation, you have to be able to imagine a future that doesn't have you inhaling salt water. You imagine the future you want, then you inhabit it.

If our bodies, our minds, our hearts, and our spirits are the instruments, then we can think of our imagination as the conductor. It's a tricky thing, imagination. Everyone has one. Everyone uses it. But no one knows quite how it works. I like to think of my imagination as the best part of me operating at peak capacity. It's not only the thing that makes me better, it's the thing that makes me *want* to be better, it makes me *believe* that I can be better.

That's what change-proof resilience is based on: imagining a better world for yourself and for your people. Though it seems like a mystical, intangible idea, it's actually a powerfully practical tool that you can use to activate your body, mind, heart, and spirit, and what's more, you can use it to activate your organization.

As a leader, the most important resilience tool you have at your disposal is your imagination. Even if you don't use it as much as you did when you were small, you use it every day you're blessed to be able to sit at the big desk and make the big decisions that will impact your organization in the short term and will live on after someone else is seated where you are right now.

That's our trick. As human beings we have the ability to imagine a future in which we may not even get to take part. The company you're leading today will not always be led by you. So you have to use your imagination. You have to imagine a future where your organization is growing no matter what happens and no matter who is in charge.

As I've stated many times over, no one can predict the future nor can anyone control it, but to be a change-proof person and leader, a healthy, thriving imagination is the tool that will help you survive any rip current you may face.

Every day your organization or team exists is a new day, a new opportunity to create the kind of place you dreamed about working in when you were a newbie, before quarterly reports, human resources spreadsheets, data mining, the cloud, the market, and a thousand daily pressures were threatening to drag you into the abyss. If you really think about it, the organization you lead today began as an idea that somebody (maybe it was you) dreamed up out of the clear blue sky. The very next thought was, "Am I crazy to think this is possible?" Imaginative creativity defines the futures we inhabit.

Many, many years from now, when you and I have passed out of the memory of the people who come after us, when the entire history of the world is written, it's likely that the kingdom of human imagination will have been dominated by two creative forces: William Shakespeare and Walt Disney.

Separated by almost 400 years, both men had more than a little in common: though they came from relatively modest circumstances, they left home and made their way to a capital of industry, London for Shakespeare, Hollywood for Disney, to make their fortune in show business. Both were creative men who were also business owners, and they knew full well the value of the real estate between their ears.

Shakespeare revolutionized theater in such a way that even today's Hollywood blockbusters are structured like his plays.

Disney took an art form in its infancy, cinema, and helped create and monetize the animated films we still watch with our children today. Arguably, Shakespeare and Disney both have created the most successful characters in the history of the English language that have and will continue to stand the test of time. If someone owned the rights to Shakespeare's plays today, they'd likely be in possession of the most valuable artistic resource in the world. It generates enormous revenue every single day. When it comes to content, the sun still hasn't set on the Disney empire, which is a cultural behemoth the world over.

Shakespeare and Disney were united by one thing: their shared ability to harness the potential of the human imagination. That's what the great ones do. Now, in your line of work, you don't have to be operating on the level of William Shakespeare or Walt Disney. But you do need to do the one thing they are best at: you need to imagine the future you want for yourself and your organization so you can thrive in the face of uncertainty and change.

Change was one of the bedrocks of Walt Disney's philosophy in terms of his relentless focus on reinvention. It's as we've said, you have to self-disrupt from within before your organization is disrupted from without. His consistent embrace of change was adopted by the company that would eventually renew Disney Animation: Pixar. In the more than 25 years since *Toy Story* changed the face of animated film forever, Pixar has churned out hit after hit after hit. Other than a couple of creative missteps, the company is damn near undefeated at the awards podium and the box office.

In his book documenting the rise of Pixar Animation, Ed Catmull writes about building a company culture designed to release the collective imagination of the thousands of people who work for years on a Pixar film. He lays out all the various reasons and bullet points of how and why the Pixar culture is so imaginatively innovative, but they can all be boiled down to one core idea: They do not fear change. At any level.

That creates a culture where risk and failure are something to be sought after instead of run from. Managers don't fear change, so their teams don't fear change. From that, every data point they mine in their organization is about creating a better product. They give power to creatives, they give and take honest feedback in a way that's not personal, they examine and innovate without the expected fear of repercussions.

It doesn't matter where the ideas come from, all that matters is the idea. That's truly change-proof leadership. It's ego-less and empowering, and it's how they've been able to adapt and grow in every single cultural environment. If you don't fear change in your own life or in your organization, then every decision you make will be about imagining a better way through the inevitable uncertainties that every business faces.

Catmull writes:

> *Here's what we all know, deep down, even though we might wish it weren't true: Change is going to happen, whether we like it or not. Some people see random, unforeseen events as something to fear. I am not one of those people. To my mind, randomness is not just inevitable; it is part of the beauty of life. Acknowledging it and appreciating it helps us respond constructively when we are surprised. Fear makes people reach for certainty and stability, neither of which guarantee the safety they imply. I take a different approach. Rather than fear randomness, I believe we can make choices to see it for what it is and to let it work for us. The unpredictable is the ground on which creativity occurs.*

Your organization might not be in the business of creating magical films that parents and children alike can enjoy and celebrate, but no matter what your business is, you need to be creative. Harness the power of your organization's resilient imagination by pausing, asking, and choosing to use what is and what will be, and you'll be around for the long haul. Like the US Coast Guard did in the 1990s.

In the summer of 2020, J. Peter Scoblic wrote about this very thing in the *Harvard Business Review* in a fascinating and instructive article called "Learning from the Future," where he correctly analyzes the tendency of organizations to focus on small-bore, short-term solutions that seem easily controllable in the moment but ignore the long-term implications of expansive innovation.

It's the classic leader's dilemma where you're constantly forced to act in the present and simultaneously plan for a future where you might not be the leader anymore. The trouble with most leaders is they find that drilling down into short-term decisions is more comforting, but it's really like being in a rip current and focusing on a more efficient swimming stroke instead of the counterintuitive decision to simply float with the current and let it spit you out on the other side. As I've said, there's no swimmer alive who can survive the Suck by just swimming better.

Scoblic writes:

> *Now the tyranny of the present is supreme. A lot of organizations have had no choice but to focus on surviving immediate threats. (There are no futurists in foxholes.) But many business and political discussions still demand farsightedness. The stakes are high, and decisions that leaders make now may have ramifications for years—or even decades. As they try to manage their way through the crisis, they need a way to link current moves to future outcomes.*

The solution, he goes on to say, is something he calls "strategic, foresight" which ". . . doesn't help us figure out *what* to think about the future. It helps us figure out *how* to think about it." It's the fundamental difference between goals and systems. Goals give us intentional direction to survive in the present, but systems help us thrive into the future by allowing your organization to make better decisions.

Scoblic issues a challenge to all of us leaders when he writes:

> *If companies want to make effective strategy in the face of uncertainty, they need to set up a process of constant exploration—one that allows top managers to build permanent but flexible bridges between their actions in the present and their thinking about the future. What's necessary, in short, is not just imagination but the institutionalization of imagination.*

That's the key to being a change-proof leader capable of leveraging uncertainty into something powerfully and creatively useful: you have to develop and cultivate your organizational imagination so that your entire organization is imagining a more flexible future.

Seems tricky, doesn't it? Maybe not just tricky, but pretty impossible. Right? Yet that's what the US Coast Guard did in the late 1990s, which enabled them to thrive in the tragic and turbulent events that would occur just a few short years later on a bright, cloudless New York morning.

In response to the end of the Cold War and the shifting ecopolitical landscape, according to Scoblic, the Coast Guard ran an operation, the aptly named "Project Long View" in 1998 and 1999, with the intention of "future-proofing the Coast Guard" so they could strategically plan for a future that was becoming more complex by the moment. The article goes on to talk about the concept of being organizationally "ambidextrous," which means that organizations need to be able to walk and chew gum at the same time; they need to efficiently function in the present while at the same time planning for a variety of futures. Scoblic writes, "The problem is that these two imperatives compete for resources, demand distinct ways of thinking, and require different organizational structures. Doing one makes it harder to do the other."

As a leader, you know full well about the competition for resources that's happening every single funding cycle in your organization. Right now, you probably think that imagining your future is a luxury you can't afford. But when you focus on strategic foresight and develop your institutional imagination, according to Scoblic, "The programs didn't reduce the organization's ability to attend to the present. If anything, the opposite occurred."

And then he offers a bullet point we can all use: "Exploration enabled exploitation." Who wouldn't sign up for that right at this very moment? We all want to find solutions that are profitable. That's the paradox we're dealing with here. Against all engineering principles, the bumblebee still flies.

You want to survive a rip current? Don't fight. Don't swim. Don't try to survive. Lift your feet and float. That's about as paradoxical as you can get, in life and in business. Your instinct may be to fight to survive. Hell, that's probably how you got to where you are. But that's not what we're talking about here. What we're talking about is imaginative foresight that can literally inhabit the time and events that are coming.

Reframing your concept of time is the simple trick for businesses, organizations, and leaders. Scoblic says:

> Humans tend to conceive of time as linear and unidirectional, as moving from past to present to future, with each time frame discrete. We remember yesterday; we experience today; we anticipate tomorrow. But the best scenario planning embraces a decidedly nonlinear conception of time. That's what Long View did: They took stock of trends in the present, jumped many years into the future, described plausible worlds created by those drivers, worked backward to develop stories about how those worlds had come to pass, and then worked forward again to develop robust strategies. In this model, time circles around on itself, in a constantly evolving feedback cycle between present and future. In a word, it is a loop.

In its way, strategic foresight is like building a time machine where you visit a number of plausible futures and, like Marty McFly and Doc Brown, bring back the knowledge that will make your organization change proof in the present and the future.

Scoblic breaks the process of strategic foresight into the seven distinct steps you can take with your organization to discover what it means to future proof your organization:

1. Invite the right people to participate.
2. Identify assumptions, drivers and uncertainties
3. Imagine plausible, but dramatically different futures.
4. Inhabit those futures.
5. Isolate strategies that will be useful across multiple possible futures.
6. Implement those strategies.
7. Ingrain the process.

Like Pixar and the Coast Guard, you have to make it your company's business to constantly be imagining the future. You have to do the work. And then once you do it, you can't just store it in a drawer to take out on a rainy day, because as we've said, over and over again, when it starts pouring down rain and you need an umbrella, your suit is going to get wet. Resilience has to be built before you need it so that it's there when you need it. You can't stop the rain, but you can make sure you've got the best and the biggest umbrella. That's what the future can provide for your resilience.

That's because some of these futures might not happen. None of them might happen. It's not even about the plans that organizations come up with that are integral to becoming change proof, it's in the act of planning, not the plan, that defines an organization.

Like so many other things, just the act of awareness creates a sense of uncertainty that can be frightening, because we all fear change. We're human. Of course we do. By becoming aware of the possibility of multiple futures, you're already broadening your perspective on the world. The uncertainty is the hump we all have to get over. Not Wednesday.

Every child is an imagined future. Because that's what they're doing all the time, at every moment. They don't worry about the future. They imagine it.

That's what I learned from my future-seeking daughter, Eden, who, as she always does, summed up the truth of our change-proof journey without realizing that she was doing it. She says:

> *I feel like in this moment my life's challenge is to sit with my uncomfortability and to really pay attention to the situations that make me uncomfortable, or rock me. And really examine, "Why am I feeling uncomfortable? Why can't I step out of my box right now?" Really getting to the core of that. It sounds stupid, but when I was talking to you the other day about planning, and I felt that uncomfortability, like it was the shift between like recognizing that and then running away from it, and recognizing it and running toward it, and running into it and tackling it, because that's what got me over the hump. And now I feel like I have this thing that I'm letting into my life. That's so amazing. So it really is just sitting with those feelings and not trying to be happy all the time and not going to this status quo of, "I feel uncomfortable. How can I make myself happy again?" It's actually, "How can I get to the core of this? How can I live in a state of uncomfortability? Because that's just life and that doesn't go away."*

Twenty-somethings like Eden know at an intuitive level that the future is change. Change is the future. And like change, the future is inevitable. They don't question it. As a leader, you need to imagine multiple futures so that your company can exist in whatever future arrives, stronger, more efficient, and more aware than ever before.

The same as you. You're going to turn that page and this book will be over. The world is changing right now, and there's a thousand years of thought that says no one can prove what will happen in that future world. The question is: When that future comes, will you be change proof?

I look forward to meeting you there.

> *O heaven! that one might read the book of*
> *fate, and see the revolution of the times.*
> **—WILLIAM SHAKESPEARE**

Resources for Building a
Change-Proof Culture

Keynotes and Workshops

https://AdamMarkel.com/Keynote-Speaker

 Adam supports organizations through engaging and interactive in-person and virtual keynotes, workshops, open space meetings and masterminds. Adam will skillfully motivate and inspire your team and attendees. But that's not enough—they will leave with practical and meaningful tools that can be immediately applied. Adam's support materials ensure that the audience remembers and can easily apply the takeaways. Adam handcrafts his talks for your specific audience and your intended results and objectives. View Adam's core talk abstracts at https://AdamMarkel.com/Keynote-Topics/.

Individual and Organizational Support

https://AdamMarkel.com/Become-ChangeProof

 Adam and his team are dedicated to building a more resilient world, one individual and organization at a time. No matter what type of support you're looking for, we are here to help you . . .

Create a Change-Proof You

- Leadership and Executive Coaching
- Adam provides an exclusive and holistic approach to business mentoring and leadership development, expertly integrating personal growth with business mastery.

Change Proof Your Team

- Facilitated Trainings, Workshops, and Offsite Retreats
- Group Coaching Programs

Build a Change-Proof Culture

- Organizational Training and Support
- Consulting with HR and C-suite to Build Cultural Resilience a Change-Proof Mindset.

Resilience Assessment

https://AdamMarkel.com/ResilienceRank

 Building Resilience and Becoming Change Proof go hand-in-hand. Are you and your business as resilient as you need to be? Take our Resilience Assessment and find out. Along with your results, you'll receive a link to our Resilience Kickstart Kit, full of information to get yourself back on the resilience track and create new resilience rituals.

Resilience Kickstart Kit

https://AdamMarkel.com/ResilienceKit

 Cultivating resilience is a daily practice. This guide contains strategies and tips for building holistic resilience—mind, body, and spirit. It's an amazing resource to start focusing even more on creating master resilience habits. These rituals will allow you to show up in life with higher levels of energy, passion, and focus.

Becoming Change Proof Podcast

https://AdamMarkel.com/Podcasts

 Life isn't always going to be what you expect. . . . What if that was a good thing? Every single day you wake up, you face change, uncertainty, stress. Become Change Proof and easily use each one of those to your advantage. Resilience is the key and the thing *Change Proof* host, Adam Markel, knows best. Enjoy insightful discussions with Adam and leaders and innovators who share breakthrough guidance to fully embrace new opportunities and master today's disruptive marketplace.

Change Proof in Bulk for Teams & Organizations

https://AdamMarkel.com/ChangeProof-Teams

 The best way to create a "Got Your Back" culture of resilience is through a common set of values, priorities, and goals. Providing your team members with a copy of *Change Proof* is a great place to start. Bulk purchases receive a 40 percent discount off the hardcover list price. Discounts are also available for bulk ebook and audiobook purchases.

Connect with Us

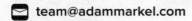 team@adammarkel.com

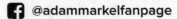 @adammarkelfanpage

 +1.877.MY.PIVOT

 @adamdmarkel

/adammarkel

@adammarkel

Acknowledgments

It truly took a village to bring this project to fruition. What a glorious journey, made all the more special by Cheryl Segura, Adam Seybold, Deanna Crimmins-LeBlanc and Bill Gladstone. To be sure, this book would never have been born without the unconditional acceptance of my parents, Irene and Kenneth, the brilliant and beautiful love of my life Randi and our inspiring "big kids" Chelsea, Lindsay, Max, Eden, Connor and Matthew.

Index

277

About the Author

Adam **Markel** is a number-one Wall Street Journal, USA Today, Los Angeles Times, and Publisher's Weekly bestselling author of *Pivot: The Art & Science of Reinventing Your Career and Life.*

A leading international keynote speaker, for companies like Equitable, P&G, The Home Depot, Cannon, and Citibank, Adam has reached tens of thousands worldwide sharing how to create resilience one individual and one organization at a time. An attorney, CEO, and business development trainer and mentor, Adam is a sought-after business culture catalyst who inspires, empowers, and guides organizations and individuals to become resiliently "Change Proof." Adam is also the cofounder of More Love Media, a keynote speaking and workshop facilitation platform that helps leaders raise the bar on performance without perpetuating talent turnover and costly burnout.

Adam credits much of his success to the principles he learned during his 8 years as a Jones Beach lifeguard in New York. As a first responder in a life-and-death environment, he learned the importance of cultivating a high-performance capacity, impeccable teamwork, and leadership. He's found that the principles of first-responder culture also apply to any business that wants to build a sustainable competitive advantage for the long-term.

For over a decade, Adam has trained and led programs around the globe in the areas of business and entrepreneurship, resilience, leadership, transformation, relationships, and public speaking. As a self-proclaimed "recovering attorney," he has shared his unique content and heart-led leadership style on four continents, in dozens of countries, and throughout hundreds of cities.

Adam's powerful and practical talks offer a unique bridge between self-development and business mastery. They are crafted to inspire, empower, and guide people to achieve a greater impact through greater awareness, authenticity, and action. He is a recognized expert in reinvention, thriving through change and the integration of business and personal development. Adam has been interviewed by many media outlets, including: *Inc.*, *Forbes*, *The Wall Street Journal*, Fox News, and *Entrepreneur*.

Adam holds a degree in English from the University of Massachusetts at Amherst and a Juris Doctorate from St. John's University School of Law. He has been married to his college sweetheart for more than 30 years and has four wonderfully heart-centered and inspiring children.

For more on Adam, visit www.AdamMarkel.com and listen to *The Change Proof Podcast* on your favorite player or at https://adammarkel.com/podcasts/.